Wakefield Press

The Defiant Anti-conscriptionist

Helen Hennessy experienced a varied career as a library manager, teacher, local historian and a community engagement officer with the CFS. Helen Hennessy is now able to devote her time to researching and writing history. In 2019 she was awarded the title of South Australian Regional Historian by the History Council of South Australia.

Patricia Booth is the great-granddaughter of E.H. Coombe and she spent her early years with his second son James Bright and his wife, Alma (née Sauer). Many stories were told about Harry and the Coombe family, which she took to heart. Even as a child, it was obvious to her that her great-grandfather's tragic death had changed the course of her grandfather's life. Now Harry's story can be told to a wider audience.

The Defiant Anti-conscriptionist

The curious life of E.H. Coombe

HELEN HENNESSY and PATRICIA BOOTH

Wakefield Press
16 Rose Street
Mile End
South Australia 5031
www.wakefieldpress.com.au

First published 2022

Cover designed by Michael Deves, Wakefield Press
Edited by Maddy Sexton, Wakefield Press
Typeset by Michael Deves, Wakefield Press

This publication has been assisted by:
The History Trust of South Australia – South Australian History Fund
The Historical Society of South Australia
The Town of Gawler, Community Grants program

ISBN 978 1 74305 961 6

A catalogue record for this book is available from the National Library of Australia

This publication was supported by the History Trust of South Australia's South Australian History Fund

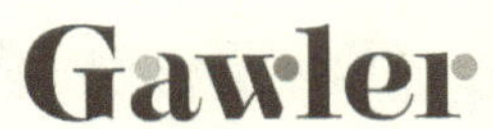

The Town and Citizens of Gawler and the Residents in the surrounding districts owe more to you than they can repay, but we sincerely trust that the memory of your good works will live on and be an inspiration to others.

Gawler will always be richer because E.H. Coombe has lived and worked therein a loyal, patriotic, self-sacrificing citizen.

Illuminated Address presented to E.H. Coombe in June 1914 on the occasion of his relocation to Adelaide[1]

Mr. Coombe had two great characteristics – high ideals and an infinite capacity for hard work.

Memorial to the late Mr E.H. Coombe MP in the Advertiser, 23 September 1919 [2]

What a splendid representative you have in Mr. Coombe; he is the best all-round man in the House. At times he is a nuisance because he is so persistent in his requests. I can put anyone else off, but he won't take 'No' for an answer.

South Australian Premier Tom Price speaking at Lyndoch, 1 February 1907 [3]

Walking along the main street of Tanunda, in the Barossa Valley of South Australia there is a substantial and elaborately carved monument located on the corner of Murray Street and Julius Street. It was dedicated in 1930 as a mark of respect to Ephraim Henry Coombe MP. While his name may not be widely known today, this man worked tirelessly to ensure South Australians lived in a society free to express their ideas and with every opportunity to pursue their own path through life, just as he had done.

Family records[4]

Contents

E.H. Coombe, 1902
SLSA B3987-14

Foreword

The name Ephraim Henry (Harry) Coombe is possibly not well known outside of the Gawler, Barossa and surrounding districts, except among local history enthusiasts or those with an interest in the political and social history of the area.

This fact is both sad and an injustice, as Harry Coombe was a man who, while embedded in the Gawler community, made a significant contribution to the progress of our state.

This book will hopefully bring to the attention of a larger audience the life and times of Harry Coombe.

While the book follows his life journey, we also meet several family, friends and political associates who had an impact on Harry; including his wife Sarah and Catherine Helen Spence, who had a major influence on him.

These intersecting stories are just as interesting, and the book effectively invites the reader to further explore their lives. The book provides a social commentary of the times and captures the mood of the day.

Harry's family came from a very humble beginning in England, and despite his own modest formal education, he was motivated to keep learning eventually becoming the editor of the local Gawler newspaper, the *Bunyip*, and also the Member for Barossa.

Through his family and his community involvement Harry was well connected to the region and used those contacts to improve the lives of people in the Gawler, Barossa and further afield.

He was a man of great principle, which he demonstrated in his political life.

This book needs to be read more than once to gain the full benefit of the extensive research that lies behind this fascinating story of one of Gawler's greatest citizens.

Tony Piccolo MP
Member for Light

Preface

Helen Hennessy

How did this book come about? The answer begins nearly 40 years ago when I first moved to Gawler, and promptly began work as the Chief Librarian for the soon to be opened Gawler Public Library. This service, provided by the council and subsidised by the State Government, is located within the Gawler Institute, an organisation that has a proud tradition of providing library services to the town since 1857.

Part of my induction was to spend time with Mrs Hilda Heinrich, the last of the institute librarians. Hilda was a fount of information on the town, its history and its influential people. She carefully mapped out a reading program for me, which included E.H. Coombe's *History of Gawler*. What a book. I became intrigued by its author, especially as we soon made the connection that the house we were renovating was his family home.

The Local History Collection of the Gawler Public Library was established, and attracted many contributions and conversations. I kept a notebook of these gleanings, especially those pertaining to Coombe. This gathering of resources was a factor in my decision to undertake studies in local history from the University of New England during 1989–1991. One of my research projects was to map and describe the historic area around the Willaston Bridge including, of course, the Coombe's General Store and the family home next door.[1]

It became obvious that Coombe had been highly active and well respected for all that he had achieved. However, there seemed to be a mystery regarding some of his story. Gawler has a proud history of commemorating its famous sons (but sadly, few of its daughters) through public monuments or paintings. Within the Institute Reading Room there were many such memorials with fine oil portraits and marble busts. But where was the Coombe memorial? In the main street of Tanunda! What was that all about?

I continued keeping notes as I read more about South Australian history, thinking that one day there might be a story to be told.

By 2015, I was lucky enough to have more time to devote to my interest in local history and attended many of the events offered during South Australian History Month. It was at one such event that Karen Redman, the Mayor of Gawler, introduced me to Patricia Booth, the great-granddaughter of E.H. Coombe. The stars had aligned, and I found myself with an enthusiastic primary source of information on Coombe and his legacy.

Over the next few months Patricia and I swapped stories and agreed to continue our research and commit our discoveries to book form. This grew to be a greater project that would commemorate Coombe's untimely death in April 1917. We gained the support of several other important community leaders, including the Member for Light, Tony Piccolo, and the then editor of the *Bunyip*, Rob McLean. (Rob's successor, Grady Hudd, and his successor, Sara Gilligan, have been equally supportive.)

We created a detailed project plan, and in December 2015 we were successful in receiving a grant from the Historical Society of South Australia.

In December 2016, we were fortunate to receive a Town of Gawler community grant to aid in the creation of an E.H. Coombe Walking Tour of Gawler, to be launched at a ceremony to mark the 100th anniversary of Coombe's death in April 2017. Enlisting the help of local photographer Janette Menhennet, we set about choosing 16 sites that would give a glimpse into Coombe's life. These ranged from the Gawler Railway Station through to the Wesleyan Church in Willaston. A brochure was created, printed and published to the Town of Gawler website. Mayor Karen Redman launched this publication at a civic gathering at the Gawler Uniting Church in Todd Street, adjacent to the original church where Coombe's parents were married.

The E.H. Coombe Walking Tour of Gawler now appears on the Walking SA website and has been converted into an interactive program on the Town of Gawler Visitor Information Centre's website.

The project's second outcome is this book. The third outcome is an archive of all of the research that has underpinned the project. This, we hope, will find a home in the Gawler Cultural Heritage Collection for future researchers to use.

Patricia Booth

Having lived the first 24 years of my life with my Coombe grandparents, James Bright Coombe and his wife Alma Helena Martha (née Sauer), my childhood was steeped in the stories of my great-grandfather, Ephraim Henry Coombe. My grandfather had some very bitter memories of the way his father had been treated, and we spent many hours together talking about him.

I had often thought about putting something together, and had nearly put some of my friends to sleep talking of my ambition.

To collaborate with Helen in finally having Coombe's story told is a wonderful gift, for which I thank her.

With my grateful thanks also to Mayor Karen Redman, the Historical Society of South Australia, Anthea and Andrew Buxton, Denise Schumann for hosting the historical event which brought Helen and I together, and all of my long-suffering friends!

Launch of the E.H. Coombe Walking Tour April 2017
Left to Right: Mayor Karen Redman., Patricia Booth, James Booth, Anthony Coombe, Stuart Coombe, Paul Booth, Helen Hennessy, Tony Piccolo MP

1

Anti-conscription

History certainly does repeat itself. Anti-conscription is a rallying cry that has reverberated through our country on more than one occasion and made agitators of the most unlikely people.

Who remembers the birthday lottery? Little balls tumbling around in a cage, spitting out numbers certain to bring sadness, fear and the prospect of death into many homes. Prime Minister Harold Holt's decision to send national servicemen overseas as part of Australia's commitment to the war in Vietnam had consequences the Government should have foreseen. Marches, disobedience, rallies, burning of draft-card papers, gaol for protesters and draft dodgers traumatised the community just as it had 50 years earlier.

In 1914 Australia followed the United Kingdom in proclaiming war against Germany. Newspapers had been reporting of the deteriorating situation in Europe for some time. In Australia this concern was magnified by the proximity of German colonies in part of New Guinea and several nearby island groups. The declaration of war brought a wave of patriotic feeling and the hope that hostilities would soon be over. As a newly federated country, Australia had already sent troops to the Second Boer War and the Boxer Rebellion in China, but this was to be a larger, more coordinated commitment.

By 1915, the loss of life on the battlefields of Europe caused the then Australian Prime Minister Billy Hughes to consider the need for conscription in order to bolster the ranks of Australian troops in Europe.

Hughes had spent six months in London and on the Western Front, where he had listened to the arguments presented to him on the need for reinforcements. How he was to supply reinforcements, given the flagging enlistment numbers, was a matter of some concern. The idea of conscription appealed. The United Kingdom had imposed compulsory active service in January 1916, New Zealand had introduced it in September 1916 and Canada, after much public debate, followed suit in July 1917.

However, his party was split over the issue of compulsory overseas military service. Because of a hostile Senate, Hughes was not able to amend the *Defence Act 1903* to allow for overseas service outside the Commonwealth. So, on 30 August 1916, at the National Labor Conference, Hughes announced his intention to take the matter to the public by holding a referendum on conscription hoping to gain public support. Such support would have no legal force, but Hughes felt it would give him a mandate with which he could pressure the opposition as well as opponents within his own Cabinet. A fine orator, driven by the belief that this action was essential if the war was to be won, Hughes was able to persuade caucus to allow the referendum to proceed. The enabling legislation was passed, but only with the support of opposition members.

The vote was technically a plebiscite as the Australian government already had the power to introduce overseas conscription for service in the Commonwealth. Now he wished to include outside the Commonwealth. All Australians including those serving overseas were eligible to vote.[1]

The date of the referendum was set for Saturday, 28 October 1916. Australians were asked:

> Are you in favour of the Government having in this grave emergency, the same compulsory powers over Citizens in regard to requiring their Military Service, for the term of the war, outside the Commonwealth as it now has in regard to Military Service in the Commonwealth?[2]

The lead up to the referendum was bitter and controversial, a situation not helped by Hughes requiring all young men aged between 22 and 40 to immediately register for and attend military training camps in readiness for what he anticipated was to be a straightforward matter. Hughes seemed to be forgetting the strong and immediate objections that came from many sectors of society on the introduction of universal military training under the recent *Defence Act 1911*.[3] High unemployment, widespread industrial unrest, severe drought, anti-Catholic and anti-Irish sentiment all came into play as both sides lobbied for the vote. Broadly speaking and at a national level, Anglo-British Protestants and Scottish Presbyterians supported Hughes, while Irish Catholic Australians, led by the outspoken Melbourne Catholic Archbishop Daniel Mannix, aligned themselves with the trade unionists, most feminists, pacifists (including Australia's Quakers), socialists (including many Labour rank and file supporters), and atheists against the proposed compulsory service.

Hughes had a keen sense of the power of publicity, and soon a conscription propaganda campaign was launched. Recognising the power of the female vote, it included an appeal to the patriotism of Australian women. As the debate grew heated many prominent anti-conscription activists were gaoled in Melbourne and Sydney under the *War Precautions Act 1914*.[4]

In Melbourne, union secretary and prominent anti-conscription speaker John Curtin was charged with failure to enrol and sentenced to three months' gaol. Suffragette Adela Pankhurst, who was married to trade unionist Tom Walsh, was sentenced to three months gaol for leading a demonstration against high food prices in Melbourne as part of a campaign against both conscription and the war. In Sydney, members of the Industrial Workers of the World were prosecuted for uttering 'inflammatory and seditious' words denouncing the war.

South Australian Premier Crawford Vaughan, who attended the Labor conference and who had held anti-conscription views before the conference, announced on his return home that he was in favour of the referendum while remaining personally against compulsory service. The 66 members of the South Australian parliament were free to express their own view. Of these, 59 were regarded as being pro-conscription.[5]

State Labor parliamentarians Lionel Laughton Hill and Ephraim Henry Coombe, then editor of Adelaide's Labor *Daily Herald*, championed the anti-conscription position, becoming president and executive officer of the Anti-Conscription Council of South Australia, respectively.[6] They also had the support of John Gunn, who emerged as another leading figure in the anti-conscription struggle.[7]

While Coombe, Hill and Gunn communicated their anti-conscription

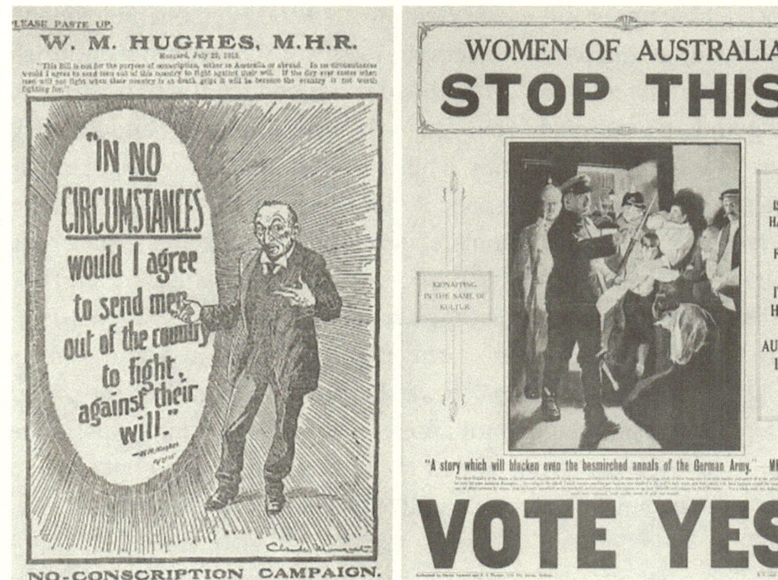

Left: Billy Hughes vote 'No' poster, 1916 State Library of Victoria;
Right: Women of Australia vote 'Yes' poster, 1915, State Library NSW FL3541603

message, the news editor of South Australia's conservative *Register,* William Sowden, ran a 'yes' campaign through the newspaper.[8]

Parliamentarians, both for and against conscription, travelled the state proclaiming their views. Public meetings were held at Booleroo Centre, Burra, Carrieton, Eudunda, Hawker, Jamestown, Kapunda, Hamley Bridge, Murray Bridge, Manoora, Naracoorte, Terowie, Yorketown, and Yankalilla, to name a few.[9] The topic generated much interest and polarised families and friends alike.

Coombe seemed hardly the type to be storming the state for the cause. Brought up in the town of Gawler as a Wesleyan and a teetotaller, he had first been elected to the state parliament in 1901 for the seat of Barossa. He held the seat until the 1912 election, before being re-elected once more in 1915. In different circumstances he was an unlikely choice to be a troublemaker or dissident.

The introduction of the 1916 referendum had a galvanising effect on him. With three sons and a son-in-law at the Front, he could hardly be seen as an antagonist to the war effort. Rather, he objected to the method and the force with which the idea of conscription was being pursued. He did not dispute the use of persuasion to encourage voluntary signing up of recruits, but the idea that men could be forced into a conflict regardless (in some cases) of their personal and employment circumstances, was abhorrent to him.

The sentiment that 'evil flourishes when good men do nothing' clearly stirred Coombe. He travelled extensively, even to Broken Hill, in the name of anti-conscription. Winning some to his cause and annoying others with his very persuasive speech, he worked tirelessly and used his position as editor of the *Daily Herald* to advantage, becoming known as 'the chief mouthpiece of the anti-conscriptionists'.[10]

He was accused of being a traitor, particularly because his circle of friends and associates included many of German descent. One of his daughters-in-law, Alma, was from a family with German heritage. She, like many of his Barossa constituents with German names, was generationally Australian. Unfortunately, it was easy for his opponents to attack him for his stance. For his family, the criticism of Coombe, while their brothers, husbands and sweethearts were serving overseas, was hard to bear.

Coombe's third son, Samuel, enlisted days after the declaration of war, and was twice wounded – first at Gallipoli and again in the trenches of France. Five months later his youngest son, Ernest, joined up and was also wounded. Less than a year later, his daughter Daisy's husband, George Arthur Ash, joined the army. His eldest son Harry Heywood, who was married with two sons, enlisted in December 1915, underwent officer training and was promoted to lieutenant. He was stationed in the Mitcham Army Camp training soldiers while awaiting his own embarkation overseas. Finally, his daughter-in-law Alma, married to his second son, James, suffered the death of her only brother, Herbert Wilhelm Sauer, after he succumbed to his wounds in an English hospital on 22 September 1916.

In October 1916, the referendum took place, with 82% of the eligible voters expressing their views. Of these, 87,924 South Australians voted 'yes' and 119, 236 voted 'no'. The states of Victoria, Tasmania and Western Australian gave 'yes' majorities while NSW, Queensland and South Australia recorded a 'no' majority. The 'no' vote had the majority by 72,476 votes, which represented a margin of 3.2%.[11] Considering that the entire

Samuel Walter Coombe
SRSA GRG2654237

Ernest John Hiscock Coombe
SRSA GRG2654235

Harry Heywood Coombe
SRSA GRG2654236

Herbert Wilhelm Sauer
SRSA GRG26541212

apparatus of government and most of the media had been campaigning for 'yes', this was a significant victory for grassroots activism.

Hughes was expelled from the Labor Party for his advocacy of conscription. The resultant party split saw members of the Party's right-leaning wing join forces with the Commonwealth Liberal Party to form the Nationalist Party of Australia, led by Hughes.[12]

In all, 31 state and federal parliamentarians had been condemned as being disloyal to the Labor Party. In South Australia just seven United Labor Party (ULP) members – Lionel Hill, John Gunn, Ephraim Coombe, John Carr, James Jelley, Thomas Butterfield and John Price were recognised as the legitimate state parliamentary Labor Party, leaving Crawford Vaughan and John Verran on the outer.[13]

Following the loss of the referendum, the bitterness did not end and harsh words continued to be directed toward Coombe in parliament. He was accused of 'making false statements' and 'criminally misleading the people' for which he 'should be awarded an iron cross'. Another parliamentarian said that he had 'betrayed his country to gain votes'. For the most part he 'gave back as good as he got'.[14]

The Vaughan Labor government to which he belonged but with whom, on this topic, he disagreed, came under heavy criticism for its pro-conscription stance. The Australian Workers' Union State Secretary, Francis Walter Lundie, launched a campaign within the United Labor Party to lobby against all in the party who had declared themselves pro-conscription.

The debates about 'the German problem' continued. The significant 'no' response was, rightly or wrongly, perceived to rest with the state's large German population.[15] Former Premier John Verran, an outspoken public representative of the anti-German feeling, introduced a Bill to disenfranchise South Australians of German descent for the third time. A Nomenclature Committee was appointed to consider substitutes for place names in South Australia 'considered to suggest foreign enemy origin'. The discussions regarding the proliferation of 'German Lutheran Schools' had commenced as early as 1912. Their resistance to proposed registration and inspection by government authorities was met in 1915 by calls for a specific kind of control of German schools.[16] By 1916, restriction was superseded by the finality of closure. Coombe led a group of clergy and peace activists in support of the Lutheran Schools, but to no avail. His impassioned speech to parliament made little difference to the result and earned him yet more harsh words from his opponents whilst consolidating his support base.[17] Fellow member for the Barossa, Sir John Downer was particularly vocal, repeatedly accusing Coombe of disloyalty to his country.

All 49 Lutheran primary schools, excluding the Koonibba Mission west of Ceduna, were closed the following year. The two Lutheran secondary schools at Concordia in the Barossa and Point Pass near Eudunda were permitted to remain open. In some cases, the South Australian Government leased back the buildings and took over the education of the children with new teachers. In others the students were transferred to the local public school. Either way, the sudden change was no doubt traumatic for the students and their parents trying to comprehend the loss of the German language teaching, their Lutheran instruction, familiar teachers, and often the amenities of their former schools.[18]

The attack on Coombe became even more focused. At an open air public meeting in Tanunda on Thursday, 26 October 1916, he was aware that there were people in the audience who hoped to catch him breaking the provisions of the *War Precautions Act* by being critical of Australia's involvement in the war. He asked one of his supporters, Hermann Juncken, to 'listen particularly to his speech, because he was being watched, and they would like to catch him'. The meeting, held beside Schraeder's Victoria Hotel, was chaired by Moritz Ernst Heuzenroeder, JP, local chemist and chairman of the Tanunda District Council. Speaking with Harry was Francis McIntyre, who was the Assistant Secretary of the Federated Carters and Drivers' Union, and Dr Clark Nikola. All three were members of the Anti-Conscription Council formed by the ULP opponents of conscription. The meeting commenced at 9 pm following on from a similar meeting at Angaston. The speakers addressed the crowd of about 500 from the back of a truck. Coombe spoke for about an hour.

Harry spent the remainder of the year replying to endless letters to the editor that criticised his championship of anti-conscription, and defending himself against a particularly vicious parliamentary attack by Sir Richard Butler when Harry attempted to have farmers and farm labourers released from the military camps in order to harvest their crops. He endured ridicule and a total lack of support from his parliamentary colleagues, led by John Verran, for his opposition to the Bill to abolish German schools and language teaching. He described all these attacks as a 'waste of time and energy, because ... personal abuse and vituperation never hurt me [and] all the anger in the world cannot alter the result of the referendum'.[19]

Predictably, early in 1917, the Commonwealth prosecuted Ephraim Henry Coombe and Francis McIntyre under the *War Precautions Regulations*, 'for offences committed at the October 1916 Tanunda meeting'.[20] The *Daily Herald* opened a Defence Fund for the two men and donations were encouraged from the readers and others who did not agree with conscription.[21] A letter was sent from the Labor Party to Prime Minister Hughes, requesting him to order the withdrawal of the prosecution, but the only response received was an acknowledgement of the correspondence.[22]

The court case was held in Tanunda on Monday 26 and Tuesday 27 February 1917 before a Special Magistrate from the city, Thomas Hewitson.[23] It was felt that as a Commonwealth case it warranted a change from the magistrate that normally heard cases in the district. Paris Nesbit, KC, appeared for the defendants, and Francis Villeneuve Smith appeared for the Commonwealth.

Barossa-born and educated Paris Nesbit was known to Coombe, for they had both been unsuccessful candidates in the 1896 election for the seat of Barossa. Adelaide-born Francis Villeneuve Smith was also well known. He had a 'brilliant reputation for eloquence and skilful cross-examination' and in 1919 would be appointed a King's Counsel at the young age of 35.[24] Magistrate Hewitson was known to both men. He had taken his articles with Francis' father and had recently been in partnership with Nesbit's son, Hubert, in a law practice in Port Augusta.[25]

Coombe was charged 'that during October, at a well-attended meeting in Tanunda he had made a statement likely to prejudice the recruiting of His Majesty's forces by having used the words 'I appeal to the people of Australia to have nothing more to do with the war' or words to that effect'. The information was laid by Detective Whittle. When questioned by Smith, Mounted Constable Lyons of Tanunda confirmed that Coombe had used the words 'have nothing more to do with the war'.[26]

Nesbit, speaking for the defence, said the tenor of Coombe's speech was in favour of voluntary recruitment. All of the witnesses for the defence, except for Francis McIntyre, were of German descent or connection. They included Fritz (Fred) Warnecke, a fruit grower from Nuriootpa; Johann Freidrick Wilhelm Schultz, a teacher at the Tanunda Lutheran School; Wilhelm Schultz, auctioneer's clerk; Albert Julius Hentschke, a monumental mason; Paul Ferdinand Zimmerman, a farmer; Paul Jarneck, a fruitgrower; Wilhelm J.C. Bietz, motor carrier; Joseph David Chandler, a distiller; Sarah Mary Graue; Hermann Julius Juncken, a builder, and Max Otto Riedel, a law clerk. Joseph Chandler and Sarah Graue had both married into German families.

The cross-examination of Coombe was reported in the press:

> Accused gave evidence that in his speech he said his three sons and son-in-law had gone as free men, and he was anxious they should he reinforced by free men. He quoted figures to show that voluntaryism had not failed, and he had spoken in favour of that system, both before and since. On the night in question he had expressed the opinion that conscription in Germany and France was responsible for the war, and it would be ridiculous for Australia to adopt the worst form of German militarism. He had appealed to the people not to adopt conscription, but they must continue to fight to the end. Voluntaryism, however, he had contended would see them through the war.
>
> Mr. Smith: You were one of the stalwarts of the anti-conscription brigade?
>
> Witness: I was one of the few legislators who opposed conscription.
>
> [Mr Smith]: You are, as a matter of fact, an antiwar man?
>
> [Witness]: I am certainly very much opposed to war if it can be avoided, I hope everybody is. If the Kaiser had been of that mind, we should not now have this war. Continuing, witness said it was not his belief that there were a large number of enemy sympathizers in the district, although he was aware that many had been interned from the vicinity.
>
> Mr. Smith: An anti-war speech would go down pretty well here, and would catch a vote or two.
>
> Witness: I do not think it would.

> [Mr Smith]: You were just as eager to catch votes that night as any other time?
>
> [Witness]: Yes. He added that the audience had been largely of German descent, but he saw no evidence of anti-British feeling. It was quite impossible that he could have made the statement alleged without knowing it. Such an idea was never in his mind. He thought Constable Lyons had made a mistake, for which he personally could not account. He suggested that confusion might have arisen by his having used the words in reference to conscription, but when asked whether he remembered the phraseology he employed he remarked that his words were, 'Have nothing to do with conscription.'
>
> Mr. Smith: What confusion could have arisen between the words conscription and war?
>
> [Witness]: None.
>
> Witness continued that he could not account for M.C. Lyons having arrived at the conclusion he had.
>
> Mr. Smith: It is incapable of any explanation, except that he invented it?
>
> Witness: No. There was some mistake on his part.
>
> [Mr Smith]: But you just admitted that there was no room for a mistake between the words.
>
> [Witness]: I cannot account for it.[27]

After nine hours of hearing plus a further hour's deliberation, the magistrate acquitted Coombe.

However, that was not the end of it. The next day a second case was held. This time Coombe was charged with attempting to cause disaffection among the civilian population, after he said, or used words to the effect, that 'It was an injustice to have certain votes earmarked. It was only done to try and intimidate people, and to try and prevent them from going to the poll to record their vote. It was very dirty work'.

He again pleaded not guilty. The only witness called was Mounted Constable Lyons. This time Nesbit pleaded for Coombe's right of free speech. In his summing up the magistrate said:

> it seemed purposeless for accused to introduce the subject of the voting provisions in his speech. If his object had not been to appeal to the passions or natural racial prejudices of some persons among his audience, what had it been? His language meant more than friendly criticism. Disaffection meant a sentiment of hostility, which the remarks were calculated to produce. The position of defendant and his influence in the community could only aggravate the offence. On the other hand, it had been argued that the language was nearly on the border line; although it was difficult to say how there could be any degrees of culpability in the matter of an attempt to create disaffection.[28]

Magistrate Hewitson declared Coombe guilty, and fined him £10 with £5/5s costs. He was further bound to enter into two sureties of £100 to comply with the provisions of Regulation 43 of the War Precautions Act while they remained in force. He had a fortnight to pay.[29]

A sad blow indeed to a man who stood by his principles regardless of the views of others and often as a lone speaker to what he regarded as a just cause.[30] The trial was widely publicised and created much debate on the use of the War Precautions Act Regulations to prevent and punish independence of thought, freedom of speech, action and the right to publish in wartime. A member of the press queried the speaker as to whether the verdict jeopardised Coombe's position as a member of parliament. In reply, Frederick Coneybeer said that he would take no action.[31] Coombe was not deterred by the negative publicity from the court cases and continued to campaign strongly against conscription.[32]

A second conscription referendum was held in December 1917. South Australia was the only state not to increase its 'no' vote. German-settled areas with a high proportion of 'no' voters in the first referendum were again subjected to a strong pro-conscription campaign by politicians and newspaper columnists. But the rural areas also included farmers who were worried about the loss of rural labour and significant Irish Catholic populations reluctant to support the English Crown. The second time around these areas did record a slightly reduced 'no' vote, but the urban votes ensured a consistent state vote of 56.1% against conscription.

However, Coombe would not witness this second referendum. The constant barrage of criticism and his passionate belief in the cause of anti-conscription proved his undoing. In late March 1917 he suffered a cerebral haemorrhage whilst addressing an evening public meeting at the Port Adelaide Town Hall and passed away a week later, on 5 April 1917 in Semaphore, aged 58.

2

Family Background

Nomenclature: From this point onwards, E.H. Coombe is generally referred to as 'Harry Coombe' to differentiate him from all of the other Ephraims in his story. His friends, family and peers knew him as Harry.

Father

Ephraim Henry (Harry) Coombe's father, also named Ephraim Coombe, was born into the small English village of Goodleigh near Barnstaple, North Devon, in 1828 and christened at nearby Swimbridge. This was an agricultural region populated by people committed to their religion and hard work.

The family records note that on 20 May 1788, Harry's great-grandfather, John Coombe married Elizabeth Howard of Landkey, Devon. They had four children – Margaret, John, Ephraim and Elizabeth. John Junior, born in 1791, married another Elizabeth, née Brook. Their children were John, Ann, Thomas and Ephraim, who would become Harry's father. Ephraim was a name used regularly within the family.

Of Wesleyan faith (a form of Methodism) Ephraim was taught to read and write, not a common occurrence at the time.[1] This gift gave young Ephraim a glimpse of what lay beyond his hometown, and in 1854, at the age of 26, Ephraim Coombe sailed to Australia as an assisted migrant.

Why would a young labourer, who began working at the age of seven, leave his village and family to travel to the other side of the world?[2]

During the first half of the nineteenth century, the United Kingdom experienced significant social, political and economic upheaval. Post war depression, famine, land clearances, high unemployment caused by industrialisation and changing farm practices led to many changes for the labouring class.[3]

The American War of Independence ended in 1783 but the cost was enormous, and the French Revolution (1788–1799) and the subsequent war with France (1793–1815) continued the drain on resources. In 1842 a series of Reform Bills were introduced, making it possible for more classes of men to vote and gain seats, thus changing the composition of parliament. In 1846, the infamous 1815 *Corn Law Act*, passed to keep the price of corn artificially high, was repealed after a period of rioting and public outcry. Acts of Parliament were passed to enclose common lands within the estates of landowners. Consequently, smallholders found it difficult to find the land for their stock to graze. The industrial revolution in the United Kingdom saw machines taking the place of workers in the fields. Also disappearing were the once thriving home-based cottage industries that enabled the women and children within families to earn extra income from weaving and other crafts.

As a generational farm labourer and the youngest in a family of three sons and a daughter, Ephraim was one of many who felt that their prospects and standard of living could be improved elsewhere. Farm labourers occupied the lowest rung of the rural workforce. Their employment was itinerant, seasonal and paid by the day. A bad harvest, poor weather or being replaced by inventions such as a threshing machine, meant no work and no money. Free passage to South Australia, via a 'bounty scheme', drew many to contemplate emigration. Under this arrangement an incentive (a bounty) was paid to recruiting agents in the United Kingdom to find suitable skilled labour, mechanics, agricultural labourers and tradespeople, and then safely ship them out to the new colony that was in urgent need of these skills.

The Bounty Immigration Scheme developed from a colonisation scheme first suggested by Edward Gibbon Wakefield, a man whose ideas were to be instrumental in the establishment of South Australia. Wakefield proposed that the Australian colonies' system of free land grants should cease and Crown land should instead be sold. The revenue from these sales should be used to boost emigration rather than transportation from the United Kingdom, with certain conditions applying to the type of immigrant accepted. These conditions required that applicants must be in good health, free from all bodily or mental defects, of good moral character, sober, industrious, and in the habit of working for wages at the occupation specified in their application. (These were requirements far from Wakefield's own life, which saw him imprisoned for kidnapping and marrying underage heiresses.) Character references would be sought from responsible persons such as the local magistrate or clergyman. The applicants would also need to prove their age through a certificate of baptism. Age limits were set with payment penalties for those over 40. Commonly selected immigrants included shepherds, ploughmen and agricultural labourers, followed by a lesser number of tradespeople such as brickmakers, carpenters, blacksmiths, tailors and needlewomen.[4]

Ephraim applied for and was accepted under the Second Bounty Scheme that had commenced in 1847. He set sail on the *Ebba Brahe*, departing from the port of Plymouth on Saturday 14 October 1854, having travelled from Goodleigh, possibly via the newly opened North Devon Railway's Barnstaple station. After a 12 week voyage, he arrived in Sydney on 6 January 1855.[5]

His experiences over the next eight months are unknown. There is speculation within the descendant family that Ephraim may have gone chasing gold on the NSW gold fields. Given that he arrived mid harvest, maybe instead his skills as a farm labourer were sought to fill the gaps left in the local workforce by the absence of others who had gone gold hunting. Whatever his adventures, we do know that the young Ephraim did not leave England without some knowledge of his destination. Like many others he had family members already in the new country and after some months in Sydney earning money for his fare, he travelled to join them.

On 22 September 1855, he set sail from Sydney on the cargo ship *Eugene*. He arrived with two other steerage and two cabin class passengers in Port Adelaide on 12 October 1855.[6] No doubt his first contact was with his uncle (also called Ephraim Coombe) who was doing well at Walkerville. The now 27-year-old Ephraim then travelled north to Gawler, probably via a paid passage on the regular mail coach. This was a van-shaped vehicle covered with canvas as protection from the sun and dust. This horse-drawn cart took from four to five hours, on a good run, to travel the 35 miles of rough track.[7]

Paternal Uncle

His paternal uncle, Ephraim Coombe, had arrived in South Australia on board the ship *Lloyds* on 1 December 1838, nearly two years after the proclamation of the colony.[8] In his emigration records this Ephraim was listed as a 34-year-old blacksmith who travelled with his wife, Susannah, aged 28, and their eight-year-old son. Sadly, a four-year-old daughter died shortly before migration. Ephraim applied for a free passage to South Australia on 22 June 1838, under the first bounty scheme. In order to meet the emigration age limit, Ephraim reduced his and Susannah's real age by ten years. Family records show Ephraim's actual year of birth as 1794 and Susannah's as 1800.[9]

By 1840 he owned a property in Melbourne Street, North Adelaide, and farmed on the banks of the nearby Torrens River. The property was in Ephraim's name alone, as until the South Australian *Married Women's Property Act* was passed in 1883, married women could not acquire, hold or dispose of property. The farm was an enterprise that in February 1849 was producing newsworthy potatoes.[10] A month earlier another newspaper item reported the damage caused to this property by a bushfire 'in barley, fencing, grass-feed, and clothes, more than 40 pounds in value' and that 'Mr and Mrs Coombe wish to thank their neighbours, friends and visitors who helped fight the flames'.[11]

Ephraim's ownership of property entitled him to vote, stand for parliament, and, under the 'nomination' scheme introduced in 1852, to nominate three migrants for the journey to Australia for every £80 spent on Crown land purchases. Nominated people had to be eligible for selection under the Colonial Land and Emigration Commission regulations, but the choice of the person lay with the land purchaser or his agent. His niece and nephew are likely to have been two of Ephraim's nominees.

Ephraim Coombe became a prominent and active resident of the Walkerville area, involving himself in public affairs. In 1845 he signed a petition against a proposal put forward by David McLaren, Manager of the South Australian Company, to introduce convict transportation to South Australia.[12] In 1859, he successfully nominated a local solicitor, William Charles Belt, to become the council's chairman and a fellow farmer, Samuel Barker, to be one of the four other councillors.[13] In 1862,

Ephraim himself became an elected member of Walkerville Council under the chairmanship of Edward Angus Hamilton and again in the company of Samuel Barker.[14] These were significant associates indeed. Edward Angus Hamilton was the Colonial Architect and Supervisor of Works who later became a member of parliament. Hamilton was responsible for the design of many important Adelaide buildings as well as St George's Church in Gawler and the Telegraph Station, later to become the Gawler School of Mines.[15]

Ephraim Coombe's wife, Susannah, died aged 67 in 1867. Two years later, he remarried 60-year-old Eleanor Emily Morrell at St Luke's Anglican Church, Adelaide. Now 75, Ephraim set about putting his affairs in order. He had become the owner of quite some considerable property in Walkerville, even then described as a 'better class of village' where land was sold at much higher rates per acre than, for instance, in Bowden. Land title records show that by 1858 Ephraim Coombe owned six acres at Gilbert Town (now Gilberton) and occupied a house of six rooms, outbuildings, gardens and paddocks at 17 Walkerville Terrace. By 1862 he was the owner/ occupier of part of Lot 19 in the same area, which he initially rented to a clerk, J. Thomas Senior and in 1866 to J.C. Presgrove.

In his last will and testament, dated July 1869, Ephraim Coombe, gentleman of Gilbert Town, near Adelaide, bequeathed £200 at 'their arrival at age' to Alice Coombe Godfrey, daughter of the late John Bond Godfrey, with the same amount to be shared by Henry Ephraim and Thomas, who were sons of Ephraim Coombe.[16] The property was left to his wife, Eleanor Emily Coombe, for the term of her natural life. The rest and residue of his estate was held on trust to William Ephraim Coombe Hillier and Mary Jane Hillier who were children of his niece, Adelaide Hillier. There is no mention of the son who was listed when he emigrated, suggesting that he had died. Ephraim therefore left his not insubstantial estate to the children of a niece and nephew and someone given the middle name of Coombe, possibly another relation. When Ephraim Coombe died on 25 April 1871, his obituary records him as being in his 77th year, a veritable age for the period.[17]

According to his wishes, part of Lot 19, together with Lots 20 and 21, became the property of Mrs Eleanor Coombe following Ephraim's death. Eleanor later moved to Church Terrace. She died on 27 February 1886 at the age of 77, at which time she was listed as living at White Street, Walkerville.

Paternal Aunt

The other relation that newly arrived Ephraim Coombe had in South Australia was his married sister, Ann Pope, née Coombe.

On 21 March 1849, 25-year-old Ann Coombe had arrived in Port Adelaide on board the *Pakenham,* having set sail from Plymouth on 17 December 1848.[18] Under the conditions of her emigration, Ann, as a single woman, had to travel under the care of her family (parents or a near relative) or that of a married couple. It is likely that her paternal uncle Ephraim sponsored her for emigration and that she travelled with a married couple. A diary written by fellow passenger, Stephen Richards, provides details of those on board, many of whom were headed toward the Burra mines.[19] One family, though, headed for Gawler. This was Richard and Harriet (née Dawe) Pinson and their children, two-year-old Samuel and baby Ann Elizabeth, who had been born on the voyage. Like Ann, the Pinsons boarded at Plymouth. Richard is recorded as a timber merchant, although he later worked in Gawler as a stoker.[20] Perhaps Ann befriended the Pinsons, or as a single woman who wished to travel to Australia, maybe she was introduced to them prior to leaving as a travelling companion who could help with their children? Maybe the Pinsons' baby born on board was named for her? After a short stay with her uncle and his wife in North Adelaide, she possibly travelled with the Pinsons to Gawler.

Somehow, she made the connection with Gawler because two years later, on 13 April 1851, Ann, spinster of Gawler South, married Samuel Pope, bachelor of Gawler South, at St George's Anglican Church in Gawler.[21] The Pinsons were active in this church.[22]

Ann's husband, Samuel Pope, was also an assisted immigrant. He had arrived in Melbourne in 1844 before travelling on to Port Adelaide in 1845.[23] He too was from Devon, from a town named Topsham. In Port Adelaide, he began working for the miller, Stephen King, a member of the syndicate who had commissioned the Gawler Special Survey and a trustee of St George's Church. Later Samuel worked for Walter Duffield, another Gawler based miller.[24]

After his arrival in Gawler, Samuel built and briefly lived in a red brick cottage on Finniss Street. It was the first brick house to be built in the Church Hill area of the town at a time when there were only pine cottages along the main street.[25]

In May 1846 Samuel was involved in the founding of the Loyal Gawler Lodge of Oddfellows, a nineteenth century social organisation that provided mutual assistance in cases of personal difficulty in an era before government funded community and social services. Ann's brother, Ephraim, would later join him in this organisation. Samuel was also involved in his church, and by Easter 1855 he had become a warden of St George's Church. In 1858 his name was listed on the parchment beneath the foundation stone of the 'new' St George's Church as one of the 19 members of the Building Committee that both coordinated the work and raised money to fund it. Two years later his name appeared among 66 others making a monetary presentation to the Reverend W.H. Coombs. These two lists are a veritable 'who's who' of Gawler and show that Samuel was mixing in influential circles. Also appearing on both lists was James Harris, who would employ Samuel's brother-in-law, Ephraim, six years later. Gawler was even then a highly networked community.

In 1847 Samuel acquired two acres of land on Lyndoch Road, Gawler East, then known as the Barossa Highway (and today as the Barossa Valley Way). Two years later Samuel bought an adjoining 106 acres which he farmed for the next 14 years. He built the Wheatsheaf Inn on the original two acres with the first liquor licence being granted to a Thomas Henry in March 1859. In 1861 Samuel and his brother, Abraham, were listed as farmers of Gawler.[26] However, in March of that year, Samuel supplemented his farming with innkeeping by taking over as the licensed proprietor of the Wheatsheaf Inn. This was a role he held until June 1866 when he then passed it on to a series of short-term landlords.[27]

Ann was also involved in running the Wheatsheaf Inn. In 1864 she and Samuel were listed in a court case arising from one of their employees, Sarah Elven, accusing Ann of striking her. Both Ann and Samuel were individually fined.[28] By then Ann had given birth to three of her five children; Samuel, Charles and Susannah, all born while she was in her thirties. Her youngest was born when she was 43.

In 1868, two years after Ann and Samuel handed the running of the hotel on, gold was discovered in the Barossa and the establishment was 'upon the direct route to the diggings [and] travellers [were] assured of every attention'.[29] But despite the potential for an increase in trade the business did not flourish. In 1873 Samuel Pope was declared bankrupt and the *Bunyip*, Gawler's local newspaper, records the sale at auction of the Wheatsheaf Inn and the farm property. The Wheatsheaf Inn then lost its licensed status.

After Samuel's death in 1892, his obituary reported that after having been a very successful farmer, 'a series of reverses left him in comparatively poor circumstances, and he was never able to make up lost ground'.[30]

Ann died on 25 February 1898, at the Williamstown residence of her youngest daughter Harriet and her son-in-law Thomas Worden. Her obituary described her as 'a colonist of 49 years'. There is no mention of Ann and only a cursory mention of her husband in her nephew's *History of Gawler.* Their involvement with the selling of liquor may explain a perceived distance from her Wesleyan temperance Gawler Coombe relatives. Yet this is somewhat counterbalanced by the championing of E.H. Coombe by his Williamstown cousins.[31] This extended into the 1950s with a letter to the *Bunyip* from Mary Worden, Harriet's daughter, in which she expressed her concerns about the state of the graves in Pioneer Park including the graves of the Coombe family.[32]

With both Ann and Ephraim emigrating to Australia, their parents back in Devon had the support of their remaining sons, John and Thomas. Like most families divided by the miles, it is likely that there was a regular exchange of letters between Australia and England. Unfortunately, none of these have been discovered.

Father's arrival in Gawler

Harry's father Ephraim arrived in Gawler in late 1855 and began work as a manual farm labourer. During this time, South Australia has been described as 'the granary of Australia', and together with the early copper discoveries, the colony experienced an era of almost continuous economic expansion.[33]

One of Wakefield's tenets for a self-supporting colony was that land should be priced so that labourers might buy it, but only after working

Samuel Pope,
Gawler Branch National Trust SA

Ann Pope née Coombe,
Gawler Branch National Trust SA

Henry Lock,
family records

Hannah Lock
family records

for others for two years.[34] Ephraim Coombe preferred instead to invest his money into his own business. But the colony's prosperity did extend to his Uncle Ephraim, who owned land and provided mortgages to several people in country areas.

Perhaps influenced by his uncle's experience ten years earlier, Ephraim Coombe donated five shillings in March 1859 to the Bushfire Relief Fund organised in Gawler by a committee led by the local politician Walter Duffield.[35] The February fire had started in the Adelaide Hills at Macclesfield and burnt fiercely southwards into the Hindmarsh and Inman Valleys. Many homes, crops and stock were destroyed and a colony-wide relief campaign was organised for the victims.

Upon his arrival in the area Ephraim Coombe joined the Salem Bible Christian Church, located on the Gawler Plains, but transferred his membership to the Gawler Wesleyan Church.[36] Research on Methodism on the Gawler Plains showed that there was a free-flowing cooperation and overlap between the members of the different Methodist streams of Bible Christians, Wesleyans and Primitive Methodists.[37]

His farming connection or perhaps his membership of the Wesleyan Church led Ephraim Coombe Senior to meet his future wife, Mary Lock.[38]

Mother

Mary was the daughter of Henry and Hannah Hatherway (née Riggs) Lock. The farm labouring Lock family emigrated from Dorset in 1851 on board the *Marion* with two sons and four daughters. The land they farmed at Gawler River, leased from the Ragless family, is now known as the Food Forest.[39]

Gawler Plains was the name given to the area to the southwest of Gawler and now encompasses Smithfield, Edinburgh, Angle Vale and Virginia. Gawler River is an area to the west of Gawler. The use of these regional geographic names sometimes overlapped.

Hannah's parents, Henry and Mary (née Bishop) Riggs, after whom Mary Lock was named, soon joined them, emigrating in 1853. They farmed in the nearby Gawler Plains. By 1855 seven of Henry and Mary Riggs's nine children had emigrated – three daughters and four sons – with two daughters remaining in England. This made Mary Lock one of a very large local farming family.[40] It is highly likely that when Ephraim Coombe arrived in 1855 he found work either on the Riggs or the Lock farms.

Two years after his arrival in Gawler, 29-year-old Ephraim married Mary Lock, 21, in the Gawler Wesleyan Chapel on 27 October 1857.[41] This church, built in 1850, is located at the junction of Tod Street and Scheibener Terrace.[42]

Just three weeks before the wedding, the railway from Adelaide to Gawler was opened.[43] Married, with a wife to support, Ephraim supplemented his farm labouring work with employment as a porter at the railway.[44] For convenience, the newlyweds took up residence close to the railway station, in Elizabeth Street, Gawler South.

Railway porters, in the days before bulk handling of grain, were bag handlers. These were men employed to manually handle the heavy, grain-filled jute sacks from the farm carts into stacks at the station and later onto the trains. Porters were employed on a piecemeal basis by farmers to undertake this seasonal task. This explains why his name does not appear in railway employee lists for that period.[45]

Married life for Mary Coombe was also physically demanding. Homes for the most part were basic, with external bathrooms, and laundries and kitchens under a lean-to. Women were expected to undertake all of the household chores including those requiring heavy lifting. Tasks such as setting pots over the fire, washing and cleaning were all done by hand, work made more difficult by constant childbearing.

Between August 1858 and November 1863 Ephraim and Mary had four children, with all births registered in Gawler South. Only Henry Ephraim, the first child, and Thomas, the third child, survived infancy. The other infants, William and Elizabeth Ann, died within two weeks and then six months of their respective births. William's death was recorded in Gawler South while Elizabeth's death was at Gawler West, possibly indicating that Mary took baby Elizabeth home to her parents' home at Gawler River for them both to be nursed.

There were no hospitals in Gawler at that time. Private cottage hospitals provided by local nurses and doctors did not come into existence until close to the turn of the twentieth century. Births, as well as most injuries and illnesses, were instead treated at home. There were a number of medical doctors in Gawler in 1858, however giving birth was considered a natural, if hazardous, part of a woman's life, and she

Original Gawler Wesleyan Church,built 1850
Photo: J. Menhennet

Far right, Gawler Store c. 1845
From a sketch by Samuel Calvert SLSA B-9483-8

1856	SUSAN ADAMS JURY	22	
1857	JOHN FOTHERINGHAM (SON OF DAVID)	9 MTHS.	
	GEORGE T. WARD	1 YR.	8 MTHS.
1858	STEPHEN SHUTTER	10	
	ANGELINE FORBES	9 MTHS.	
1859	GEORGE JAMES GLEN	5 MTHS.	
	ELIZABETH JOHNSON THOMAS	29	
	ELIZA JANE GILBERT	1 YR.	5 MTHS.
	JAMES DAVID GILBERT	29	
1860	ENGELBRECHT ALPHONS	6	
	JOHN ROBERT GREY	5 YRS.	
	JAMES PATERSON	47	
	ISABELLA ANNE GLEN	12 MTHS.	
1861	THOMAS FORGIE	11 MTHS.	
	PATRICK FLANAGAN	32	
1862	MARY ANN McEWEN	18	
	JAMES RUSSELL	24	
1863	ELIZABETH ANN COOMBE	6 MTHS	
1864	MARY COOMBE	28	
	FREDERICK WEBB	1 YR.	4 MTHS.
	ELIZABETH ANN WEBB	19	
	JAMES RUSSELL MICHAEL	1 YR.	8 MTHS.

Pioneer Park Cairn listing early burials
Photo credit J. Menhennet

Willaston Main North Road, c. 1900

Ephraim Coombe, the father
E.H. Coombe *History of Gawler*

Phynella and Thomas Coombe
Courtesy Cynthia Beare

would be supported through the experience by other women. Twenty-one-year-old Mary could rely upon her mother Hannah, grandmother Mary, sister-in-law Elizabeth (who was a Riggs cousin and married to her brother William) and younger sisters Elizabeth and Edith, all of whom who lived at Gawler River. There was also her older sister, Harriet who was married to James Parks Woods and lived at Willaston with their son.[46]

Tragically, Mary died of 'decline' in February 1864, barely three months after her baby daughter Elizabeth's death. 'Decline' may well refer to an infection resulting from the childbirth that is known as childbirth fever or puerperal sepsis. This was the cause of high mortality rates for women of the era. With no antibiotics available to treat the infection, the mother's life ebbed away as her family stood helplessly by.

Mary, 28, had been married for six years. Her death left behind two sons, five-year-old Henry Ephraim and two-year-old Thomas. Both Mary and baby Elizabeth were buried in the original cemetery in Gawler, now known as Pioneer Park. This cemetery closed in 1870 after a decade-long community controversy over its impact on public health. Mary's burial occurred four months before the Council resolved to prohibit further burials. Thirty-six-year-old Ephraim was left a widower, with the need to continue working to support his two young boys.

Stepmother

Two years later, on 22 February 1866, Ephraim remarried. Elizabeth Tall of Willunga was single and at 46, seven years his senior. She was also Wesleyan in faith and had come to South Australia in February 1852. Their marriage took place in the Wesleyan Chapel in Brompton, Adelaide.[47] Susannah Coombe, his uncle Ephraim's first wife, signed as a witness to the marriage. The network of family and faith seems to have found a solution for a man who needed a mother for his children as well as a companion.

Elizabeth Tall was born in Plympton, a small village near Plymouth in Devon on 12 September 1819. Before her emigration she was employed by a retired naval officer as a live-in domestic servant, eventually rising to the position of cook. As a domestically skilled single woman she was among the most eagerly sought category of immigrant for that period but the conditions of her assisted passage still required that she travel under the sponsorship of a family member. This would be her paternal uncle, Samson Tall. Samson and his wife Elizabeth were pioneers of the Willunga/ McLaren Vale district, and it was at their farm that Elizabeth would reside for 14 years before her marriage to Ephraim Coombe.

The question arises as to why Elizabeth moved from the Willunga district to Gawler, a not inconsiderable distance, to marry so late in life? When Elizabeth arrived in 1852 the Talls were relatively elderly, at 61 and 62 respectively. Their adult children were Mary, 35, Sarah, 31, and Samson Junior, 22. As a 32-year-old, Elizabeth would have fitted neatly into the family unit. Samson Junior had recently married and within two years produced the first of his ten children. Elizabeth was a useful pair of hands in the shared household.

Mrs Elizabeth Tall died in February 1861 and just over a year later, in May 1862, the widowed 74-year-old Samson Tall married 67-year-old Ann Pilkington.[48] The marriage was performed by the Reverend Robert C. Flockhart. In 1863–1864 Flockhart transferred to work in the northern circuit that included Gawler, and may have had a hand in connecting Ephraim and Elizabeth, for two years later it was he who married them. The changes in the Tall family dynamics and the encouragement of her minister may have contributed to Elizabeth's decision to move north and marry Ephraim Coombe. While she was a welcomed member of the Tall household, she had no formal standing in their family. With marriage she stood to gain her own household and the opportunity to become a mother to Ephraim's two boys.

She was almost old enough to be the boys' grandmother, but Elizabeth became the only mother the boys remembered. Her new family recalled her as 'active in disposition and thoroughly devoted to the claims of her home'. Upon her death at the age of 82, at her residence in Willaston, her obituary notice, probably written by Harry, records himself and Thomas as her 'two sons', rather than, more accurately, her stepsons.[49] It is Elizabeth who shares Ephraim's grave at the Willaston Cemetery, while Mary and baby Elizabeth remained at Pioneer Park.

At the time of his second marriage Ephraim was described as a 'storeman of Gawler Town'. We know from his son's writings that Ephraim worked for James Harris at the Gawler Stores in Murray Street for a long period.[50] The general store was located where Ned's now stands, south of the National Bank.

Move to Willaston

In 1867, Ephraim became a trustee of the soon to be erected Willaston Wesleyan Methodist Church, marking the start of the Coombe family's long association with Willaston. Among the other six trustees was John Lock, Ephraim's brother-in-law.[51] Ephraim had been a Sunday school teacher and occasionally a steward at the Gawler Wesleyan Church. Within three years he was appointed a superintendent of the Sunday school that was associated with the new Willaston church.[52]

Both in 1868 and 1872, Ephraim Coombe was listed as a 'storeman at Willaston'. There were two stores operating in there: the Willaston Store (later known as the Willaston General Store) and the Willaston Grain (or Wheat) Store. Both of these were built by 1858.[53]

In 1862 Job Harris purchased the Willaston General Store from the first owner's widow, Mrs James David Gilbert.[54] It is very likely that Job Harris made the purchase with the help of his stepfather, James Davies, a lime burner of Bertha. In November 1864 Harris opened a post office within the store.

In May 1867 Job Harris gave up the Willaston General Store and Post Office to become the licensee of the Sandy Creek Hotel.[55] At the same time, he purchased the land on which the Sandy Creek Hotel stood, against which he gained a mortgage a year later, from Ephraim Coombe's Uncle Ephraim.

Some sources then have a Mr Willington taking on the running of the Willaston General Store, but the ownership of the business and the running of the post office remained firmly in the Harris/Davies family hands. Perhaps Willington was employed to run the store for them? An advertisement of the time had the company of James Davies & Co listed as the postmasters.[56] Job Harris' younger sister Hannah Harris became the postmistress until her untimely death in 1868, followed by his elder sister Ann Harris until her marriage in 1869, when his stepsister Hannah Davies took on the role. She married Thomas Henwood in 1871.[57] Thomas Henwood put the business, associated with the store and post office, up for sale in December 1874. It took nearly a year for he and Ephraim Coombe to conclude the transaction for the transfer of the business (but not the premises).[58] So, in November 1875 Ephraim became the storekeeper and postmaster of the Willaston General Store, finally purchasing the premises in 1889.[59]

The mystery existing around when Mr Willington worked in Willaston comes from a reference in Loyau's *Gawler Handbook* that did not appear in Coombe's *History of Gawler.*

Thomas Humpstone Willington, a confectioner and storekeeper in Melrose, moved south around 1867, with an Adelaide meeting of his creditors in January 1868 and the dissolution of his Melrose-based business partnership in February 1869.[60] It is likely that he was employed during this period to manage the Willaston General Store with Ephraim Coombe as the incumbent storeman. By June 1870 Willington had moved on to become the postmaster at Smithfield, where he remained until 1876, when he returned to Willaston to set up a confectionery business. As Ephraim Coombe now ran the Willaston General Store and Post Office, the confectionery business was probably located in the Willaston Store. This shop, located opposite Coombe's store, was owned by the neighbouring publican Henry Johnson.[61] Willington also took a six-year lease on the cottage north of the Coombe's store. It was when Willington was forced to sell his business in 1879, due to ill health, that E. Coombe & Son subsumed the confectionery business and the house lease, and it was into his former premises that Harry moved in 1881. A complex mix of business names, ownership and working relationships provides clues to why Ephraim's son later made no mention of Mr Willington.

Mr Willington had a secret past. He had been a convict sentenced in 1830 to seven years transportation to Van Diemen's Land. Once he gained his ticket of leave, he married and set up a business but found the stigma of his convict past socially stifling. A year after his wife died in 1851, he emigrated to South Australia where he remarried, had ten children and moved several times. He kept his past to himself, perhaps another reason for his low profile in the history books.[62]

Residences (see also Appendix A)

Ephraim and his new wife moved to Willaston from Gawler South shortly after their 1866 marriage. This is shown by his involvement in the new church and the commencement of his new job working for Thomas Henwood. The question is, where did they live?

There are three residences associated with the Willaston General Store and Post Office, all located on parts of Lot 8, which has led to difficulty in sorting out their tenancies.

One of these is a cottage that no longer exists. It was located immediately behind (or east of) the Willaston General Store and Post Office until it was destroyed in the April 1889 floods. As the flood waters rose it was reported that Ephraim had to relocate his goods from the cellar of this cottage into his new premises.[63] It is likely that Ephraim and his family lived in this cottage since 1875 and perhaps even for some years beforehand.

Another of the residences is the house located immediately to the north of the Willaston General Store and Post Office. Immediately behind (or east of) this house there is another older cottage. The two cottages were probably on the same alignment and built about the same time.

Title records indicate that the second cottage was built between 1867 and 1872 for the flamboyant and controversial businessman Orlando Adcock.[64] He was the third licensee of the Willaston Hotel and a 'racing celebrity' who successfully trained and raced horses.[65] Colonial in style, this cottage was built of local stone and rubble with a hip roof, no eaves and brick quoins. The house in front is a more substantial residence, indicative of a house built in the 1880s or 1890s.

Orlando Adcock died in 1872. In 1876, the land with cottage was leased to the shopkeeper Thomas Willington by Orlando's widow, Ann. Three years later this lease was transferred from Willington to the new storekeeper, Ephraim Coombe. In 1887 the Adcock family sold the property to John Matthews, who operated a commercial garden on the land. When Matthews sold the property in 1896 it was described as:

> two acres of garden land, on which is erected a substantial and well-built Stone House of six rooms, cellars, outhouses, coach House, stables, & ... well of good water.[66]

The successful Willaston butcher Edwin Gartrell bought the property. It is likely it was he who had assisted Matthews in having the substantial house built. He certainly had the money. He had operated his butchery business across the road from the Willaston General Store and Post Office since 1874.

The houses and land become the property of the Coombe family when Thomas Coombe bought it from Edwin Gartrell in 1909, soon after his father Ephraim's death. Thomas then named the house *Goodleigh* after Ephraim's birthplace in North Devon.[67]

It is likely that Ephraim Coombe and his small family lived in all three residences over the period of his 40 plus years' association with Willaston. However, except for the cottage that was destroyed almost as soon as he owned it, Ephraim Coombe senior did not own any of the houses he lived in.

The Willaston General Store

The Willaston General Store was located north of the second North Para Bridge, on the traffic route from the mining towns of Kapunda and Burra to Port Adelaide. This bridge, built in 1848, replaced a bridge upstream that was washed away in the 1847 flood.[68]

It is estimated that at least 100 drays a day passed through Willaston, and within a year a hotel was built on the western side.[69] This, the original Willaston Hotel, provided ample camping ground on the river flat for the bullock drays and mule teams whilst their drivers and passengers sought rest, refreshment and provisions. To meet the demand, other businesses were soon established, including a wheelwright and a blacksmith, which set up next to the hotel. Within a couple more years, a shoemaker's business began operating from buildings constructed on the opposite side of the road.[70] All these trades were essential to a hard working bullock driver or teamster. However, the type of traffic soon changed because of a road diversion. From 1850, the use of the alternate Port Wakefield route reduced the amount of mining traffic, however the growth and prosperity of the surrounding agricultural district continued to send loaded vehicles on their way to the flour mills, markets and, from 1857, to the railway junction in Gawler. The Willaston General Store and Post Office and the other neighbouring businesses were all well placed to take advantage of the busy trade route.[71]

Ephraim, with the later aid of both his two sons, Harry and Thomas, ran the Willaston General Store and Post office for 33 years. Ephraim Coombe remained in Willaston until his death, aged 80, in 1908.[72] He was buried with his second wife, Elizabeth, in the Willaston Cemetery.

Thomas continued to run the business with the aid of his sons for another 27 years after his father's death, creating a total of 60 years of the Coombe family's association with the Willaston General Store and Post Office. During that time there were various ownership name changes – E. Coombe & Son in 1879, E. & T. Coombe in 1903 and T. Coombe & Sons from 1910 to 1922.

Thomas died, aged 73, while at work in the store. His second wife, Phynella, assumed the official role of postmistress until the sale of the business six months later in September 1935.[73]

In 2009 the Willaston Post Office relocated away from the General Store and in 2019, the Willaston General Store ceased trading.

3

Birth, Growing Up, Education and Marriage

Ephraim Henry Coombe, born 26 August 1858, was the first son of Mary and Ephraim Coombe.[1] His birth certificate indicates that his mother registered him as Henry Ephraim Coombe, and he was certainly referred to in this manner in his Great Uncle Ephraim's last will and testament, dated 27 July 1869. Having two living male relatives named Ephraim, it is little wonder he was given the first name of Henry, a name that honoured both Mary's father, Henry Lock, and her maternal grandfather, Henry Riggs. Although it cannot be exactly determined when the name order change occurred, he was recorded as Ephraim Henry Coombe when he married at 21. His birth certificate was formally changed to Ephraim Henry by the District *Register* in July 1906. Throughout his life he was colloquially referred to as 'Harry Coombe' and went on to name his eldest son Harry.

Harry's birth was registered at Gawler South, as the family then lived in nearby Elizabeth Street, Bassett Town, close to his father's place of employment as a railway porter. The official plans for the townships of Gawler South and Bassett Town had been deposited in the Lands Titles Office just months before. Developed in response to the arrival of the railway and associated businesses, these subdivisions became a popular and affordable area for agricultural and industrial workers to live.

The death of Harry's mother in 1864, when he was five years old, had a lasting impact upon him. There is evidence of this when in 1909 Harry, as the editor of local newspaper, rebuked the council for the poor treatment of graves in Pioneer Park, the site of his mother's and younger sister's final resting place.[2]

Schooling

In 1866, one of the likely first tasks for his stepmother, Elizabeth, after setting up a new home in Willaston was the selection of a school for the boys.

Education in colonial South Australia was very different to today. The first *South Australian Education Act*, passed in 1851, set out to assist secular education in various ways. There were enormous challenges in creating a consistent approach to education across the fledgling colony. This included a lack of trained teachers and inadequate resources. There was also a lack of reliable transport, communication and little parental funding, especially in communities existing on subsistence level farming.[3] As a growing regional centre, Gawler was more fortunate, and a number of successful schools emerged. One of the earliest was built in the mid-1840s by Henry Calton, proprietor of the Old Spot Hotel, at the junction of Scheibener and Fotheringham terraces.[4] It was followed in 1850 by the St George's Day School created by Canon Coombs in Orleana Square on Church Hill.[5]

State aid was limited, parents were expected to pay for their children's education and there was no compulsory attendance, nor standard hours. As a result, many children attended sporadically, if at all.

It is not known at what age Harry began school. With the trauma associated with his mother's death, it is likely that he did not start until aged seven or eight, which was not uncommon at the time. Sunday schools often provided introductory reading and writing skills to young children.[6] The 1875 *South Australian Education Act* made school attendance compulsory for children aged seven to thirteen years. The same Act set school hours at four and a half hours a day.[7] Harry's schooling lasted for five years, at the most; he left school in 1869, at the age of eleven.

In 1866, a new building was erected for the expanding St George's School, now run by the popular teacher Leonard Samuel Burton. Headmaster Burton was known to be a strict disciplinarian. A focus on the three Rs, as well as personal application to duty, would have been on the curriculum. Classes were large and segregated between girls and boys.

It was here that Harry was sent to be educated, a matter that he remained proud of all his life. His father, having progressed from farm

Thomas, Ephraim, Harry and Elizabeth Coombe c. 1866
family records

Tom and Harry Coombe, school aged, c. 1868, Gawler Branch National Trust SA

Ephraim Henry (Harry) as a young man, c. 1879
family records

Harry Coombe c. 1880
family records

Sarah Coombe c 1880
family records

labourer to storeman, was keen to ensure his sons were as well educated as they could be within his financial limitations. His Wesleyan faith valued the virtue of good education. However, in fitting with the wider landscape of the time, this did not extend to a secondary or higher education. Harry had at best four or five years of formal education, but the Sunday school where his father taught, would have assisted in his early and ongoing learning.

Early Employment

After his school days ended, Harry went to work as an assistant for James Harris' Gawler Stores in Murray Street, the same establishment where his father had worked. The Gawler Stores was a large conglomeration of showrooms that included a drapery, grocery, ironmongery and other items of use to the farming community. The shop, opposite the Old Spot Hotel, had been in existence since the beginnings of Gawler.[8] Here Harry would learn the basics of running a small business, including customer service, stock ordering, display, delivery and money handling.

After a few years under Harris' watch, Harry left to join his father in the Willaston General Store and Post Office. There he may have remained but for a generous benefactor and 'an ambitious turn of mind'.[9]

In May 1879 Harry bought eight and a half acres of land north of Bertha, a northern section of Willaston, from James Davis, a lime burner of Bertha and stepfather of Job Harris. Harry now farmed his own land.

When Harry turned 21 on 26 August 1879, he came into possession of the £100 legacy from the estate of his Great Uncle Ephraim, who had died eight years earlier. The equivalent of nearly a year's wage for a grocer's assistant, this much-anticipated gift would result in him being made partner in the family's business that traded as E. Coombe & Son of Willaston, General Storekeepers and Manufacturing Confectioners.[10] (Harry's brother Thomas would receive his £100 legacy when he turned 21 in 1882.)

In December that year he ambitiously entered a colonial government funded competition for a £4,000 bonus for an improved reaping machine. He entered the design for a machine that could reap, winnow and bag wheat in one operation. Although the device had been invented by John Croft of Willaston, it was Harry who lodged the patent and entered the competition. He was among 26 competition applicants from across the colony that included the agricultural implement firms of James Martin & Co and W. Bodley & Co, both of Gawler.[11] Improved machinery trials were regularly held at Gawler and helped create enormous interest in agricultural invention.[12]

Harry didn't win the princely sum but his application showed his willingness and ability to work with both his hands and his mind. It would not have been every 21-year-old who would have the knowledge or the skills necessary to apply for a patent. John Croft had sought assistance in obtaining a patent through the Chamber of Manufactures and reports of his request had appeared in the newspapers in May 1878. Perhaps it was this advertisement that saw Ephraim and John join forces?

Marriage and Fatherhood

The next year, 1880, was to be a monumental year for Harry.

On 1 March 1880, 21-year-old Harry married 18-year-old Sarah Susannah Fraser Heywood at the Wesleyan Chapel in Pirie Street, Adelaide. The wedding was a noteworthy event, reported in at least four local newspapers.[13]

> Frazier and Fraser are names of Scottish origin and interchangeable. Sarah's parents chose the simpler spelling for their daughter. Fraser continues to be used within the Coombe family.

Sarah was born on 9 July 1861 in Footscray, Victoria, to Samuel Walter and Mary (née Frazier) Heywood. Another daughter, Mary Elizabeth, had died at 11 months in 1860. Sarah's mother Mary died on 23 December 1873 when Sarah was 12. Samuel married again two years later. He died aged 51 in 1881, a year after Sarah's marriage to Harry.[14] In the probate of his will Samuel was described as a railway employee, married to Charlotte Eliza Ryan Heywood both of Melbourne Road, Williamstown, Victoria.[15]

It appears that Charlotte and Samuel's relationship preceded the death of his wife. Birth records detail children born to Samuel Heywood and Charlotte Eliza Ryan Baldock as William Henry, born 1871, died 1873, and Kate Mary, born 1872, died 1873. Perhaps these children and Sarah's mother were all victims of the same epidemic, for smallpox, typhoid and diphtheria were rampant in Melbourne during this period. Charlotte and Samuel went on to have Charlotte Baldock Heywood, born 1875, Samuel Walter, born 1876, and Ada Eva, born 1880.

In 1879 Sarah Heywood lived with her father, stepmother and two stepsiblings with another one on the way. Was this the reason she looked to leave her home and reached out to relations interstate?

Sarah travelled from one Australian colony to another to visit her childless paternal aunt Sarah and her husband James Bright, a brick maker at Willaston.[16]

Sarah Bright, née Heywood, after whom Sarah Susannah Heywood was perhaps named, was to become a mother figure in her niece's life. They lived not far apart in Willaston and attended the same church. In 1854, the Brights relocated to the home of Sarah's brother, William Heywood at Glanville, hoping for a seaside recovery for the ailing James. After her husband's death in January 1895 Sarah returned to live in Gawler. She died in 1904 at the home of her niece.[17]

While on this visit, young Sarah met and married Harry. At 18, she was not yet legally an adult but betrothal and marriage at a young age was not uncommon. At that stage the marriageable age in the Australian colonies was set at the age of consent: 12 years old for females and 14 years old for males. Perhaps the good prospects of her young man, their similar faith background and, more pressingly, the arrival of their first child on 10 October that year, contributed to their union.[18]

Their marriage lasted 37 years and produced seven children. They were Harry Heywood (1880), James (Jim) Bright (1884), Samuel (Walt) Walter (1889), Daisy Neville (1890), Mary Lock (1892), Ernest (Ernie) John Hiscock (1895), and Catherine (Nell) Helen Spence (1898). All but Mary, who died just weeks after her first birthday, survived to adulthood.

The couple followed the family tradition of naming children after their forebears (Heywood, Bright, Lock and Neville, the latter being Sarah's paternal grandmother's maiden name). Their last two children, though, were named for people known and respected by Harry. The first, Ernest John Hiscock, was a former resident of Gawler, fellow journalist, state level cricketer and social reformer who had died tragically young at 26 in 1894.[19] The second, Catherine Helen Spence, was a high-profile South Australian social reformer who Harry had encouraged to come to speak in Gawler and surrounding towns.

Little information about Sarah is available, other than family memories of a tall, imposing woman who had a 'capable and sympathetic manner' and who worked with many charitable organisations.[20] Giving birth to seven children (over the course of 18 years), raising six of them to adulthood, and supporting Harry in his concurrent business, journalistic and political endeavours, gave her little time for many pursuits outside of the home and shop. This was consistent with the cultural expectations of women of the era.

Not that she was completely invisible. As early as 1883, when she was 21, she was asked to be one of the judges for the annual Friendly Societies' Picnic associated exhibition. Sarah was also involved in the Women's Christian Temperance Union (WCTU), established in Gawler in August 1889; the governance of and fundraising for the District Trained Nursing Service that formed in Gawler in 1894 just a year after its commencement in the city; the Adelaide Children's Hospital Gawler Cot Committee, established in 1899; and in 1911 she became a member of the Hutchinson Hospital Board of Management.[21]

Harry was also involved in these organisations, but with society's acceptance of women's growing independence, Sarah became interested in many social and political matters of the day.[22] Given that one of the WCTU special areas of interest was 'Hygiene and Influencing the Press', Sarah would have been well placed to contribute.

Another WCTU area of interest, 'Legislation and Franchise', addressed the matter of women's suffrage. When the superintendent of the South Australian WCTU division, Elizabeth Webb Nicholls, spoke to large crowds on the matter in the Gawler Institute in 1889, 1890 and 1892, Sarah accompanied Harry to these gatherings.[23]

Elizabeth Webb Nicholls visited the town again in 1896 where she spoke to the Barossa Temperance Electoral Committee. She revisited many times during that election year and her name and cause became the focus of ridicule by one of the election candidates, Paris Nesbit.[24] 'A woman was out of place cackling and strutting about the place attending these woman's unions ... It was not for Mrs. Nicholls to say whether he should have a glass of wine.'

Elizabeth Webb Nicholls returned to Gawler in 1898 to attend the week-long Tenth Annual South Australian WCTU Convention, held in the town and attended by over 70 visiting women. Harry was invited to speak on gambling at the convention.[25]

Sarah's public appearances increased as her husband's political aspirations grew and the campaign for the emancipation of women evolved. She often accompanied Harry when he addressed campaign meetings for newly enfranchised women voters.

She was granted the privilege of christening the new Gawler Bridge when it was opened in January 1908 by the Governor, Sir George Le Hunte. The bridge was built from iron and steel by Gawler's James Martin & Co had been a major achievement for her now parliamentarian husband.[26]

In November 1909, Sarah opened the Good Samaritan's Convent Catholic Bazaar in the Institute in her husband's place. She did so again in October 1916.[27]

On several occasions Harry spoke appreciatively of his wife's contributions to his career. In 1914 he publicly acknowledged that half of the credit for what he had achieved should be directed to her for her cooperation and assistance.

E. Coombe & Son of Willaston, General Storekeepers and Manufacturing Confectioners

For the first three decades, most of the colony's industry was focused on the growing and exporting of raw materials, but from the 1870s these raw materials were turned into produce for local consumption, fostering an increase in wages and the general prosperity of the population.[28]

With more than two thousand residents in 1880, Gawler had many service industries. Foodstuff and beverage manufacturing through baking, confectionery, brewing and cordial making as well as the production of building materials by brickmaking and lime burning were all prominent.[29] The businesses were intrinsically linked, both commercially and socially, often through extended family ownership.

In 1880 there were three flour mills in Gawler, employing 65 people between them. The mills diversified their trade to include the sprouting of grain to produce starch and glucose for sale, the ingredients needed for a confectioner's business.[30]

Confectionery making may seem at odds with the rest of the retail business E. Coombe & Son were conducting. However, when Ephraim, aged 47, and his wife Elizabeth, 55, progressed from storeman to storekeeper of the Willaston General Store and Post Office in 1875, their sons were 17 and 14 years of age. As parents they sought ways to secure their sons' future by generating more income to both finalise the purchase of their business, achieved in 1889, and provide a role for the young men within the business.

Harry had spent the years since he left school learning the grocery trade from his father's former employer, while Thomas learned the trade of wheelwright from John Allen of Gawler.[31] Thus, Ephraim and Elizabeth ensured one son was trained ready to work in the store and the other was able to earn his own wage as well as help repair the delivery vehicles used by the business.

In 1879 they decided to extend their business by taking on their former neighbour's food manufacturing operation. George E. Loyau described the expanded business in his Gawler Handbook:

> Messrs. E. Coombe & Son combine with the business of storekeepers that of manufacturing confectionery. Their goods enjoy a good reputation in the country, and they supply Gawler, Angaston, Kapunda and surrounding districts. The establishment, if not pretentious, is compact and neat. The articles used in their business are of first quality, and the chemicals which produce the orders of a harmless quality. The business was formerly in the hands of Mr. Willington. Since passing onto the possession of the present proprietors the trade has materially increased.[32]

Where had the idea and skills for taking on this new enterprise come from? We may recall that Harry's stepmother Elizabeth Coombe emigrated as a cook from the household of a retired naval officer in Devon.

Cookbooks of the day described confections as a 'grace note to any table, indispensable to those who meant to entertain handsomely'. Initially seen as an activity to be undertaken by female domestic servants, confectionery was then taken up by women wanting to start a home business.[33] It was one of a narrow range of socially sanctioned ways for a woman to make money. This is borne out by the fact that five of the seven confectioners mentioned in the 1908 *History of Gawler* were women, most of whom had operated their businesses for many years.[34]

The term confectionery covered a very wide range of products including cordials, comfits, sweetmeats, preserves, preserved fruits, compotes, fruit jellies and jams, brandy fruits, marmalades and fruit pastes, candy and rock works, boiled sugar and caramel work, drops, biscuits, wafers, creams and ices, syrups and cooling drinks, liqueurs and ornament making.[35]

Gawler's Mediterranean climate was conducive to the growing of a range of citrus and stone fruits as well as figs and grapes. Most early colonists grew a great variety of fruit and vegetables in their home gardens, since the distance to travel to markets made it a practical necessity.[36]

For the new confectioners, what couldn't be sourced locally could be easily obtained from outlying areas. Home delivery of shop products and the practise of bartering or accepting goods in exchange meant that Elizabeth had a ready source of ingredients and was well placed to guide the family business toward meeting the demand for readily stored and transportable confectionery items.

Branching out into the confectionery business, or perhaps the new partnership, didn't go to plan. On 5 February 1881 E. Coombe & Son advertised in the *Gawler Standard* for the sale of a confectionery plant and an advertisement also appeared for the sale of Harry's land at Bertha.[37]

The business obviously was in transition. At a meeting of creditors held in Adelaide on 7 February 1881, it was clearly indicated the assets of the business exceeded the liabilities (assets £947, liabilities £796 7s 6d).[38] This would allow the business to trade out of its problems if assets were sold off. And sure enough, another advertisement appeared in the city press on 12 February for the stock of a general store and confectioner plant indicating that tenders would close a week later. An assignment notice (a term used in contract and property law to indicate the intent to transfer rights) then appeared in the *Register* newspaper on 15 February for Ephraim Coombe and Harry Coombe, trading as E. Coombe & Son, of Willaston, storekeepers.[39]

On 25 February there was another sale under the name of E. Coombe & Son, this time for two horses, farming equipment including a reaping machine, household furniture and eight tons of hay.[40]

The strategy worked. On 26 February 1881, E. Coombe, without the term '& Son', advertised that their business had reopened almost immediately opposite the Willaston Store and Post Office in the property next to the original Willaston Hotel.[41] This shop, once known as the Willaston Grain Store, was now owned by the widowed Mrs Johnson. She had let the property and moved to Adelaide.[42] This was where Thomas Humpstone Willington had run his confectionery business from circa 1876–1879.

Within a period of three weeks one business was wound up and a new one started. It is hard at this distance to understand exactly what had happened, but it was likely an early version of the process of going into voluntary administration to finalise the trading of a business. Such a decision provided an opportunity for Harry and his wife, Sarah to start a separate business while Ephraim and Elizabeth continued running the Willaston Store and Post Office.[43] Street directories of the time continue to list E. Coombe & Son as trading until 1885, after which E. Coombe, storekeeper and postmaster in Willaston, was listed separately.[44]

This second confectionery venture was also short lived with another assignment notice appearing just 18 months later in August 1882, followed in January 1883 by a creditors' notice for the estate of E. Coombe & Son.[45] The estate was wound up in May 1883 with creditors being paid out with a second dividend of just over a shilling in the pound.[46] Interestingly, this time the advertisements did not appear in the local Gawler press. The part payment of creditors indicates a less healthy financial situation than at the first winding up. However, as the business name of E. Coombe & Son continued to be advertised it appears that again the business was permitted to trade its way out of debt and restructure for a third time.

This bumpy time in their business ventures matches the general economic situation experienced by the colony. The drought between 1880–1884, coming after a run of exceptionally good seasons, saw many farmers unable to meet their commitments and the government was obliged to allow them to surrender their holdings and select land in other areas, or convert their credit land purchase agreements to leases. The flow on effect to local businesses must have been equally difficult. This might explain why little public fuss was made of the fluctuating fortunes of E. Coombe & Son.

E.H. Coombe Confectioner with Murray Street National Australia Bank,
Gawler next door c. 1884
Gawler History Team Deland collection

E.H. Coombe, Confectioner

By January 1884 Harry was running a wholesale and retail confectionery outlet at 296c Murray Street, Gawler. This property, emblazoned 'E.H. Coombe, Confectioner', was located on the western side of the main street, opposite the Town Hall and just north of the recently built (in 1881 or 1882) National Bank. James Harris' Gawler Stores, where both he and his father had worked, was located on the other side of the National Bank.[47]

Harry was putting into practice all he had learned about the retail trade including its ups and downs. He took a series of calculated risks of moving out onto his own into an industry that relied upon better economic times and then relocating the business into the main street of Gawler. His choices proved wise: the new location proved busier than the Willaston location, something he may have known from his experience working just a few doors down.

Adult Learning

Harry was probably assisted in the confectionery business by his wife, Sarah, who had been trained by her mother-in-law, Elizabeth.

His wife's support meant that it was during this period that Harry became proficient in shorthand, despite the time demands of the business and a growing family. This ability to record the spoken word verbatim in a series of altered characters and symbols is a skill used by reporters in the media, court and parliament both then and today.

He was already familiar with another encoded system of communication, that of Morse code. Part of the knowledge that young Harry acquired while working with his father in the Post Office, was a thorough understanding of the role that the telegraph system played in the reporting and receiving news. The completion of the Overland Telegraph Line in 1872 linked Adelaide direct with London, via a submarine cable between Darwin and Java. This gave Adelaide and Gawler (through which the telegraph line passed) an Australian monopoly, being the place where overseas news arrived first. Access to overseas news revolutionised newspaper reporting, in a time when the gathering and printing of daily news was highly competitive.[48]

Harry learned shorthand and typewriting at adult education classes provided by the Gawler Institute, conveniently located just across the main road from his confectionery business.[49] This he later confirmed in an autobiographical speech recorded in the Institutes' Association Journal. 'He ... left school when he was 11 years of age and had to thank the facilities offered by a well equipped institute for much of his education.'

The Gawler Institute owed its formation to the work of local business leaders and the educated Germans at the nearby settlement of Buchsfelde. After an inaugural meeting in July 1848, the Gawler Institute was finally formed in October 1857, just ten months before Harry's birth.[50] Established in 1857, the Gawler Institute provided a raft of cultural and educative services to Gawler and its regional community.

Harry was not alone in the pursuit of an adult education. Sir Henry Parkes, Dame Nellie Melba, Henry Lawson, Joseph Furphy (Tom Collins), Edmund Barton, Billy Hughes, Ben Chifley and Sir Robert Menzies all used Mechanics Institutes to further their education. Aimed at popularising science and providing a medium for educating skilled workers, then known as artisans or mechanics, it was part of a workingmen's movement rooted in the socialist developments of the nineteenth century. However, as historian Denise Schumann outlines:

> The Gawler Institute was not merely established like other 'Mechanics Institutes' for the self-improvement of the working classes. The Gawler Institute and its operations reflected the aspirations of a unique group of educated free settlers whose constituency was unlike any other group at that time in Australia. Their object was to satisfy intellectual pursuits regarding the arts, philosophy and the pursuit of science.[51]

The Gawler Institute also provided a library of several thousand volumes, as well as a range of other cultural pursuits that was just the thing for an ambitious young man looking to further himself. Leonard Samuel Burton, Harry's schoolmaster, was the treasurer of the Institute Committee for many years, and it is very likely that he encouraged his former student to continue his education by these means. Later in life, Harry returned the favour by teaching classes in shorthand and typewriting at the Gawler Institute from 1894–1902.[52] He would also act as the secretary to the Burton and Warren memorial committee upon their untimely deaths in 1895.[53]

Journalism

With access to this form of self-improvement, and perhaps by practising in the evenings or when trade in his shop was quiet, Harry acquired new skills. And it paid off. In February 1888, whilst still conducting his confectionery business, he was appointed as the local correspondent to the *Register*, one of the major daily Adelaide newspapers of the time.[54] This was quite an achievement for a young businessman, husband and father of two young children. He was well on his way to earning his reputation as a self-made man.

Newspaper correspondents were outsourced as community-based reporters of local interest stories. Gawler was an important regional centre relatively close to Adelaide and with a reliable train and telegraph service connection. The town boasted many cultural, sporting and benevolent societies. The institute provided a venue for many local and travelling entertainments and the local police court provided a steady stream of news. As a main street trader, Harry was well positioned to keep in touch with the activities of local commerce and the town hall. He also had useful familial connections through his Lock, Riggs, Pope, Woods and Bright relations.

Harry would have been paid on a piecemeal basis, probably at a rate per published word. Having shorthand skills meant that he could gather information efficiently, edit it and then submit it via telegraph, daily post or, with the February 1889 arrival of the telephone link between Adelaide and Gawler, by phoning it through. Until then telegraph was the quickest medium and the transmission of long messages was not uncommon. Eight to ten thousand word reports were regularly sent overseas by newspapers; the *Argus* reportedly once sent a twenty thousand-word piece. The use of telegraph also helped increase the number, regularity and circulation of South Australian newspapers and reduced their price.

Harry's reporting would not have paid enough to support the family but the two roles, shop owner and correspondent, would have complemented each other. (Interestingly it was claimed that at one stage he was offered a position on the *Register*'s literary staff but he 'preferred to make a pecuniary sacrifice than limit his usefulness in Gawler'.[55]) Time management became even more critical when he was also appointed as a Hansard reporter for the same newspaper, a role that meant catching the train to attend parliamentary sessions. His education continued as he became immersed in political and parliamentary intrigue.

Hansard, the record of parliamentary debate, commenced with the beginning of the South Australian parliament in 1857. For the first fifty years Hansard reporting was contracted to the Adelaide newspapers. In 1907 a Government Reporting Division took on the responsibility. Only in 1987 did Hansard reporting move under the control of parliament.[56]

Today's requirements for a Hansard reporter provide insight into Harry's skills: an ability to transcribe and edit to a specified standard in an efficient manner; superior knowledge of English grammar, syntax and usage; an ability to communicate clearly and effectively, both orally and in writing; the capacity to work long and irregular hours during parliamentary sessions; a successful record of working under pressure to meet exacting deadlines; an ability to adapt quickly to changing circumstances and to schedule work, whilst maintaining work performance and output; an understanding of the practices and procedures of the Westminster system of parliamentary democracy as practised by the Parliament of South Australia; and a comprehensive working knowledge of South Australian and Australian politics, current affairs and a wide general knowledge.[57]

Livelihood diversification to ensure multiple sources of income was common during this period but for Harry, something had to go. He and Sarah gradually withdrew from their small business responsibility. The last published advertisement of the E.H. Coombe confectionery business appeared in December 1886, and we know that the family relocated to Finniss Street by 1892.[58] There was no public notice of the sale of the business nor its contents, however in January 1892 the *Bunyip* advertised that the Misses Roney had opened confectionery and coffee rooms across the road in Murray Street, and at about the same time a Mrs Wilson had set up a confectionery business opposite the Gawler Stores, in the vicinity of the Old Spot Hotel.[59] It is entirely possible that he sold the ladies the confectionery equipment, allowing Sarah more time to care for the young children and him more time to concentrate on his journalistic responsibilities. Harry had transitioned from a shopkeeper to a person who earned his living from his writing.

In 1894 his younger brother, Thomas, left his job at James Martin & Co to join their father in running the Willaston General Store and Post Office. The family partnership of E. Coombe & Son re-emerged.

Thomas Coombe was also educated at L.S. Burton's school. He then trained as a wheelwright with fellow Wesleyan, John Allen, before working for James Martin & Co. His departure from the engineering business coincided with the onset of a colony-wide economic depression that resulted in cancelled orders for rolling stock and a subsequent large reduction in staff. This was a fortuitous time for Thomas to change trades to join the family storekeeping business. After his father's death the business would become Thomas Coombe & Sons.[61]

Well, almost, because in July 1891 he took on the role of auditor for the District Council of Mudla Wirra South, a paid position that he held for two years.[60] Maybe the costs of a steadily increasing family (four by this stage) was having an impact.

Gawler had its own local newspaper, the *Bunyip*, owned by the Barnet family with offices located in Murray Street. In July 1890, just two years after his first journalistic role, Harry took over the editorship of the *Bunyip*, a role he would hold for nearly 25 years.[62]

At the age of 32, Harry was now a businessman, a city newspaper correspondent and Hansard reporter, and the editor of the local newspaper. He was to take on another role, one that would take the last decade of the century to achieve, but more of that in another chapter.

4

Journalism and Writing

By 1890, Harry had become well known for his articles in the *Register* based on the political news emanating from North Terrace.

He was familiar with the process of writing descriptively, concisely and to a deadline, having come under the mentorship of the *Register*'s sub-editor, Charles John Stevens, who became the Leader of the Reporting Staff and ultimately the Associate Editor.[1] Ambitious Harry felt he had the professional experience to take on the responsibility for the entire production of a weekly broadsheet.

Five years later Harry would invite his mentor to submit a weekly column as an Adelaide based correspondent to the *Bunyip* under the pseudonym of 'Cit'. This contribution continued for 22 years, long after Stevens retired from daily journalism to live a semi-rural life at Enfield where he established a literary society and continued his Masonic membership, other areas of common interest with Harry.

Harry was also well connected in his own community. As a representative of the press, he had attended the first annual meeting of the Gawler Branch of the Amalgamated Society of Engineers at the institute in January 1890. An event that attracted over 100 men, including such notables as Sir John Downer, the Honourable James Martin, Mayor John Jones, Frederick and Albert May, and David Thomson, he described it as 'a red letter day [when] … masters and employees met together to hold a sociable evening [with] three [engineering] firms represented there that night'.[2]

Harry played chess with the mayor and became a committee member of the Gawler Institute.[3] He associated with influential people beyond Gawler, people like George Frederick Hussey, a city baker and confectioner, who later became a printer and politician and with whom he shared an interest in literary societies, cricket, chess and institutes.[4]

Politically, Harry grew increasingly active, becoming the Secretary of the Friends and Supporters for the candidacy of George Berry for the Barossa in the 1890 election. Reverend Berry, formerly of Angaston but now of Burnside, was unsuccessful, losing to James Hague of Robertstown and the incumbent, Sir John Downer; an experience from which Harry no doubt learned.[5]

He provided his assistance to a council subcommittee that included the former mayor, and now Member of the Legislative Assembly, James Martin. Formed to investigate a Barossa Water Scheme, the committee launched a major lobbying campaign that resulted in the construction of the Barossa reservoir to supply Gawler with much needed water from 1902.[6] In September he was on hand to report on a public meeting in Gawler regarding a union strike that was addressed by the same James Martin.[7]

With his change of occupation and increased status, the family of six relocated from the cramped premises behind the confectionery shop in Murray Street, to Finniss Street. This was a four-roomed house previously owned by his maternal grandfather, Henry Lock, who had died, aged 80, in May 1891. On Henry's death the property transferred initially to William Riggs and then to his daughter Amelia Louisa Riggs, Harry's second cousin. It was from Amelia that Harry and Sarah rented the house that was within walking distance of his work.[8]

Their next two children, Mary and Ernest, were born in this house. Mary Lock Coombe was born on 23 September 1892, the same day as her cousin Arthur Whicker Lock Coombe, the son of Thomas and Lucy Coombe.[9] Tragically, both children died a year later of 'whooping cough, bronchitis and congestion of the brain' and 'whooping cough, teething and diarrhoea' respectively. While whooping cough is a highly infectious, airborne respiratory disease currently treated by antibiotics and prevented by vaccination, little could be done in the 1890s.[10] Their deaths in October and November 1893 were poignantly recorded in the *Bunyip* newspaper by Harry.[11]

The *Bunyip*

What did the editorship of the *Bunyip* involve?

The *Bunyip* newspaper covered a large economically productive region that included Gawler, the Adelaide Plains, the Barossa Valley and beyond. After the short-lived *Northern Star* produced in Kapunda from 1860–1863, it was the earliest newspaper in the area.[12]

Its originating body, the Humbug Society, was founded in 1859 on an impulse by Jefferson Stow and George Isaacs. Their belief was that there was too much pomposity and 'stuffiness' in the town and it needed to be addressed. The club gained notoriety, not only in Gawler but in the wider public arena. The society's favourite meeting place was the Globe Hotel (now the Kingsford) and meetings were decidedly entertaining. One of the rules stated:

> That any member guilty of puppyism, hawhawing, murdering the Queen's English, or any conduct unbecoming a gentleman, be summarily expelled from the Society, and as a mark of contempt, be elected a member of Parliament on the first vacancy occurring.[13]

Within four years the society generated its own newspaper which they called the *Bunyip*. Intended as a satirical monthly publication, it was produced by a Scotsman named William Barnet, who ran his own printing business in Murray Street. The first editor was Dr George Nott, a man who, with a lively mind and an acute sense of humour, made the *Bunyip* 'sparkle'.[14] The first issue resulted in a libel case, also irreverently reported. William Home Popham, a local doctor who had set up a hospital in the town, felt he had been mocked for his enthusiastic advertising of his new venture. Jefferson Stow appeared for the defence in a trial marked by much laughter. The jury found for the plaintiff, awarding damages of just one shilling.

Within three years, the business was a financial success. By January 1866 the *Bunyip* had evolved into a weekly newspaper and had had no trouble in attracting good editors. After George Nott, there was a run of prominent early South Australian journalists, including Edward Lindley Grundy, George Isaacs and George Loyau.[15]

From 1885 Henry John 'Harry' Congreve became the editor after the merger of the short-lived Gawler *Standard* with the *Bunyip*.[16] The *Bunyip* then became the first South Australian country newspaper to sell at the low price of one penny per issue. But in July 1890, 61-year-old Congreve resigned due to poor health, and William Barnet appointed the much younger Harry as editor.

William Barnet himself died unexpectedly at 60, just five years later. His wife Hannah became the proprietor and she made their son, Robert, manager.[17] Robert had been apprenticed, at the age of 13, to the printing office and four years later, in 1885, became foreman. He was ten years younger than Harry.

It is hard to say how much editorial interference the Barnet family imposed on Harry, but the traditional model was for the proprietor to set the tone of the newspaper and outline to the editor what was required of them. Harry would then control the written content of the newspaper while Robert, as manager, would oversee the commercial management including the advertising, marketing, printing and distribution of the newspaper and the business's other printed material. Both reported to Hannah as the proprietor. This situation was to remain stable for the next 19 years, suggesting a good working relationship was soon established.

What mandate was the editor given? Like all country newspapers there was a requirement to relentlessly promote the district's advancement.[18] As the business owners, the Barnets were obviously invested in encouraging development and prosperity in the communities they served. Yet from the start both William and Hannah supported a genuine radicalism in thinking and encouraged their editors to promote a range of socially progressive literary and political causes as well as celebrate the literary arts, self-education and community contribution.

The post 1875 expansion of elementary education meant that the *Bunyip* had a large audience of readers. Initially, they were provided with editorials, reprinted political events and speeches, and excerpts from novels and poetry, sometimes written by the editor. (Nott, Isaacs and Loyau were all published poets.) By Harry's time, this was supplemented with detailed reports of local events, politics, correspondence, court reporting, sports, games and public entertainments. All added to the developing sense of community in the town. Even the advertising section expanded beyond farming and business requirements to include items of interest for women readers.

Left: William and Hannah Barnet, and *right:* Robert Barnet
History of Gawler

W. Barnet, Printer, Lot 10 Murray Street, Gawler

The fourth site of the *Bunyip* Printing Office, and its present location

Physically the *Bunyip* office consisted of a:

> front shop fitted up for carrying on the business of bookseller and stationer, a large back room, the composing-room, the *Bunyip* press-room, and two jobbing rooms behind. Underneath the shop and the press-room was a large cellar which was used for jobbing ... there were five presses used in the establishment.[19]

In February 1885 these premises burnt down and the business was re-established on the other side of Murray Street, next to its present location.

> William Barnet operated from four separate premises along Murray Street. The first, at 6 Murray Street (where the BP Service Station now stands), was a small printing shop. The second was at number 14, the corner of Walker and Murray Street. The third, the one that burnt down, was at number 197. The destruction caused by the fire necessitated a fourth move to number 118, immediately adjacent to today's *Bunyip* premises at 120–122 Murray Street, Gawler. The final relocation was made in about 1915 by the descendant family of William and Hannah Barnet.[20]

To determine how many staff were employed, the mention of five presses provides a clue. In 1840, when the *Register* was running five printing presses, it employed a staff of 21: an editor, ten compositors (type was then set by hand one letter at a time), three pressmen, two binders, a collector, a clerk, a deliveryman and two boys as runners. By the 1880s the city newspaper, the *Register*, had moved to automatic typesetting and printing presses presumably with fewer staff.[21] However, we know that the *Bunyip* still used a hand printing Albion Press well into the twentieth century. The two-storey *Bunyip* office would have been filled with a lot of people and when the presses, located on the ground floor, ran it would have been very noisy.

As editor, Harry was the predominant writer and news gatherer but he engaged others to contribute too. From the by-lines we can see that he supported an active group of journalists and correspondents who shared and supplied the colony's newspapers with written copy.

In a biographical piece for the *Register*, Harry was described as having 'considerably added to its [the *Bunyip*'s] vitality and popularity'.[22] Many years later he was again portrayed as having 'added very considerably to the value of what was then the most influential paper published outside the metropolitan area.'[23]

It was a time of much social change including women's suffrage and discussion around federation.

Women's Suffrage

Harry's initial reporting of the case for women's suffrage was highly suspicious of early attempts to link it to property ownership, and in 1890 he reflected the tone of the period:

> We are far from saying that a woman is incapable of exercising her franchise, and it would be sad indeed if she did not attain to the average ability displayed by the majority of the stronger sex in these matters. That her influence might be exerted for good occasionally we do not question for a moment, but can she not be accomplishing a greater good elsewhere than in the polluted atmosphere of the political arena? We have a very high appreciation of the graces and abilities of womanhood and think it would be calamitous to society if she were to descend from her more exalted pedestal and become amenable to the relatively degrading influence of political life.[24]

However, under the influence of the likes of Mary Lee, Catherine Helen Spence and the Women's Temperance League, he changed his position to one of strong support. We can find Harry's father, Ephraim Coombe, as one of over 10,600 South Australians who signed the 1894 Women's Suffrage Petition in favour of women's suffrage.[25]

> The Women's Temperance League's grounding in a Protestant Evangelical Christianity provided its members with the determination and skills for their campaigns. Many women of middle and lower middle class background were dissatisfied with the limitations of their parish work and the Women's Temperance League and the Women's Christian Temperance Union offered new possibilities for women to engage in public life and social reform.[26]

Adelaide Federation Conference, 1898

When the Adelaide Federation Conference was held in 1898, Harry was the only country journalist to cover the proceedings. His experience as a Hansard reporter meant that he was well versed in politics, and was a swift and accurate exponent of shorthand. He was familiar with the background to federation, having reported on the case since the first Australian Federation Convention was held in 1890. It was a topic that he had actively debated as a participant in the Gawler Literary Society.[27]

Besides his continuing editorial and correspondent roles, Harry branched out into other publications.

The *South Australian Institutes' Journal*

From 1904 to 1907 Harry edited the *South Australian Institutes' Journal*, the monthly publication produced by the South Australian Institutes Association. This organisation was formed in January 1899 as a result of a long-standing dispute about the erosion of the centralised system of support for the institutes in South Australia.[28]

Since self-government in 1856, the country Institutes had received a range of services including bulk purchasing, circulation of books via travelling boxes, monetary subsidies for supplementing lecturers' fees and other expenses. These were to replicate what was provided to city residents from the South Australian Institute on North Terrace. The central Board of Governors often clashed with local Institute committees with dissension commonly led by the larger Institutes of Port Adelaide, Gawler and Kapunda. Astute lobbying then resulted in the dispute being taken up by parliamentarians who were ultimately responsible for the budget allocation for the annual grant. In July 1888 a parliamentary committee was formed to oversee the interests of country institutes.

Among the first members of this parliamentary committee were Thomas Burgoyne, MP, who became the committee's chairperson and James Martin, MLC, president of the Gawler Institute. The Honorary Secretary to this committee was Arthur Rose who was later replaced by Frederick Edward Meleng. Rose and Meleng were the first and second librarians at the Port Adelaide Institute who used their position to continue to campaign vigorously for continuing subsidies for country institutes.

In 1898 the committee recommended the establishment of an Institutes Association to better represent the suburban and country institutes. A convention of Institute representatives was held and an interim committee of five was elected that included Thomas Burgoyne and Harry, now president of the Gawler Institute. When the association was formalised in March 1899, Burgoyne became president and Harry one of two vice-presidents, with Meleng elected as general secretary and treasurer. The association supported the reappointment of the parliamentary committee that had proved such a useful lobby group.

The *South Australian Institutes' Journal* was first published in August 1900, edited by Thomas Burgoyne, with the aim of keeping member institutes informed of association news and providing other matter of general literary interest. Harry took over as editor in July 1904 and focused more on the institute matters by actively soliciting contributions from institute committees. Both men worked with the dedicated and very successful business manager Meleng who raised revenue through advertising and subscriptions.

History of Gawler

But Harry's magnum opus was the 1908 *History of Gawler.* There had been earlier histories of the town: the first preceded the publishing of the *Bunyip* and was entitled *A Short Sketch of the Rise and Progress of Gawler.* Written by Dr George Nott, it accompanied *A General and Commercial Directory for Gawler* that was published, both in 1860 and in 1861, by William Barnet of Murray Street, Gawler. It described itself as 'a concise, authentic, and very readable account of the history of the town from the laying out of the Gawler special survey in 1839 until the stirring times of 1860'.

The second history, *The Handbook of Gawler: a record of the rise and progress of that important town, to which are added memoirs of McKinlay the explorer and Dr. Nott,* was written in 1880 by George Ettienne Loyau, editor of the *Bunyip* from 1878–1879. By including Dr Nott's earlier history, a span of 41 years of the town's history was achieved.

The catalyst for Harry's history book came from the approaching 50th anniversary of the Gawler Institute and a fundraising scheme created by F.E. Meleng to supplement the income of the *South Australian Institutes' Journal.*

The first issues of that journal carried a series of profiles of individual institutes and the personalities associated with them. With an eye for economy, Meleng charged the institutes for these articles and offered them a copy of the accompanying photographic portrait to keep. The journal was then able to reuse the material in many ways.

To celebrate the 50th anniversary of his own Institute in July 1901, Meleng offered the committee the opportunity to use the Port Adelaide Institute article to add to the Institute's proposed new supplementary catalogue. In this way the Institute Committee could produce a celebratory book.

When *Fifty Years of the Port Adelaide Institute* was released in 1902 it was described as a:

> curious melange of articles and photographs of the Port, prominent Portonians, the Institute and its work, together with the supplementary catalogue and more than twenty pages of advertising. Some articles had been written specifically, but others were reused from the *South Australian Institutes Journal* or newspapers.[29]

By January 1903, Meleng was able to report successfully to the Port Adelaide Institute Committee on publication costs and a steady sale rate.

Other communities took up the idea, with the Town of Kensington and Norwood Council producing its own *Fifty Years' History* in 1903 to celebrate its jubilee.[30] Two years later Thomas Gill produced *The history and topography of Glen Osmond* for the Glen Osmond Institute.[31]

Harry knew Thomas Gill well. He was a fellow governor of the Public Library, Museum and Art Gallery of South Australia. Gill was also a member of the Library Association of Australasia and for its 100th meeting, he wrote a paper entitled 'A few notes respecting the statistics of suburban and country Institutes of South Australia', which of course included information sourced from the *South Australian Institutes' Journal*.

Harry's decision to compile a history was also influenced by the journalist Henry Thomas Burgess, the editor of the two volume *Cyclopedia of South Australia*, published in 1907 and 1909. This publication was also a compilation of articles, photographs and advertisements. While individual contributors were not acknowledged, Harry's style is recognisable in the three articles written about himself as a parliamentarian, the South

Australian Literary Societies' Union and the town of Gawler and its prominent citizens. In researching and writing these articles Harry was already preparing material for his own publication.[32]

> Henry Thomas Burgess was 19 years older than Harry and came from a similar family mercantile background. At the age of 20 he became a travelling Wesleyan minister. His country circuits included both Willunga and Gawler so it is likely that Burgess knew the Coombe family from this time. He supplemented his stipend by prolifically writing for the daily press, contributing to many Australian and American periodicals, and editing the local Methodist paper.[33]

Harry had already written the profile of the Gawler Institute for the 12th issue of the *South Australian Institutes' Journal* in July 1901, so the seeds for the creation of a Gawler history publication were sown. As the *Bunyip* editor he had the means for collecting information and he had a proven model for charging a fee to those whose portraits and advertisements would be included.[34] He even had a willing assistant, Miss Ray Matilda Trigar, a former star shorthand pupil who had taken over teaching Harry's institute classes.[35]

The jubilee of the Gawler Institute was to be celebrated in 1907, and despite the town experiencing a marked economic downturn with financial problems at the Martin's factory, there was still plenty of enthusiasm to celebrate the event.

> After 1900 demand for mining machinery lessened and the government railway workshops took business away from Gawler. Agricultural expansion outside Gawler's hinterland widened the market for agricultural machinery and competition became keener with many more manufacturers appearing. In 1907 Martin & Co. went into liquidation.[36]

At the January 1906 Gawler Institute committee meeting, Harry raised the idea of collecting photographs that could be used to illustrate a future history of Gawler. He duly reported the concept in the *Bunyip* and the *South Australian Institutes' Journal,* as a way that country institutes could prepare and preserve historical records for their respective towns.[37]

Next, Harry introduced the idea of a jubilee celebration to the institute committee at their March meeting and again reported on it in the *South Australian Institutes' Journal*.[38]

By the April meeting, Harry proposed that the celebration have three main goals: firstly, the issuing of a history of Gawler; secondly, the increase of the Institute's membership by 100; and finally, the addition of £100 worth of literature to the Gawler Institute reference library. This amount was to be raised by conducting multiple events – a jubilee demonstration at the town's recreation ground: a *conversazione* (a scholarly social gathering held for the discussion of literature and the arts) and a jubilee social, both to be held in the Institute Hall. There was unanimous agreement to his proposal and a subcommittee was formed.[39]

By May 1906, both the historical photographic collection and the planning for the jubilee celebrations were well underway. The Gawler Institute committee formally asked Harry to undertake the compilation of the history of Gawler. He would be supported by a business sub-committee. Four more subcommittees would organise the other celebratory events. Harry again reported this outcome in the *South Australian Institutes' Journal*:

> Gawler has adopted a comprehensive scheme to celebrate its jubilee next year. The art of setting ourselves a task and making ourselves do it is a valuable one, both for discipline and development.[40]

The project received a major boost when, early in 1907, the Gawler Council joined the show. The municipality's jubilee coincided with the Institute's and a combined celebration was felt appropriate.

The *History of Gawler* took longer than expected to produce. It was finally published in mid-1910, three years after the jubilee year.[41] However, there was great excitement and anticipation of its publication. An article in a July 1910 issue of the *Bunyip* (probably written by Harry), describes the history, its purpose and its layout in glowing terms:

> It was stressed that despite the Institute covering the cost of publishing the publication was not a net cost to the Institute but instead, and as was planned, it raised a surplus which was to be devoted to the strengthening of the Institute's reference library. The book consisted of upwards

> of 450 pages, capitally printed on art paper, and including 148 pages of splendidly reproduced photographs, including likenesses of pioneers, past and present residents and a few scenes. It was available in cloth bound at 5 shillings and cardboard bound at 3 shillings both at The *Bunyip* Office and in the city.[42]

Reports of copies being bought and sent to families overseas appeared as part of the *Bunyip*'s marketing campaign. Sections were reproduced in other newspapers, and advertisements and reviews were similarly distributed.[43]

Presentation copies were made to Thomas Burgoyne, MP, as the president and F.E. Meleng as the secretary of the South Australian Institutes Association.[44]

Six months after the book's release Harry received a lengthy letter from Mrs Eliza Sarah Mahony, née Reid, widow of the late Dr David Mahony, who now resided in England. While she was very interested in the book and admired its accuracy and coverage, she took him to task for not mentioning the role that her family played in the history of Gawler. This she outlined in some 1,400 words, which Harry faithfully reproduced in December 1910 edition of the *Bunyip*. Another such letter was received from Mrs Mahony giving more details and this appeared in print in the following September.[45]

A year later a celebration was held at which the president of the Gawler Institute, Robert King Thomson, presented Harry with a leather-bound copy that was one of 20 such copies ordered in September 1910. Harry's copy contained all the signatures of the officers and members of the Institute Committee (and is now part of the Gawler Cultural Heritage Collection). He was also presented with an engraved gold watch.[46] In the many tributes that followed, it was noted that 'his labour of love and untiring efforts on all his many endeavours would be a lasting monument to Mr Coombe's determination and ability'. Diplomatically, they also thanked Mrs. Coombe, 'for she must have been deprived of a good deal of her husband's society when he was writing the book'. It was not only the book that kept him busy. In his reply of thanks Harry mentioned his recent visits interstate visiting towns in Victoria and New South Wales.[47] It was little wonder that he gave up the editorship of the *South Australian Institutes' Journal* in 1907.

Throughout all of these writing pursuits, Harry continued in his role as editor of the *Bunyip* and a correspondent for the *Register.*[48] Even after his defeat at the 1912 elections, when he was casting about for other avenues for his talents, he retained the roles. A major change occurred from 1914 to 1916 when Harry left the *Bunyip* to edit the *Daily Herald*, a newspaper published by the Labor Party in Adelaide.

The *Daily Herald*

South Australia's *Daily Herald* was another groundbreaking newspaper. From its inception, the South Australian branch of the Labor Party, like its interstate counterparts, had hoped to have the resources to produce a daily newspaper. In 1910, with a state election looming, it was decided to take a risk and turn the *Weekly Herald* into the *Daily Herald.* This was the first metropolitan daily Labor newspaper in Australia, just two years after Broken Hill's *Barrier Truth* became Australia's first Labor daily.[49]

In its initial years the *Daily Herald* reached a circulation of almost twenty thousand. At the time there were two other two morning daily newspapers in Adelaide – the *Register* and the *Advertiser.* The *Register* was very much the conservative newspaper, while the *Advertiser* was only a degree less so. The *Daily Herald* took a genuinely socialist stance, reporting enthusiastically on industrial issues that drew much popular attention in the years immediately before the First World War.

Under Harry's editorship, the newspaper gained a reputation for obtaining cable news of events ahead of the bigger newspapers and for issuing 'War Specials' – special editions that appeared in the early afternoon. These were followed up by obituaries to the soldiers killed in action. The newspaper also contained extensive reporting on sports and like the *Bunyip,* the *Daily Herald* undertook job printing to make ends meet.

A report appeared in the *Mail* on Saturday 25 April 1914 announcing that Mr Ephraim Henry Coombe had been appointed editor to succeed Mr Cam Pratt. He was described as 'a specially interesting choice' and that there would be plenty to challenge him in this new role. The question was raised as to whether the managing committee would 'allow him the privilege of a free hand'.[50]

This remark proved to be prophetic. Two years later it was reported that the Adelaide Branch of the Australian Workers Union threatened to withdraw their patronage from the *Daily Herald* if Harry was retained as editor.[51] This move was supported by the United Trades and Labor Council. Worryingly, his even-handed approach to articles appearing in the newspaper did not suit everyone, a tension pithily referred to by the editor of the South Australian Methodist weekly newspaper:

in spite of his possessing journalistic abilities unequalled among his associates [Harry's] occupancy of their editorial chair was short-lived. With an extreme party paper an editor's business is to find out the wishes of his masters and to give them the most eloquent expression of which he is capable. He has no right to express his own opinions or to exercise his own judgment, even in things, unessential.[52]

Henry Kneebone, former editor recently returned from an overseas posting, was brought in to replace Harry at the newspaper. This left Harry to concentrate on his role as a politician, having won re-election in March 1915, and to undertake a vigorous campaign against conscription.

5

Parliamentary Career

Until 1891 and the formation of the United Labor Party (ULP) as a political body, there were no permanent or clearly defined divisions in the South Australian parliament. Instead, and in keeping with its British heritage, there existed two main political groupings: those of a liberal persuasion, and those that considered themselves conservatives. Politics was fluid and governments formed and reformed in response to internal alliances. This resulted in the formation of 28 governments in the 20 years of self-government since 1856. Despite this fluidity, South Australia was successful in passing significant social legislation, and the local politicians had a reputation for handling their disagreements relatively politely.[1]

Labor had made its first move for parliamentary influence in South Australia in the 1887 elections. The United Trades and Labor Council (UTLC), formed in 1884, backed nine liberal candidates sympathetic to many of its aims. There had been a few politicians loosely bound to the cause of trade unionism since the late 1870s, but this was the first time they stood under a common platform.

Seven of the UTLC candidates were successful, and through their influence, payment for all politicians, not just ministers, was introduced in 1887. Prior to this, aspiring country-based politicians found it costly and difficult to spend time away from their home. As a result, most politicians were city-based and had a family or professional income.[2] Now candidates who better understood the plight of the working classes, a sector dominated by rural workers, and knew how to advocate their wants could be attracted. This did not necessarily mean the candidates were working class, but rather that they would support candidates in electorates where there were working class majorities and thereby influence the passage of legislation that suited their aims and aspirations.[3]

Labor looked to hold the balance of power between those political groups that championed either Free Trade or Protectionism, both conservative in their outlook. It could then achieve its aims of improved social conditions by offering either side its support in return for concessions. This was entirely in line with the shifting political patterns of the time.

In response to the appearance of the ULP, a second party in South Australia also formed in 1891: the National Defence League (NDL), created by the conservative forces in the colony. The remainder of politicians were generally referred to as independent members.

> The very earliest Australian trade unions, dating back to 1840, were essentially craft union associations that had little political significance but rather acted like Friendly Societies with an industrial bent. This type of collective social support was recognisable in Gawler with its proliferation of Friendly Societies that included Oddfellows, Foresters, Rechabites, Hibernians, Druids, Sons of Temperance and Good Templars.[4]

The seat of Barossa covered the Barossa Valley and beyond, extending into the surrounding hills as far as Williamstown and Keyneton, then east to Sedan, and on to a section of the River Murray near Blanchetown.[5] Electorally it was dominated by Gawler, which provided 30–40% of the votes in an otherwise largely rural electorate. This voting pattern contributed to the Barossa electing both a city and an electorate-based representative as their two members, with Gawler generally supporting a city-based politician. Two notable exceptions until this point were Gawler's support of Walter Duffield (1857–1868 and 1870–1871) and James Martin (1865–1868).

The Barossa electorate existed from 1857 to 1938 and again from 1956 to 1970. During that period, it was represented by 29 individuals, many of whom were farmers, lawyers, millers or people associated with newspaper production. Two representatives served as premiers during their terms of office (Downer and Butler). Two fathers and their sons

From left: John Jones, John Downer and James Hague
History of Gawler, SLSA B-9586 and SLSA B-24267, respectively

Paris Nesbit, SLSA B-16966

served (Basedow and Hague). Only one representative, the last, was a woman – Molly Byrne.[6]

Labor's first candidate for the seat of Barossa in 1893 was businessman, wheelwright, former chief magistrate and mayor of Gawler, John Jones. He was the second president of the Gawler District Trade and Labor Council. He made a very creditable challenge to the two sitting candidates, Sir John Downer, the then premier, and James Hague, both members of the National Defence League (NDL). City based lawyer Downer had represented the seat for 16 years and served as premier twice. Angaston shopkeeper Hague had represented the seat since 1890.

In 1894, Harry became involved in the founding of the Barossa Political Reform League, signalling a growing interest in politics.[7] This was a progressive political association whose aim was to foster the cause of liberal candidates in an area that was dominated by conservatives, many of whom ran under the auspices of the National Defence League. An earlier Political Science Association had been established by James Martin.[8] Established at the instigation of the Gawler Institute Sociological Class and the Gawler District Trades and Labor Council, the Barossa Political Reform League became a vehicle for a broader discussion of politics as well as Harry's possible candidature for the seat of Barossa.[9]

With the strength of his convictions, the availability of remuneration and the support of his capable wife Sarah, Harry could now contemplate politics as a future career. He also had the advantage of an hour long train ride for travel to and from Parliament House.

1896 Election

The next South Australian election, to be held on Saturday, 25 April 1896, saw 37-year-old Ephraim Henry Coombe stand as the Barossa Political Reform League's candidate for the seat of Barossa.[10] His opponents were the sitting members Sir John Downer and James Hague who were again both affiliated with the National Defence League. The fourth candidate was Edward Pariss Nesbit who was running as an Independent. Harry was considerably younger than the other candidates, Downer being 51, Hague 61 and Nesbit 43.[11]

Harry knew his opponents. He, along with his father and his wife's uncle, James Bright, had been a member of Downer's Gawler support committee in 1884; a committee chaired by his mentor and then Mayor of Gawler, L.S. Burton.[12]

For many years Downer had been heavily involved in the federation discussion, leading him to spend much time away from his electorate, travelling interstate and overseas. He was overseas for the 1887 and 1893 elections and was now unable to campaign for this election due to his wife's ill health. Elizabeth Downer was diagnosed with cancer in 1895, and despite an operation, her condition deteriorated. She was admitted to a nursing home in Glenelg in January 1896. Sir John Downer contemplated retiring from politics but some of the electorate's leading citizens, including James Martin, MLC, convinced him to stand again. As with the previous elections, Downer sought the assistance of James Martin to address many local voter meetings on his behalf. Seventy-five-year-old Martin, who had been mayor of Gawler several times and who had held the seat from 1865–1868, was an impressive champion.[13]

Harry was also very much aware of James Hague, who had been an early member of the Country Institutes Parliamentary Committee that had assisted country institutes, including Gawler, in receiving additional funding. Hague had been invited to address the 1891 annual social gathering of the Gawler Literary Society of which Harry was a member.

Edward Pariss Nesbit (who later shortened his name to Paris Nesbit) was another lawyer. He had been born and educated in Angaston but was now resident in Adelaide. In 1893 he was made a Queen's Counsel, in spite of having been twice committed for lunacy. He was an articulate but controversial character whom the Adelaide gossips described as an 'absinthe-drinking, woman-loving, tobacco-enslaved ... Prince of Bohemia'.[14]

The 1896 South Australian election was the first in Australia in which women were eligible to both vote and stand for office. These rights had been won after a lengthy suffrage campaign two years earlier. Great efforts were now made to encourage this new stream of voters to participate. Candidates found themselves attending organised 'afternoon teas' in addition to the more traditional, male-dominated, evening presentations.

The candidates often had ladies' and men's support committees A local woman, Jane Deland, claimed that first-time women voters in Gawler were perceived to favour Harry as were 'all the labourers', and that there were women in Murray Street 'pulling the people in to vote for him'.[15] This preference by Gawler's women voters for Harry over Downer was confirmed by the *Bunyip* columnist Cit.[16]

At an electioneering meeting for ladies Harry reminded the audience that he was the only candidate who agreed with the passing of the Act that granted them suffrage. Downer, Hague and Nesbit all voted or spoke against it. Downer was an early supporter of women's suffrage spending part of his early career amending the *Marriage Act* and formulating the *1883 Married Women's Property Act*, but he would not support the right of women to become members of parliament. Nesbit had similar views. Many years earlier he presented a public lecture supporting women's suffrage but by the time the Bill passed, he had changed his mind, stating that women didn't deserve the vote because 'they didn't have the brains for it'.[17]

The election was held concurrently with the first referendum to be held in Australia. It dealt with matters relating to secular and religious education. The South Australian public would affirm the system of free, secular, state education in place at the time but reject scriptural instruction in state schools and a capitation grant for religious schools.[18]

From reports in the *Bunyip* it is possible to see Harry's appeal to the voter. As a first-time candidate he dealt with interjections with great aplomb and quick wit, while setting out his arguments in a reasonable and down-to-earth manner.[19] In answer to a woman interjector who stated that he knew nothing about politics because he had made lollies, he confidently replied, 'surely there was no reason why a man who made good lollies should not make a good legislator'.

He spoke eloquently on topical issues such as taxation, the locomotive contract dispute and subsequent strike at James Martin Foundry, as well as the introduction of coloured workers. Even though Harry chose to run as an independent, James Martin accused him of being a socialist and warned that if his views were carried out the works would close. Martin went on to say that while he could not support Coombe, he was, 'as good a reporter as he had ever met'. In return Harry replied that 'businessmen often are too busy to study political science' and that the class who made the most intelligent study of political science was the labouring class.[20]

And Harry was able to call upon strong allies. The 70-year-old

Catherine Helen Spence visited Gawler at the invitation of the Barossa Political Reform League on Friday, 7 February. She addressed afternoon and evening public meetings at the institute and spoke on electoral reform and the single tax, both items on Harry's campaign.[21] In her autobiography, Catherine later reported that Harry had initially had difficulties in accepting the Hare system that she propounded until he undertook further experiments that changed his mind, after which he 'became a convert to effective voting and an able advocate'.[22]

Regardless of the absence of the premier in the electorate campaign, both he and Hague were re-elected by the voters of the Barossa. Harry won the polling booths of Gawler and Williamstown but lost at the other booths of Tanunda, Angaston, Lyndoch, Keyneton, Sedan, Truro, Stockwell, Nuriootpa, Moculta, Blanchetown and Anna.[23]

According to John Bannon's *Supreme Federalist*, a recent biography of Sir John Downer:

> It was perhaps fortunate that the credible local candidacy of the editor of the Gawler *Bunyip*, Ephraim Coombe, born and raised in Gawler, was diluted by the adventurous intervention of the colourful and eccentric lawyer Paris Nesbit, QC, who campaigned on an anti-Kingston vendetta.[24]

Harry was not successful at this, his first attempt at running for parliament, but he learned from the experience and had made quite an impression in the community. At an evening social function held in his honour, he was presented with an illuminated address and many people rose to praise his efforts and encourage him to re-nominate at the next election. The speakers included several politicians who were all pleased to have the opportunity to espouse their own views knowing they would be duly recorded in the local and city newspapers. They spoke glowingly of Harry's talents as a communicator, and the high regard that the community had for him. The speakers included King O'Malley and William H. Carpenter.[25] William Henry Carpenter & the colourful King O'Malley were both Labor politicians for the House of Assembly electorate of Encounter Bay. Carpenter had been a locomotive boilermaker and foreman at James Martin & Co from 1891–1896, and was active in the Barossa Political Reform League.

The costs to the candidates were released after the election. Running for his first election had cost Harry just over £23, which was significantly less that Downer's £104, and Hague's and Nesbit's £67.[26] It was still a considerable sum for an editor supporting a family with five children.

1899 Election

Not daunted by his loss, Harry decided to stand again for the April 1899 election. His previous election experience and his established reputation in Gawler and the surrounding districts stood him in good stead. His editorial role at the *Bunyip* made him very familiar with local issues and his involvement in the South Australian Institutes Association made him well known by over 60 country and suburban institutes. His role as a Hansard staff member for the Federal Convention in Adelaide had given him close access to politicians and political thinkers from South Australia and from interstate.[27]

This time Harry opposed just the two sitting members of Hague and Downer. He polled strongly in Gawler and Williamstown but again he did not make an impression in the German settled country areas. Downer did not win a booth in the electorate but still won enough votes overall to be returned.[28] It was his eighth time running for office, and for more than half of those, he was either the leader of the opposition or the premier. He sustained his reputation as a powerful and well connected representative for the seat. When James Martin again campaigned locally on behalf of Downer, he described Coombe as 'a land reformer and teetotaller'.[29] He was right: with a Wesleyan background, Harry taken the temperance pledge when he joined the Sons of Temperance at aged 19. He made no apology for his stance but made it clear to his potential constituents that he did not begrudge others the pleasure of drinking in moderation. Given the number of public houses and wineries in the Barossa electorate this was a wise move. (Harry was also later described as a non-smoker and vegetarian and hence totally lacking in vices!)[30]

Harry was supported by a campaign committee in Gawler led by prominent citizen Edward Potter and elected council members, Charles Alfred Horne, George Bright, Charles George Rebbeck and Robert King Thomson, soon to become mayor.[31]

During this election the public debate between Harry and James

Martin took on a slightly less convivial tone. Battling against the respected 'father of Gawler' took courage but it was time for younger and less conservative challengers to step forward. Martin, who died later that year, was cautious about social reformers and the theories they espoused. He said, 'he was not sure about him [Harry]' as he was 'afraid that by electing him they would be destroying a good citizen and making a dangerous legislator'.[32] Not perturbed, Harry would later recommend that the upstairs School of Design room in the Gawler Institute be dedicated as a memorial to the late Honourable James Martin.[33]

Harry campaigned on several issues. He railed against the government adopting the state manufacture of locomotives, refuting the Commissioner of Public Works' assertion that locomotives cost less from the Islington works than from Martin & Co. He promoted his support for the Barossa Water Scheme, another venture he had shared with James Martin. He spoke of his support for the mining industry and that he was strongly in favour of land values taxation, which he believed to be fair, but he was not in favour of any increase. In his address to a large audience at the Institute Hall he reminded voters that 'he was a local' with their interests at heart.[34]

The vote in Gawler took place on Saturday, 29 April, in the Town Hall. This was a room with a single point of access leading someone to later suggest that any polling booth should always 'have a separate door for ingress and egress'. The total electorate contained 4,906 enrolled voters, 2,628 men and 2,278 women; 3,220 of these voted with almost a third choosing to 'plump'.[35]

Plumping', based on English common law, is a traditional form of plurality (first-past-the post as opposed to preferential) voting that gives voters the right to vote for only one candidate in a multi-candidate electorate. Voters limit their votes to those candidates they support, rather than being constrained to also vote for those they oppose. When voters concentrate their votes in this way, it increases the chance of their choice of representative winning. 'Plumping' was a part of South Australian elections from its first election in 1857 until 1929, when contingency voting was introduced for both houses utilising a system of preferences for the first time.[36]

Harry benefitted most from these 'plumped' votes but it did not help.

The final election count was Hague 1,936, Downer 1,786 and Coombe 1,567.[37]

The result was again disappointing for Harry, as both James Hague and Sir John Downer retained their seats. After two attempts at trying to oust Downer, Harry must have despaired. Good things come to those that wait though, for when the election for members of the first Commonwealth Parliament was called in March 1901, Downer ran for the Senate and was successful. He was one of seven members of the South Australian Parliament who moved to federal politics, and as a result, a series of by-elections for June were called.

1901 By-election: third time lucky

The by-election for the seat of Barossa was held on Monday 8 June, which was also a local race day, inspiring the following advert in the *Bunyip*:

> To the racing men of Gawler – Coombe is the correct tip for the Barossa Cup tomorrow. He comes of good stock, has been well trained, starts quickly, has heaps of pace, never wobbles across the track, never loses his head, tries right up to the winning post, has any amount of pluck, never disappoints his friends, is always reliable and always in good temper. Then invest on Coombe in the ballot machine tomorrow.[38]

Harry's opponent this time was James Fergusson, who at 50 years of age was another well-known resident of Gawler. Fergusson, the conservative candidate, had worked in a supervisory role for James Martin for 35 years, rising to become a director of the firm. With James Martin now dead, Fergusson was supported by no less than the Leader of the Opposition Hermann Homburg.[39] Harry's teetotaller habits were again raised but the fight was described as 'friendly'. He reassured the audience that the two candidates were old friends before and would continue to be afterwards. Harry's support committee was again chaired by Edward Potter assisted by Charles George Rebbeck who was now the mayor of Gawler, and Percival Trimmer, a vigneron from Tanunda whose father had been a politician in the early days of the colony. Throughout his campaign Harry actively appealed for the support of women voters, having a ladies' organising committee as well as a men's.

This time Harry won not only the booths at Gawler and Williamstown

Left: Mayor James Rebbeck, and right: James Fergusson
Gawler History Team

The extended Coombe family c. November 1901.
Back row: Daisy, Samuel, Harry, James, Herbert, Lena, Norman
Middle: Alick, Margaret, Sarah, E.H., Ephraim, Tom, Phynella
Front: Ernest, Catherine, Doris, Rita, Muriel. Family records

but Nuriootpa too. James Fergusson polled best in the other 10 more conservative country booths throughout the electorate. Despite this, the final election count was Coombe, 1,515 votes, and Fergusson, 1,360 votes. Just under three thousand of the nearly five thousand enrolled voters cast their vote, with 27 of them making an invalid choice. This time there was no plumping.[40]

Cartoon in *The Express and Telegraph*, 24 August 1901, p. 5

As at the last election a crowd had gathered under the balcony of the *Bunyip* offices in Gawler to hear the election results. The news was also announced later to a cheering crowd gathered below the Gawler Town Hall balcony. At his Tanunda campaign's headquarters, the Victoria Hotel, the banner over the verandah announced 'Good old Coombe. Successful at last' and he and a large number of his supporters sat down to a celebratory lunch prepared by the publican, John Shanahan, and Mrs Shanahan.[41]

A social was held in the Nuriootpa Institute to congratulate the new Member for Barossa. He was given an ovation as he entered to meet over a hundred people including some from Angaston, Truro and Tanunda. The Minister for Education, Thomas H. Brooker MP, William H. Carpenter MP (with his wife, Alice) and the Mayor and Mayoress of Gawler, Charles and Elizabeth Rebbeck, were among the many notables attending. In the speeches that evening he was described as 'a true liberal' fighting great odds but never giving up: 'Known as an excellent cricketer he would be hard to get out.' In response, Harry spoke of his desire to ensure the district received attention to the needs of its constituents so that it 'could compete with Encounter Bay for the title of the Arcadia of South Australia', a nod to his now parliamentary colleague, William H.

Carpenter, the Member for Encounter.[42]

Finally, Harry had succeeded in his quest to enter the South Australian Parliament.[43] He and Sarah had five children at home, the youngest of whom was just three years old. Their eldest son was now married and living in Gawler South.

Richard Butler
SLSA B-10798

The victory was to be tempered by the death five months later of Harry's beloved stepmother, Elizabeth Coombe, aged 82.

Harry threw himself into his new role. Given the honour of seconding the address-in-reply to the governor's speech at the opening of the new parliament, Harry used the phrase, 'We live in exciting times'. With the commencement of federalism, and the beginning of the Edwardian era, change was certainly underway. He made it clear that he remained a great advocate for adult suffrage in both Houses of Parliament believing it was the right of every man and woman in the state to have full and free voting rights.[44]

The members of the House of Assembly soon became familiar with his great ability to use sarcasm and wit to make a point. At the Budget debate on 24 September 1901, he directed his remarks toward his political opponent, Richard Butler, the member for Yatala:

> [he] congratulated the Treasurer upon his business-like and straightforward statement of the finances. While he could not concur with his conclusions, he could admire his application and painstaking efforts to master the details and overcome the difficulties of his office. All was satisfactory, no deficit, no increased taxation. Most of the budget guesswork. No one could blame the Treasurer for putting down £660,000 for customs, but only a guess.[45]

He did not forget the rural workers in his speeches, especially those finding it difficult to gain employment. He asked the Commissioner of

Public Works if it would be possible to take-on extra men in the Barossa and elsewhere as there were sixty to a hundred men out of work in Gawler.[46]

Harry strongly supported the Angaston Railway project stressing how vital it would be to the region's and state's economic growth. He highlighted the expansion of winemaking in his area by Seppeltsfield, Chateau Tanunda, W.H. Smith and others. Vintages were increasing, producing a valuable commodity for export, prompting Seppelt to claim to be the largest establishment of its kind in the world. Barossa grown apples also represented a profitable overseas trade, as did the local canning and jam-making industry. He also cited the output of the wheat and the flour mills at Angaston, Stockwell and Tanunda and dairying at Lyndoch. The *Angaston Railway Bill* was successfully passed on 19 November 1901.[47]

Harry again took aim at Butler in his role as the Minister of Agriculture, decrying the loss of Professor Lowrie, Head of Roseworthy Agricultural College, because of a difference of opinion with Charles Owen Smyth, Superintendent of Public Buildings. Harry admired the professor, but to some he was rather irascible and overbearing. Professor Lowrie returned to New Zealand, his home country, to a position with a salary commensurate with the salary he was receiving at Roseworthy.[48]

In December 1901 Harry criticised the government, stating:

> As a young member of the House – it seems a peculiar procedure to allow the session to advance so far and then tackle one of the most important items of parliamentary business and attempt to get through the work in one night. They were being asked to vote 15 items in one night ... The Audit Commissioner's Report was late and ought to be at hand before estimates were entered upon.[49]

He took every opportunity to speak for his electorate and the agricultural sector. The allowance for the Dairy Instructor came under scrutiny, and was deemed by him to be too little. He saw the Dairy Instructor's work as valuable and of lasting benefit to South Australia, comparing unfavourably to the recognition given to this work in other states.[50]

Less than a year later a full parliamentary election was called in South Australia.

1902 Election

One of the promises made to the public in the lead up to federation was that the costs of setting up and operating another layer of government would be offset by a reduction in the State Legislature. In April 1902, both the number of ministers and the number of members in both chambers of the South Australian Parliament was subsequently reduced and a redistribution of electoral boundaries carried out. The lower chamber dropped from 27 to 13 districts and there would be 42 instead of 52 representatives. Barossa increased from a two to three seat electorate.[51]

These changes triggered the election of the state's seventeenth parliament in May 1902. It was to be a 'new start' for the state's parliament.

Standing for the seat of Barossa were four candidates: Richard Butler, from Maylands, farmer and grazier; Ephraim Henry Coombe, from Gawler, journalist; William Copley, from Black Rock, farmer; and William Gilbert, from North Adelaide, merchant.[52]

Gilbert and Butler had represented the seat of Yatala since 1881 and 1890 respectively, but it was one of the seats that was abolished with the redistribution. Yatala had covered an area stretching from the River Torrens in the south to the Little Para River in the north and spanning from the coast in the west to the Adelaide foothills in the east. It was considered a rural district.

As a result of the redistribution, Barossa gained booths at Salisbury, Smithfield, Gilles Plains, Dry Creek, Enfield, Buchsfelde, Two Wells, Virginia, Dublin, Mallala, Redbanks, Dublin and Wasleys. Gawler became the centre in the new electorate and the chief polling site.[53]

Butler grew up at Yattalunga, a property near Gawler that was owned by his wealthy uncle, Philip Butler. He would later manage the property for his uncle. After his marriage he bought his uncle's sheep station at Mallala and become a prominent member of the Mallala community. He was a councillor and chairman of the Grace Council, before entering parliament as a conservative. By the 1902 election he had already served as the Minister of Agriculture and Education and was the current Treasurer.[54]

City-based Gilbert ran a successful milling business in the city but later, in partnership with his nephew, set up chaff and fodder mills in Gawler and Wasleys. He was not the William Gilbert, pastoralist and vigneron from Pewsey Vale. Gilbert was another conservative, affiliated the National League, which would go on to become the Australasian National League.[55]

Copley also had parliamentary experience. He represented the seat of Frome from 1884–1887. From July 1887–1894, he moved to the Legislative Council representing the northern division. After a two-year gap he returned to the House of Assembly as the Member for Yorke Peninsula until the seat was abolished in 1902. During his time in parliament Copley had served as the Commissioner for Crown Lands and Immigration and the Minister for Agriculture and Education. He was a strong farmers' advocate and introduced 'homestead block' measures, based on New Zealand legislation that led to the inauguration of ten-acre holdings at Gawler Blocks and other places.[56]

Harry was by far the youngest and least experienced of the four political candidates. All were known in the electorate except Copley, who, by his own admission, was an outsider.[57]

Harry had used his ten months in office well extending his influence to all parts of the electorate. He had lobbied to get Tanunda and Wasleys supplied with their own town water and the Gawler water supply had been extended to the Gawler Blocks. He had improved the delivery of mail services to Tanunda resulting in a chorus of 'for he's a jolly good fellow' being sung in his honour at the Tanunda Club.[58]

Despite the 'new start', this election seemed far less energetic in the electorate than the earlier by-election, with the *Bunyip* columnist Cit seemingly paying as much attention to the returning Second Boer War veterans as to the candidates.[59]

Coombe, Butler and Gilbert were elected.

The final tally was Coombe 2,880, Butler 2,848, Gilbert 2,525 and Copley 2,104.[60] In the multi-member system that existed, the candidate with the most votes was considered to be the senior representative for the seat, a position that presumably held some sway. Harry, with the highest number of votes, won this position in the 1902 election. He went on to win the position again in 1910. Butler was the senior representative in 1905, 1906 and 1915.[61]

In his speech at the declaration of the poll, Butler expressed his disappointment at the number of Gawler people who had plumped for

Harry, their local man, rather than give him their preferences.

It was Harry alone who addressed the crowd from the balcony of the Gawler Town Hall, the other two successful candidates having already returned to Adelaide. He made a point of telling his audience that he wasn't thinking of moving his abode elsewhere.[62]

1905 Election

Two months before the next election, Richard Butler became the Premier. He replaced John Jenkins, who resigned in order to become the Agent General in London.[63] The date set for the election was Saturday 27 May.

The major issue in this election was to be the long-standing problem of franchise reform for the Legislative Council. Franchise reform sought the removal of property ownership requirement for voters to the Legislative Council. This had been disputed since 1893 when Charles Cameron Kingston began his strong advocacy for progressive social policy and reform of the Legislative Council. The ownership of property was a requirement seen as class-divisive, with the Legislative Council only representing a proportion of the community. The alternative, often termed Household Suffrage, allowed working, non-propertied men and women the right to cast their vote for the Upper House. The debate strengthened when it became clear that such a distinction would not appear in a new Federal Constitution. However, as the House of Review, the Legislative Council repeatedly blocked any attempt to reform its power base.[64]

There were four distinct blocs: the United Labor Party (ULP); a Liberal group (to which Harry belonged) of franchise reformers led by Archibald Peake; the Butler Conservatives who had Farmers and Producers Political Union (FPPU) support; and an 'extreme conservative' group led by John Darling at the core of the Australasian National League (ANL).[65]

The FPPU was a new party formed before the election. Formed by rural stockowners and graziers who felt that the focus of the ANL was now on the metropolitan electorates and urban issues, it had a conservative political agenda and was adamantly opposed to franchise reform. It was essentially the rural wing of the ANL.

The three sitting members, Coombe, Butler and Gilbert were joined by Albert Maynard Dawkins, Paris Nesbit and Samuel Bruce Rudall in nominating as candidates for the seat of Barossa. Gilbert ran again as an

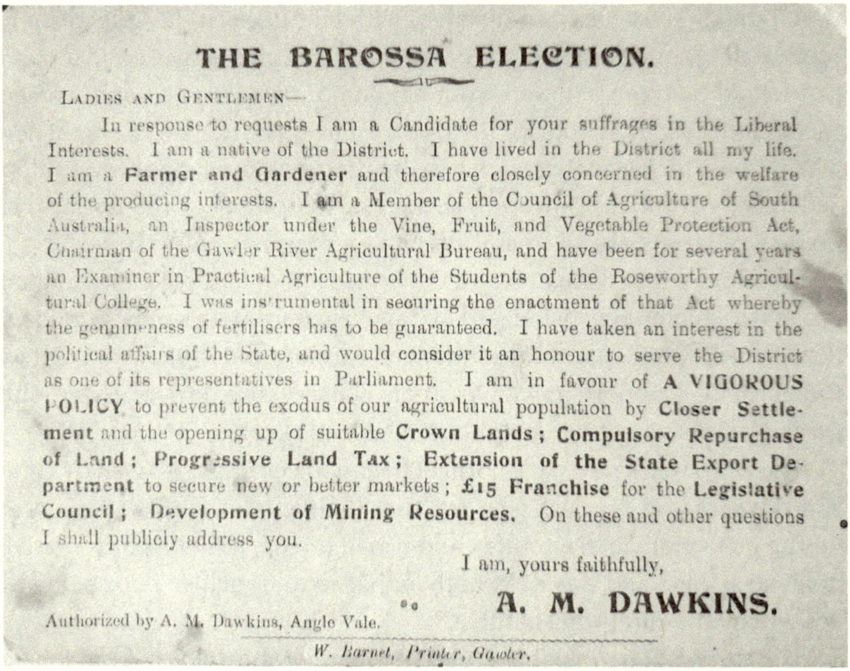

THE BAROSSA ELECTION.

LADIES AND GENTLEMEN—

In response to requests I am a Candidate for your suffrages in the Liberal Interests. I am a native of the District. I have lived in the District all my life. I am a **Farmer and Gardener** and therefore closely concerned in the welfare of the producing interests. I am a Member of the Council of Agriculture of South Australia, an Inspector under the Vine, Fruit, and Vegetable Protection Act, Chairman of the Gawler River Agricultural Bureau, and have been for several years an Examiner in Practical Agriculture of the Students of the Roseworthy Agricultural College. I was instrumental in securing the enactment of that Act whereby the genuineness of fertilisers has to be guaranteed. I have taken an interest in the political affairs of the State, and would consider it an honour to serve the District as one of its representatives in Parliament. I am in favour of **A VIGOROUS POLICY** to prevent the exodus of our agricultural population by **Closer Settlement** and the opening up of suitable **Crown Lands; Compulsory Repurchase of Land; Progressive Land Tax; Extension of the State Export Department** to secure new or better markets; **£15 Franchise** for the **Legislative Council; Development of Mining Resources.** On these and other questions I shall publicly address you.

I am, yours faithfully,

A. M. DAWKINS.

Authorized by A. M. Dawkins, Angle Vale.

W. Barnet, Printer, Gawler.

Albert Maynard Dawkins and his election card
Courtesy Ross Dawkins

ANL candidate, Nesbit for the ULP, and Butler changed affiliations to join the FPPU.[66]

Albert Maynard Dawkins was a farmer from Gawler River who specialised in fruit growing. He was one of the first students at Roseworthy College and would later succeed his father, Samuel Letts Dawkins, on the Mudla Wirra South Council to sit alongside Harry's brother, Thomas Coombe.[67] As members of the Gawler Liberal League, the successor of the Barossa Political Reform League, he and Harry were invited to represent liberal interests in the election.[68]

Paris Nesbit had spent the years since his 1896 election attempt furthering his notoriety. He had launched and initially edited the very popular weekly newspaper, *Morning*. In it he defamed the equally controversial lawyer, politician and then premier Charles Cameron Kingston, and publicised his own views favouring social reform, divorce law reform, legal aid for the poor, decriminalisation of drunkenness, equal employment opportunity, and other far-sighted changes. For this election he stood as a representative of the ULP.[69]

Samuel Bruce Rudall was the son of the John Rudall, who was the first solicitor to practise in Gawler and its first town clerk. Samuel served his articles with his father, then with the legal firm, G. and J. Downer, part-owned by the John Downer who had been an earlier representative of the seat. In 1881 Samuel became a solicitor and the second Town Clerk of Gawler, a position he held for 32 years. He was also a director of James Martin's Phoenix Foundry in Gawler, a long time president of the Gawler Institute, president of the Gawler Literary Society, the first president of the Gawler Union Parliament and a keen freemason. He too was well known to Harry.[70]

Coombe and Dawkins were paired as liberals and Butler and Rudall as conservatives. Gilbert, also a conservative, was considered the 'father of the parliament' while Nesbit, the Labor man, was the outsider.

In his electioneering Harry emphasised his parliamentary achievements. In May 1905 railway fares were reduced for ordinary and excursion tickets, while student fares were increased. This placed added pressure on the many parents in his region who sent their children to schools in the city. As their elected member he had strenuously made representations for a review of the situation, resulting in the increases being rescinded.

He had been instrumental in getting plans for the building of the Gawler Blocks School (now known as the Evanston Gardens Primary School) approved.[71] Together with Gilbert, John Warren, MLC, and the relevant town clerks, he had lobbied the Commissioner of Crown Lands, Richard Butler, to increase the subsidy for the maintenance of roads in his electorate.

With Butler and Gilbert, he had lobbied the Commissioner of Public Works, John Vardon, to allow free water to flush the drains in the streets of Gawler to address the ever-present public health issues. He had also pushed for the installation of a water main to Redbanks, a small town on the road from Gawler to Mallala.[72]

He had supported the Gawler Agricultural, Horticultural and Floricultural Society's request for the Roseworthy College agricultural lectures to be given at the Gawler Institute and he was instrumental in the revival of the Wasleys Institute.

He also made sure that he was known in the 'German areas'. In the company of Premier Butler, he was present at the celebration at the Tanunda Hotel to mark the Tanunda Rifle Kingship match.[73]

He claimed to have travelled more than twenty thousand miles and written more than fifteen hundred letters in the past three years. As part of his campaign he reminded voters that during this term he had acted as the opposition whip, his first venture in an executive role[74], which involved ensuring party discipline by maintaining communication between the leadership of the party and its members, inviting fellow legislators to attend voting sessions, marshalling support for party positions on the floor, counting votes on key legislation, and persuading wavering members to vote according to the official party policy.

Harry's campaign committee, headed by his brother, Thomas, also provided support to his fellow liberal candidate Albert Dawkins.[75]

This time it was Butler and Harry who appeared on the balcony of the Gawler Town Hall to be introduced to the assembled crowd by Mayor James Fergusson. Premier Butler topped the poll by winning 17 of the 25 booths. Harry came second with very strong support from Gawler, Williamstown, Gilles Plains, Dry Creek and Lyndoch. Gilbert was third in the voting, resulting in no change in the electorate's representation.

Interestingly, Nesbit, in his post-election speech, said he had expected

Archibald Peake
SLSA B-10801

Thomas Price
SLSA B-6691-18

The Peake Ministry, 5 June 1909
From left: L. O'Loughlin, E.H. Coombe, A.H. Peake, Premier, A.R.Addison, S.J. Mitchell, J.G. Bice
Image restored by Church Hill Photography from SLSA B-10189

to receive support from Harry's voters, especially as he had joined with Coombe in speaking to voters at the institute three nights before Gilbert, Dawkins and Rudall's presentation. Nesbit also queried why, as the Labor candidate, he had received very poor support from the German areas and incurred the wrath of the editor of a German newspaper at Tanunda.[76]

As a result of the election, and despite the rhetoric around the dangers of socialism, the United Labor Party, led by Thomas Price, took office with a minority government. It then entered into a coalition Price-Peake Administration Government, becoming the start of the world's first stable Labor government. Liberal Archibald Peake, who had served as librarian and secretary of the Naracoorte Institute, was a regular contributor to the *South Australian Institutes' Journal* and well known and admired by Harry.

Archibald Peake soon agreed to pressure from within his group to form a new party, the Liberal and Democratic Union (LDU). Harry became one of the founding members and, from 1907–1909, its second president. Peake described the LDU as representing 'something not so sharply set as Labourism, not so dull in its edge as Conservatism'.[77] It drew membership primarily from small wheat farmers. At this stage, the LDU was firmly in favour of franchise reform, willing to be in coalition with the United Labor Party (ULP) and opposed to both the conservative Australasian National League and the Farmers and Producers Political Union. However, Peake did not foresee that the ULP was fast moving into the same political middle ground.

1906 Election

Another election was held just 18 months later, on Saturday 3 November 1906. This was a double dissolution election. The deadlock over the franchise issue had continued. After another attempt at reform, rejected by the Legislative Council, Price resigned his ministry. But when Butler, as leader of the opposition, was unable to form a ministry, the Price/Peake coalition remained in office. After more conflict with the Legislative Council, Price and Peake gained an early election and campaigned as a 'Ministerial Alliance'. Unfortunately, the election still did not resolve the franchise issue.[78]

The candidates for the Barossa electorate included two of the three sitting members – Coombe and Butler, with William Gilbert retiring after 26 years in parliament. They were joined by two more candidates: Hermann Bischof Junior, a farmer of Spring Gully near Gawler, and Samuel Bruce Rudall, a solicitor of Gawler.

This was Town Clerk Rudall's second election attempt while the newcomer, Hermann Bischof, was well known in the district. He played cricket and football, was vice-president of the Gawler Agricultural Show and an elected member of the District Council of Barossa that included two years as chairman.[79]

Once more, Butler stood for the FPPU and Bischof contested under the auspices of the ANL, while Coombe ran for the first time as an affiliate of the LDU. Rudall also ran for the LDU, although Harry mentioned in one speech that he felt he had three ANL candidates running against him.

Shortly before the election Harry informed the Gawler Institute Committee that although he had resigned from the Board of the Public Library he still retained the editorship of the Institutes' Journal and membership of the Parliamentary Committee on Institutes. He had spent considerable time travelling around to country institutes, resuscitating several of them. More importantly, he had begun writing the *History of Gawler.*[80] As always, his workload was demanding but he simply restructured his time to allow for this major new project.

Harry's success in Williamstown, Lyndoch, Angaston, Tanunda, Gilles Plains and Dry Creek marked great progress in the conservative country areas of the electorate.

Rudall said of Harry at the polling night:

> Nobody could help admiring his pluck and perseverance in going through a district like Barossa, where he knew the majority of the electors at most of the polling places were opposed to him politically ... so long as he was Mr. Coombe the Gawler people would support him every time. And so with regard to others, the personal element counted for a great deal.[81]

This time all three successful candidates, Butler, Coombe and Rudall greeted crowds from the balcony of the Gawler Town Hall.

Election costs published in the *Government Gazette* in January indicted that once again Harry had spent significantly less on his campaign than the other candidates.[82]

The ULP continued to govern with the support of the LDU in a

Labor-Liberal coalition government until Premier Price's death on 31 May 1909. The coalition then collapsed and Labor, as the largest single party in the Lower House, demanded it retain the premiership in the coalition. Peake refused and formed a ministry filled with LDU members, including Harry.

Peake would go on to appoint Harry as his Commissioner of Crown Lands, Minister for Agriculture and Chairman of the Royal Commission into the handling and marketing of wheat.[83] After a two-year investigation, and in spite of Harry's advocacy for bulk handing, the committee recommended against a change from bag to bulk handling. While a bulk handling system would have significantly benefitted the wheat farming sector, the wheat traders had strenuously opposed the changes.[84]

In August 1909, Harry attended the National Conference of Ministers of Agriculture in Perth and met up with Professor Lowrie, now the Western Australian Director of Agriculture. The main area of concern to all states was the introduction of diseases in fruit and vegetables via interstate transportation. These included Irish Blight in potatoes and the cross-infection of fruit fly, phylloxera, pear and cherry slug and San Jose scale between states. South Australia was fortunate not to harbour these pests and strongly supported the decision to employ inspectors at the state borders.[85]

Soon after Harry arranged for classes for farmers and farmers' sons to be presented at the Roseworthy Agricultural College. It was a very popular move with his rural constituents.[86]

The Peake Ministry survived with the parliamentary support of two conservative parties, the ANL and the FPPU. In September 1909 the LDU accepted an invitation from the two conservative parties to combine with them to form the Liberal Union (LU) to create a concerted force against the Labor Party. As president of the LDU Harry was reluctantly involved with formulating the grounds for such a pact. This uneasy union was subject to final agreement by all the LDU branches, something that would not occur until March 1910.

In Harry's own words:

> A compromise Liberal policy was adopted, including household suffrage, progressive taxation, compulsory repurchase and effective voting. No

> less progressive programme would be acceptable to the electors of the State, but it represents a substantial advance on existing legislation. The Australasian National League is displeasured at the union of the other two bodies. That organization occupies a strong position on account of its overwhelming representation in the Legislative Council, but if it persists in turning a deaf ear to the demand for reasonable political advance it will weaken its influence considerably and introduce undesirable complications into an already remarkably complex situation.[87]

In December 1909 the Peake Ministry was restructured to include opposition members from the conservative parties, now members of the LU. To facilitate this Harry stepped down from the ministry.

There is every indication that the union was proving to be unsatisfactory for Harry. Its conservative stance saw the abandonment of many of the LDU platforms including household suffrage with the dual vote and effective voting.[88] He refused to give up on franchise reform. He was offered the opportunity to run for the Senate which he declined. Instead, he styled himself as a 'democratic liberal' and prepared to continue to offer himself as the LDU rather than the LU candidate for the Barossa at the next election.

1910 Election

There were five nominations for the seat of Barossa at the Saturday, 2 April 1910 election, including the sitting members Butler, Coombe and Rudall. Hermann Bischof stood again together with a new candidate, James Robinson, a foundry proprietor of Gawler.[89]

Bischof, Butler and Rudall ran as ANL candidates affiliated with the still to be formalised LU, and Harry ran as an Independent.

James Robinson also stood as an Independent, but in his case as a conservative. He was the owner of the Britannia Foundry, having earlier been a foreman at James Martin & Co. He had lived in the town for 27 years and was active in many of its community organisations.

This election saw the entrenchment of the two-party system in South Australia and very few votes would go to candidates not affiliated with either the LU or the ALP.

Issues at this election included the future of South Australia's responsibility for the Northern Territory; water conservation and the settlement of the River Murray water distribution questions; and, as had been the case in many of the preceding elections, the offering of government tenders. With the collapse of James Martin's business this last issue was still highly topical in Gawler.

As a result of changes to the *Electoral Act* in 1908, at this election electors could receive assistance to vote while employers were required to give their employees leave of absence to vote. This increased the participation of working class voters.[90]

Harry, now an old hand, campaigned strongly on his ministerial and journalism achievements and the benefits they had brought to the electorate. He described himself as the same democratic liberal he had been since entering parliament and described the Labor Party's influence in the democratic cause, as disintegrating and therefore harmful. His electioneering speech at Gawler was reported in the *Bunyip*:

> Some of his friends had not been pleased because he had not followed the Labor Party instead of sticking to liberalism. He had done what he thought was right. He had acted conscientiously. He was a son of Gawler. He had received his education there. He had formed his habits and received his inspiration there. He had been greatly honored by the Gawler people and one of the greatest delights of his holding the positions of Chairman of Committees and Minister of the Crown was the feeling that perhaps the honor conferred upon him might be reflected upon his native town. ... If he received their support he would do his best to carry out his duties, but whether returned or not he would continue to use his energies, according to his opportunities, to advance the interests of the State and the welfare of the people.[91]

Coombe, Butler, and Rudall were returned for the Barossa, with Harry acknowledging his supporters from the balcony of the *Bunyip* offices.[92]

With Harry's help the ULP formed South Australia's first majority Labor government with John Verran as its Premier. Labor had won with the smallest constitutional majority, 21 out of 40 seats. Harry's support, as the sole survivor of the independent liberals, gave Verran a working majority of 22 seats.[93] Harry reiterated that his win and the state result came from the public's reaction to the disunity within the so-called 'Liberal' Union.

John Verran
SLSA B-21757-1

Edward Potter, as chairman of Harry's election committee, and George A. Arthur, as secretary, hosted a well-attended celebratory social for the victorious Harry at the Institute three weeks later. It was well attended by supporters from Angaston, Tanunda, Lyndoch, Mallala, Two Wells, Salisbury and other country towns. Potter presented him with a framed enlargement of his photograph, possibly one taken for display in parliament. In his speech Harry reiterated the difficulty democratic liberals like himself had in the two party system where conservatives were only too ready to strengthen their cause at the expense of the 'true' liberals. He acknowledged the support of the workers of the district but continued to distance himself from the Labor Party, saying that he saw it as being neither democratic in its organisation nor its policies. He wanted to belong to the party that would 'neither preserve the unjustifiable privileges of one class nor grant them to another, which would recognise that the happiness of each was involved in the good of all. Such a party should have as the two principal planks of its policy – household suffrage with the dual vote and effective voting'.[94]

When parliament resumed, Harry again put forward a Proportional Representation Bill, a topic much favoured by him, but not so much by other members.[95] He spoke passionately of the influence Catherine Helen Spence had had in her efforts to promote effective voting. He regarded it as a duty of legislators to secure the best instruments of government and was satisfied that this system of electoral machinery was the best that could be adopted. No other system could secure such perfect representation of the will of the people. The matter was debated at some length over the next few months, but his Bill lapsed.

It was not until 1975 that the system of effective voting, now called Optional Proportional Representation, was introduced for the Upper House in South Australia. It is the same system that is used to elect candidates to the Australian Senate, the Upper Houses of NSW, Victoria and Western Australia, the Lower House of Tasmania, the ACT Legislative Assembly and many Local Government Councils.[96]

Following the 1910 election the Liberal Democratic Union was formally amalgamated into the Liberal Union to form a concerted force against the Labor party. Peake urged the LDU members at the party conference to accept the merger, which succeeded by one vote.

Harry refused to sign up. He disputed his former leader's turnabout on the reform of the Legislative Council.[97] Instead in November 1910, with the support of the Northern Democratic Association, he formed the Democratic Liberal Union and maintained his stance as an Independent.[98] This was a decided risk in the predominantly two-party electoral system. His stand to retain the middle ground would cost him dearly.

The Verran Ministry, like many others, lasted only twenty months before another election was called.

1912 Election

At the Saturday 10 February 1912 election, Harry stood as one of five candidates for the seat of Barossa. He and Michael Lynch, jeweller of Willaston, ran as Independents. Sitting members Samuel Rudall and Richard Butler were joined by William Hague, storekeeper of Angaston, as conservative LU candidates.[99] This was the second time Harry had taken the risk of running as an Independent in the two-party system.

Newcomer Michael Lynch was Gawler born and a fellow member of the Institute. He had recently become an elected member of the Gawler Council and would go on to become mayor. They campaigned together, with Lynch declaring that he had run because he was a supporter of Harry and that their values were identical.[100]

William Hague was the son of James Hague, who had been the representative for the Barossa Electorate from 1890–1902. William was a member of the Angaston School Board of Advice, the secretary of the Angaston Agricultural Society and a correspondent of the *Advertiser* at Angaston. He had served as a Trustee of the Angaston Institute and the Chairman of the District Council of Angaston.[101] Like Harry he had strongly advocated for the railway to Angaston, believing that railways were essential to the development of the district. It was Hague, rather than the Gawler based and more experienced Rudall, who was presented to the electorate as the direct alternative to Harry.[102]

Electioneering was fierce and Harry was heavily criticised for his unbending approach. In return, he railed against the deadlock created for the reform of the voting for the Legislative Council, saying that it was the culmination of a long series of years of misbehaviour on the part of the Upper House. He preferred a second chamber based on the 'matured judgment of the people, as represented by the fathers and mothers of their homes'. The Council was on a more conservative basis than before women's suffrage, 'because the wives of well-to-do men were enfranchised, while the wives of other homes were not'.[103]

The United Labor Party Government, led by Premier John Verran, was defeated by the Liberal Union led by the Leader of the Opposition Archibald Peake, who gained an eight seat majority. Both Harry and Michael Lynch were unsuccessful.[104] As the LU had planned, Harry was replaced by William Hague. According to a later article, he felt he had been 'squeezed out of politics by the relentless demands of the party system'.[105]

Only William Hague acknowledged Harry in his celebratory speech at the declaration of the poll, with Butler and Rudall remaining silent on the topic. Harry, in his concession speech, was reported as saying that:

> He had always taken his political ideals, from the Christian principles of the brotherhood of man. He believed in political equality, in electoral equality, and economic equality, and if Christian principles were to live these things must be brought about ... He had been maligned for his refusal to join the Liberal Union. When the fusion was brought about he felt that the Liberal Union did not stand for equality. He would have been a traitor to himself if he had joined them. It would have suited him personally to go in. He would not have been opposed at this election. He might have been a Minister or had the Speakership, but he would have had to sacrifice his principles, but he preferred defeat to this. The Liberal Union were not in favour of political or electoral equality ... The Labor Party was not his ideal Party, by any means, but it was the nearest to what his ideals were, so he had nothing to do but support it. He had acted conscientiously and according to his views.[106]

E.H. Coombe 1912 election defeat testimonial
family records. Photo courtesy Joanna Robinson

Extended family, c. 1912
Back row: Alma, James, Samuel, Ernest, Harry, Margaret, George; *Middle row:* Catherine, E.H., Sarah, Daisy; *Front row;* Alick, Carl, Stuart
family records

Harry had held the seat continuously for 11 years across five elections. He had taken on the positions of Opposition Whip, Government Whip, Chairman of Committees, Commissioner for Crown Lands and Immigration, Minister for Agriculture and chairman of a Royal Commission into the handling and marketing of wheat.

Following the devastating defeat, Harry's sense of dismay was somewhat appeased by two highly complimentary socials held in his honour at Gawler and Lyndoch. These allowed his supporters to show their admiration and respect for all that he had achieved.[107]

At the large gathering in the Gawler Institute Hall, presided over by Mayor Rebbeck, Harry was presented with an illuminated address (an intricate, embossed artwork) and a purse of coins.[108] The framed artwork was created by Sydney Hobart James of the Kapunda and Gawler School of Mines, who supplemented the calligraphic text with six watercolour paintings of public undertakings that Harry had been associated with during his parliamentary career – *Jacob's Creek Bridge*, *Cutting near Angaston*, *Bridge Gawler*, *Barossa Weir*, *Embankment Rowlands Flat* and the *Tanunda Station*. All infrastructure projects were undertaken within the electorate, with three located on the Gawler to Angaston Railway. After the social the illustrated address was publicly displayed in the window of Alfred Sheard's Murray Street shop.[109]

Harry also received a letter of appreciation signed by 103 Tanunda electors that was reproduced in the *Bunyip* and the *Daily Herald*. The final clause read:

> We, the undersigned residents of Tanunda, desire to express the keen disappointment experienced by us on hearing the result in our district at the recent Parliamentary elections, which result we are confident your actions did not merit. We feel that in your Parliamentary career and also as a private citizen, you strictly followed the dictates of your conscience, and wish to assure you that there are many of us in Tanunda who are not devoid of gratitude, but who try to give honor where honor is due, and who are also able to appreciate to the utmost that excellent work you have done to further the interests of residents of the Barossa district, and the State at large. We are keenly alive to the fact that, had you sacrificed your principles to further your own personal interests you

> would have again headed the poll and we are happy in the knowledge that an inglorious victory has no attraction for you, and desire to assure you that such a victory would not have been welcomed by us. In conclusion we respectfully wish you every success for the future, and beg to assure you that our individual services will always be freely placed at your disposal should you again decide to offer your valuable services as a member for this district.

In his reply Harry wrote:

> Ladies and gentlemen – Please accept my heart-felt gratitude for your appreciative sentiments expressed in your letter. Your kindness and consideration have gone far to remove the sense of disappointment I felt at having been rejected after such a long and (to me) pleasurable service. It has been a rule all my life to give freely of my energies in the performance of duty, and I had always previously given satisfaction of those to whom I was responsible. The knowledge that I failed to do so in the opinion of a large number of my Barossa constituents is the painful part of my defeat. The loyalty and good wishes, however, expressed by you will spur me on to further efforts in the cause I have so much at heart – the whole people and not a class.[110]

6

Move to Adelaide

Harry now found himself in an entirely new situation. He was 53, no longer in office, and a grandfather with two teenage children still at home. With the support of his wife, he felt he had spare time on his hands. He was still employed as the editor of the *Bunyip* and the local correspondent for the *Register* but he looked around for other things to do.

He remained busy in the community. He continued with his roles with the Gawler Show, the Gawler School of Mines and the Gawler Institute, where he used his former contacts to source copies of the federal Hansard for the Reading Room.[1] He continued to represent the Gawler Institute on the South Australian Institutes Association.

He participated in the Gawler Union Parliament debates. He played bowls both locally and against suburban clubs. He was invited to become one of the patrons of the Willaston Coursing Club and the Gawler Fishing Club, both of which he had helped establish.[2]

As the chairman of the Board of Management for the Hutchinson Hospital he led the tendering to build process, accepting the winning bid in July 1912. And he and Sarah sat on the committee of the Gawler District Trained Nurses Society, a volunteer organisation providing desperately needed services to the town's vulnerable.[3]

Politically, he remained active. He encouraged Jeanne Forster Young, the secretary of the Effective Voting League and a friend of Catherine Helen Spence, to speak at the Institute. He travelled to Modbury to present a similar speech to their Literary Society. He also continued to support the campaign for international women's suffrage, particularly in the United Kingdom, where the vote for all women would not be achieved for another 16 years.

In June 1912 he proudly gave away his eldest daughter, Daisy, at her wedding to George Arthur Ash. The marriage took place at the Tod Street Methodist Church. Daisy went to live at Mt Barker where George was employed as a journalist with the *Courier* newspaper.[4]

Harry was invited to speak on behalf of residents at several public events including the arrival of electric light in Gawler.[5] In September 1912, he attended a public meeting where he was asked by the workers in the town to reply to statements made by Richard Butler, the Commissioner of Works, regarding the loss of the James Martin & Co (now owned by Henry Dutton) contract to supply locomotives.[6] In the same month, he attended the opening of the Lyndoch Institute in his role as president of the South Australian Institutes Association.[7]

A year later he was asked by the Willaston Vigilance Committee to speak at the planting of sugar gums along Jane Street, and in October 1913 he spoke to local farmers about the marketing and handling of wheat.[8]

Harry led the celebrations at the grand opening of the Hutchinson Hospital in November 1913. As the board chairman he presented Mr Alexander James Murray, a pastoralist and sheep breeder from Mt Crawford, with a silver key and asked him to perform the opening honours. The new hospital comprised two wards with four to five beds in each, an operating room, four staff bedrooms and other facilities – a wonderful addition to the town and the culmination of a process that had begun with a bequest by Thomas Hutchinson in 1901.[9]

He wrote political and other articles under his own name in the *Bunyip*, including one in 1912 on the proposed change to the Gawler Council's improved land value rating system. He wrote in support of the change, stating that the current situation proved a disincentive for industry and business owners to improve their premises, and that an unimproved land value system would be better. A fiery public debate ensued but the poll decided upon making the change.[10] He also submitted articles for the *Barossa News*.[11]

He and Sarah continued to be invited to social functions including the 1913 May Brothers employees' picnic where they joined the owners and other important guests for luncheon at the Angaston Hotel.[12]

In January 1914 he and his brother Thomas helped found the Willaston

Quoits Club and arranged a game against a club at Port Adelaide.[13] A month later he spoke at the farewell of the local Catholic priest, describing himself as representing the School of Mines and the District Trained Nursing Society.[14] But something was still missing.

Then, in March 1914, the position of the Gawler town clerk became available when Samuel Rudall stepped down after 32 years in the position. In his mid-February letter of resignation, Rudall cited that the role now interfered with his other work and suggested a departure date of 31 March to allow a training and handover period with his successor.[15]

With the imminent resignation, the council decided to conduct a recruitment campaign. It was a time of significant change within the municipal offices. Council had taken on the responsibility of installing and providing electric light to the town and there was a sense that the incumbent town clerk had resisted the change, mainly because of the increased workload that it brought. There were just two permanent paid staff members of the council, the town clerk and the inspector, with contractors hired to undertake the maintenance work. The inspector Philip Cheek was 77 years old and 'possibly in need of a "holiday" due to the demands of old age'.[16] (As it turns out Mr Cheek remained in his position until 1918, by which time he was 81 and had provided almost 48 years of continuous service to the corporation.)[17]

Council discussed the need for serious change in the format of both roles.[18] Given the possibility of the inspector's departure it was agreed that the town clerk's successor should not only have business ability and a knowledge of accountancy but should also be able to discharge the duties of a town surveyor. (It was a period of building growth and potential boundary change.) Up until this point the town clerk's position was purely administrative and a part-time position. Both Rudall and his father before him had been able to conduct their busy law practice in conjunction with their municipal duties.

Applications were open for two weeks, closing Monday, 16 March.[19] An unknown number were received with two applicants being short-listed – Ernest Albert Smith and Harry. It took the recruitment committee two ballots before a decision was reached and duly reported to Council on Wednesday, 18 March. Smith, formerly the clerk of the District Council of Yorketown was successful by one vote. The outcome was then reported in

MUNICIPALITY OF GAWLER.

APPLICATIONS will be received until noon of 16th March, for the position of TOWN CLERK at a salary of £175 per annum. Applications to be addressed to the Mayor of Gawler, and to be marked "Application for position of Town Clerk" Personal application to any member of the Council will disqualify the applicant Some particulars of duties may be obtained from the undersigned,

S. B. RUDALL,
Town Clerk.

Advertisement for Town Clerk, *Bunyip*, 13 March 1914, p. 5

the Friday edition of the *Bunyip*, the newspaper edited by the unsuccessful candidate.[20]

The decision was met by outrage in a community where many people had expected Harry's appointment to be a forgone conclusion. The news was picked up by the Adelaide-based press.[21] A petition, signed by 85 residents, including businessmen William Dawkins and Alfred Sheard, was presented to the next council meeting by Councillor Thomas James Wilkinson. A reconsideration was sought, especially as one of the elected members, Councillor John Tulloch, had been absent, he too having applied for the position. It was felt that Harry's qualifications and ability justified his appointment in preference to 'an outsider'. The council refused to table the petition on the grounds that the matter was now settled.

Councillors Michael Lynch and Horace Bright were vocal in their criticism of the petition. Councillor Lynch said:

> The receipt of this petition was both unusual and distinctly mischievous. It could only be regarded as an attempt by a section of the ratepayers to interfere with the affairs of the Council. It was a highly discourteous act by the gentlemen who had engineered the matter.[22]

The vote to accept the petition was lost on the casting vote of the Mayor, William Cox; Councillors Thomas James Wilkinson, John Tulloch and William Antwis voted for its acceptance and Councillors Horace Bright, Michael Lynch and John Letcher voted for its rejection.

The subsequent publication of an open letter about the petition showed considerable insider information about the selection process.[23] Anonymous letters of support further inflamed the situation causing both councillors Lynch and Bright to respond, criticising the attacks.[24]

All of this became very damaging in a tight-knit community. Horace Bright was related to Harry by marriage. He was the grandson of James Bright and his father George, a former mayor, was a member of Harry's 1899 election committee.[25] Michael Lynch had stood with Harry as an independent candidate at the elections a month earlier, and they had run a joint support committee for their campaign. He had gone on to praise and present Harry with an illuminated address at one of the socials organised by the community after the election.[26]

To shed some light on this matter, it is necessary to go back a few years. In 1881, at the age of 22, solicitor Samuel Rudall succeeded his father John Rudall, also a solicitor, who had served the municipality for its first 25 years. The handover occurred following Rudall Senior's appointment as the Stipendiary Magistrate in the new courthouse located in Cowan Street, Gawler. Father and son continued to practice law together as Rudall & Rudall until Rudall Senior relocated to Port Augusta in 1889, leaving Samuel Rudall to manage the family business.[27]

Samuel had much in common with Harry through leadership positions at the Gawler Institute, the Gawler Literary Society, the Gawler Union Parliament and the Loyal Lodge. However, politically, he was far more conservative than Harry. He stood as a conservative candidate for the seat of Barossa, unsuccessfully in the May 1905 election and successfully in the November 1906, March 1910 and February 1912 elections. During all these campaigns and his time in parliament he remained the town clerk. He campaigned vigorously yet civilly against Harry each time. (Samuel would hold his seat until March 1915, when he was defeated by the returning Harry.)

Samuel Rudall, having renounced the position of town clerk, may have had some influence with council's decision on his replacement. Was Rudall biased by his own political leanings against an application from Harry, or did he sincerely believe that he lacked the requisite skills?

Michael Lynch stated that he had made his choice of candidate based upon the experience deemed necessary to carry out the role. He recognised and valued Harry's skills and experience and looked forward to supporting him when he next ran for parliament. Lynch's belief that Harry would return to politics and that the position of town clerk now needed a full-time incumbent may well have influenced his decision.

Regardless of whether Harry encouraged the flurry of anonymous responses to the council's decision, it was very damaging both to him and to the council. The controversy raged on through weekly submissions to the *Bunyip* until the end of April.[28]

Not that the new town clerk had an easy time of it. No sooner had he been appointed, the District Council of Spalding sought Gawler Council's permission for Ernest Albert Smith to have a leave of absence for two to three weeks to complete some work he had promised for them. When this request was refused by the Gawler Council, Smith went on extended sick leave in mid-May, necessitating the appointment of an acting town clerk for Gawler.[29]

Smith returned to work in mid-July 1914 but found that the situation faced by Rudall, regarding the additional work brought about by the provision of the electric light supply, to be true.[30] Unsuccessfully, he appealed several times to the council for additional staff, even offering to reduce his wage to cover the extra cost. Despite criticism from several quarters about problems concerning the expensive supply connection, within the year he reported to council on the profitable electric light supply. During the previous year the council had lost over £40 per month but was now making a profit of that same amount within the space of six months. It seemed 'almost a miracle'.[31] In December 1916 his salary was increased by £14 and the mayor, in his annual report, spoke glowingly of his skills. Smith was now 'lent out' to three other councils to advise them on electric light supply. An engineer was soon appointed to assist Smith.[32]

Harry and the new town clerk's paths continued to cross. Smith became the secretary of the Local Recruiting Committee and in April 1916, in the midst of the anti-conscription debate, this group unanimously passed a resolution to be sent to the State War Committee, stating:

> This committee feels that ... the Defence authorities be recommended to bring in a scheme of enlistment on the basis of conscription when all eligible males should be called upon to serve their country abroad. My committee regret the necessity for passing such a resolution, but it feels that many young men view the position altogether too lightly, while many others treat the question with contempt ... Out of 140 papers received ... from the district of Barossa, 95 state that they have indifferent health. This particular district is one where nearly everyone is engaged in some kind of rural industry, usually where robust health prevails, so it can easily be seen that this number added to the number that have failed to furnish returns at all makes ... a very poor percentage of those in good health, in fact, the percentage is so poor that my committee has grave doubts as to the veracity of quite a number of the replies.[33]

He was also involved in fundraising and 'send offs' to local men going to war. For one of these, the Gawler Branch of the Mayor of Adelaide's Patriotic Fund, he served with Harry's brother, Thomas, and son-in-law, George Ash.[34]

Smith stayed with the Gawler Council for nine years, resigning in February 1923 to become the chief officer of the Broken Hill Hospital and later the superintendent of the Children's Hospital, North Adelaide. His last act for Gawler council was, ironically, to sell the municipally owned electric supply to the Adelaide Electric Supply Company.[35]

On Monday, 13 April 1914, less than a month after his unsuccessful bid, the position of the editor of the *Daily Herald* was advertised at a salary of £450 per annum (as opposed to the Gawler Town Clerk's salary of £175).[36] Amid his disappointment and the ensuing outcry, Harry applied. The *Daily Herald* was the city-based trade union newspaper. It had started as a weekly newspaper in 1894 and then moved to daily production in 1910.[37]

Harry had connections to the newspaper, having acted on several occasions as a temporary editor for the *Weekly Herald* many years earlier. The paper had been most complimentary of his maiden parliamentary speech in 1901.[38] He also knew politician Thomas Burgoyne, father of Geoffrey Burgoyne, who had been an associate editor at the *Daily Herald* until 1912.[39] When Harry became aware of the new employment opportunity, he reached out to these men for information and support.

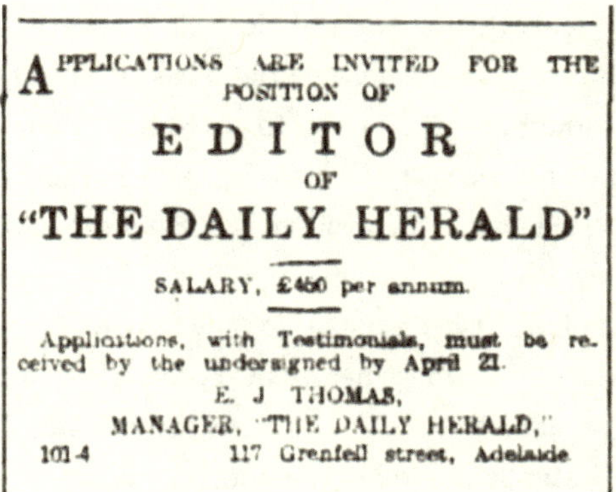
APPLICATIONS ARE INVITED FOR THE POSITION OF

EDITOR

OF

"THE DAILY HERALD"

SALARY, £450 per annum.

Applications, with Testimonials, must be received by the undersigned by April 21.

E. J. THOMAS,

MANAGER, "THE DAILY HERALD,"

101-4 117 Grenfell street, Adelaide

Advertisement for Editor, *Daily Herald*, 13 April 1914, p. 2

Thomas Burgoyne, with Harry, was instrumental in creating the South Australian Institutes Association in 1899. This organisation was set up 'to provide a body sensitive to the needs and desires of the country Institutes at a time when the Public Library was felt to be failing this role. Burgoyne had been the first president until 1911 when Harry took over the role until 1913. Burgoyne was the editor of the *South Australian Institutes' Journal* established in the first year of the Association and Harry took over this editorship in 1904.[40]

Burgoyne is very likely to have been one of Harry's parliamentary mentors. He was from Port Augusta where he had been a correspondent for the *Register* before setting up the local newspaper, the *Port Augusta Despatch*, which he then edited for three years. He was very involved in community affairs, establishing a local drama club, debating society and cricket club. From 1875–1879 he was the town's first town clerk and surveyor and later held the positions of councillor and mayor. He entered parliament as its local politician in 1884, until losing his seat in 1915, aged 87. He was involved in the establishment of the Port Augusta Institute and was later associated with the Port Adelaide Institute which, like Gawler, was large and influential. Whilst a politician, he served twice on parliamentary committees formed to monitor the interests of country institutes.[41]

Working for an instrument of the Labor Party was not at odds with his political journey. His association with the party dated way back to before the reformation of the Barossa Political Reform League, when he had worked with the local branch of the Trades and Labor Council whose financial secretary was his brother, Thomas. His son, Harry Heywood, was the founding president of the Port Wakefield branch of the Railway and Tramways Employees Union, and later the president of the local branch of the ULP.[42] Harry had been a part of the Price-Peake Labor government following the 1905 and 1906 elections, and had provided his support to ensure John Verran's Labor Party win in 1910.

Things moved quickly, and by Friday 24 April 1914 former leader John Verran, speaking at a *Daily Herald* function at Tantanoola, stated that he had received a telegram that day confirming Harry as the new editor of the newspaper. On the same day Harry made a report to the Gawler Institute Committee and included a brief notice in the *Bunyip* reaffirming the same.[43] A newspaper report in the *Mail* the next day confirmed the appointment with more detailed articles appearing a week later in the *Bunyip* and the *Daily Herald*.[44]

His appointment was surprising and to some, controversial.[45] The article that appeared in the *Daily Herald* took pains to highlight his political and journalistic strengths:

> The political significance of his accession to the editorial office, important though it promised to be, in no degree outweighed in minds of the board of management ... that 'The Daily Herald' must have in control of the paper a man of the keenest journalistic instincts, a man of tireless energy, and one whose literary gifts eminently qualified him to make the paper the best, the brightest, and the most readable daily in the State.[46]

The position meant leaving the *Bunyip* and his hometown with its strong connections, but it was an exciting new venture taking on a busy metropolitan daily newspaper rather than a regional weekly publication. It gave him the opportunity to leave behind any residual disappointment and disaffection that had come with losing both the election and the town clerk bid. Harry later claimed that the reason he left Gawler was due to his refusal to join the Liberal Union that had lost him his seat, rather than a journalistic career move.[47]

On Friday 1 May 1914 the family left Gawler for life in the city.[48] They moved to rented accommodation at 10 Morcomb Street, Stepney, relatively close to Harry's new workplace. Located at 117 Grenfell Street, Adelaide, east of the Adelaide Arcade, the *Daily Herald* office was not far from the North Terrace cultural and parliamentary institutions.

At the time of the move, Harry's dependant family was relatively small. Three of his children were married. Harry Heywood lived with his wife, Margaret, and two sons in Port Wakefield, where he worked as a fitter in the government locomotive workshops. James, his wife Alma and their two sons lived in Saddleworth, where he worked in the general store. Daisy and her husband, journalist George Arthur Ash, had recently returned from an eight-month holiday in England and had rented property in Willaston to allow him to work for the *Bunyip*.[49] Samuel was an assistant teacher at the Gawler State School, having previously taught at Peterborough.[50] Only Ernest, 19, and Catherine, 16, were still at home.

Harry and Sarah returned to Gawler several times over the next few months. One occasion, on 21 May, was to attend the fundraising fair at the Hutchinson Hospital that had been organised by a veritable who's who of women in Gawler. As his final act as the hospital's chairman, he invited Lady Butler to open the fair. Lady Butler accepted, saying that she appreciated the invitation, and that it was it was the first occasion she had been so honoured since her husband had represented Barossa.[51]

On Monday 1 June they returned for their farewell social at the Gawler Institute. This event had been planned since soon after their departure by a large committee that included politician Samuel Bruce Rudall, representing the Hutchinson Hospital committee; Alexander Philip Forgie; William Dawkins; James Beasley; William Thomas Ayling and Hermann Bischof for the Gawler Institute; James Fergusson, School of Mines Committee; S.J. Attiah, representing the town; Henry Freak, Chairman, Gawler South District Council; Andrew Phillip Armstrong, *Bunyip* staff; and Evan Gwynne, representing Willaston.[52]

Many Gawler dignitaries spoke to the large audience during the evening, highlighting the support and influence Harry and Sarah gave to Gawler. Reverend Sydney Thomas Charles Best, President of the Gawler Institute, testified to Harry's work, words with which Edward Potter, President of the Gawler School of Mines, heartily agreed. Former mayor

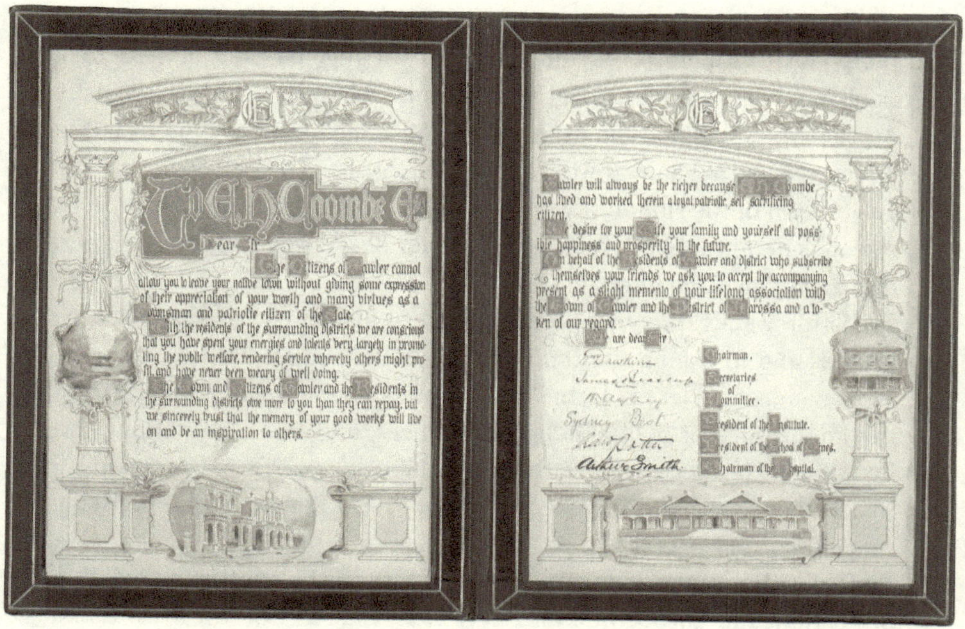

To E.H. Coombe Esq.

ear ir

he itizens of awler cannot allow you to leave your native town without giving some expression of their appreciation of your worth and many virtues as a ownsman and patriotic citizen of the tate.

ith the residents of the surrounding districts we are conscious that you have spent your energies and talents very largely in promoting the public welfare, rendering service whereby others might profit, and have never been weary of well doing.

he own and itizens of awler and the esidents in the surrounding districts owe more to you than they can repay, but we sincerely trust that the memory of your good works will live on and be an inspiration to others.

awler will always be the richer because oombe has lived and worked therein a loyal patriotic, self sacrificing citizen.

e desire for your ife your family and yourself all possible happiness and prosperity in the future.

n behalf of the esidents of awler and district who subscribe themselves your friends we ask you to accept the accompanying present as a slight memento of your lifelong association with the own of awler and the istrict of arossa and a token of our regard.

e are dear ir

hairman.

ecretaries of ommittee.

resident of the nstitute.

resident of the chool of ines.

Arthur Smith hairman of the ospital.

Testimonial for E.H. Coombe on leaving Gawler in 1914
family records

Arthur Smith, who had succeeded him as chairman of the Hutchinson Hospital, stated that the staff viewed him more as a kind father than as 'boss of the show'. In his response, Harry gave credit to his wife for anything he had been able to accomplish, and said that he hoped for a bright and happy future for Gawler. They were presented by another illustrated testimonial created by Sydney Hobart James.

Edward Potter was another of Harry's mentors. A gasfitter, plumber and tinsmith with a Murray Street business, he knew Harry from childhood. He had a close association with Harry and his family over many years as a Trustee of the Institute, a member of the Loyal Lodge of Oddfellows, the Gawler Starr-Bowkett Society, Gawler Cottage Homes, the Liberal and Democratic Union and the Gawler Tourist Association. He featured prominently in Harry's *History of Gawler* and in the second volume of the *Cyclopaedia of South Australia*, in an article no doubt contributed by Harry. He chaired Harry's first three election committees.[53]

Harry settled into his new role at the *Daily Herald* with its increased tempo of production. Within days of starting, he was invited to a ministerial lunch at Parliament House as one the three editors of the daily Adelaide newspapers: the others being Sir Langdon Bonython from the *Advertiser* and William Sowden from the *Register.* The occasion was the celebration of the Honourable A.A. Kirkpatrick's return from his term as Agent-General for South Australia. Premier Peake was not able to attend as he was travelling interstate.[54]

Within weeks Harry was reaching out to his rural contacts to source articles and to extend the *Daily Herald*'s circulation into these areas. In reply he received letters from Paul Frederick Zimmerman of Lyndoch, on the importance of bulk handling to farmers, and from Harry Heywood Coombe of Port Wakefield, on the unfair impact of patriotism as espoused by Premier Peake and the effect that the Prices Regulation Commission was having on workers.[55]

One of Harry's major tasks was to report on the continuing build-up of hostilities in Europe and on 2 July 1914, the start of 'the War to end all Wars'. The impact of war being declared was immediate with a rush among many single working men to sign up for an adventure overseas. This included his son Samuel.

Harry also used the time to prepare himself for the next election, using his platform to score points off his former colleagues that regularly drew infuriated responses from Premier Peake.[56] The premier retorted that he was dealing with a megalomaniac and had no need to use his own words to criticise the Labor Party because he could make use of Harry's words of severe criticism before he became their editor.[57] In June 1914 Harry wrote a scathing open letter to the premier, indicating that their former close relationship had been destroyed through Peake's duplicity. He published the letter on page four of the *Daily Herald* and reproduced it as a handbill to be handed out at the country locations where Peake was speaking.[58] This further enraged the premier and the Liberal Union, and the clash went on for weeks, duly reported in full detail in the *Daily Herald* and other newspapers.

He continued to promote the Effective Voting League, an organisation dedicated to the purpose of 'educating the public on the question of Parliamentary government and its dependence on just representation for its proper development'. In July 1914, Harry presented a lecture for them on 'The Development of Government in South Australia'.[59]

And he hadn't been forgotten in Gawler. In August 1914, the annual committee meeting of the District Trained Nursing Society awarded Mr and Mrs E.H. Coombe life membership.[60]

Now a member of the United Labor Party he travelled widely to branches assisting them in their governance arrangements. On 11 February 1915 he was overwhelmingly endorsed as the ULP candidate for the seat of Barossa in the forthcoming election.[61]

1915 election

This election was held on 27 March 1915, six months into the First World War. A referendum was also held on the question of new early closing hours for hotels. Austerity restrictions had already been placed on the wartime sale of liquor in the United Kingdom, France and Russia, and the concentrated efforts of some churchmen and the temperance groups would see voters support a 6 pm closing time in South Australia.[62]

Six candidates stood for the seat of Barossa: the three sitting members Butler, Rudall and Hague, as well as the former member, Coombe. They were joined by new candidates, 25-year old Norman John Oswald Makin, a patternmaker and union man who had previously worked in a Kapunda foundry and at James Martin & Co. in Gawler, and 31-year-old Max Otto Riedel, an auctioneer of Tanunda and chair of the Tanunda Branch of the Labor Party.[63] This time only two of the candidates, Rudall and Riedel, lived within the electorate.

Butler, Rudall and Hague represented the Liberal Party, the new reiteration of the Liberal Union. Coombe, Makin and Riedel were Labor Party candidates. Since before the 1912 election the United Labor Party had become the Australian Labor Party, but many branches and candidates still retained the former name.

Harry again campaigned on adult suffrage and effective voting and reminded electors of his role in bringing about the Barossa Water Scheme, the Gawler to Angaston railway extension, the debates about bulk wheat handling and the fixing of the price of wheat. He again decried the government's role in the downfall of James Martin & Co. through the awarding of tenders to interstate firms.

Norman Makin went on to have a long and successful federal political career. His death in July 1982 prompted Prime Minister Malcolm Fraser to pay tribute to him. As well as his time in parliament, Makin had served as the ambassador to the United States of America from 1946 to 1951 and the president of the United Nations Security Council in 1946 and 1947.

Max Riedel was later one of the organisers of the committee to create a memorial to Harry Coombe. He became caught up in a local scandal when he produced a pro-Labor election pamphlet circulated for the December 1919 federal election.[64]

At his campaign opening, held in the Gawler Institute, he explained why he was now a Labor man and why he had left Gawler:

> When he was first elected ... they said he was the first liberal that had ever been elected for Barossa. If the so called liberalism was what liberalism was recognised as in 1901, he would be under that banner today. At a Social given to him after his election in 1910 he said there was a proposal to form a combined organisation of the old National League, the Farmers and Producers Political Union and the Liberal and Democratic Union. At that election the three bodies were supposed to be working in conjunction, but he was opposed because he would not drop the franchise question. He declared that before he would join such an organisation, he would want to know whether they were prepared to adopt household suffrage, with the dual vote and effective voting, because the adoption of them was necessary to ensure that the new body was really liberal. His complaint against the Labor Party at that time was that it was not sufficiently democratic. It did not propose to remove electoral injustice. Shortly after the Labor Party included effective voting on its platform, and the Liberal Union declined to adopt household suffrage, with the dual vote, and only placed effective voting on its platform as an alternative. He, therefore, declined to join it.
>
> That decision cost him his seat for Barossa in 1912 and was the cause of his having to remove his residence from Gawler. He regretted the loss of his seat because it deprived him of the opportunity to render service to his town, his district, and his State. His leaving Gawler was a heartbreaking

experience to him. Did he regret having made that decision? He had thanked God a thousand times since then, in view of the development of the Liberal Union and the actions of the Peake Government, that he had had the moral courage to do as he did. He would not be in Mr. Peake's or Sir Richard Butler's shoes if he were assured of the premiership of the State for the rest of his life. The Labor Party stood for electoral equality. It believed in the sovereignty of the people. It believed in the rule of the majority. Its proposals for adult suffrage. effective voting. and the initiative and referendum would make the men and women of South Australia sovereign [65]

Crawford Vaughan
SLSA B-4528

The election results were Butler (5,082), Hague (5,001) and Coombe (4,856), with the Barossa to be represented by two Liberal members and one Labor member. Rudall came fourth with 54 votes less than Coombe, so it was a tight race. The Peake Liberal Government was defeated and a Labor Government was formed under Crawford Vaughan. Labor won 26 seats and the Liberals 20. The Barossa was one of the last seats to be decided, which meant Harry's former leader, Archibald Peake, watched its outcome very closely.[66] Harry had returned to parliament.

With news of the terrible war losses arriving, anti-German feelings throughout the state were building. As the member for Barossa, Harry protested strongly that South Australians of German heritage should not be discriminated against. He became a vocal opponent in the numerous parliamentary debates to disenfranchise people of enemy birth, to deport them, intern them and attack their religious freedom. Even those who were citizens either by birth or naturalisation were being targeted. Premier Vaughan was far less sympathetic toward South Australian Germans than the previous government had been, and Harry often found himself at odds with his leader.[67]

His was the only dissenting voice when a Bill was passed in the House of Assembly in October 1916 preventing the teaching of German

Harry and Sarah Coombe, 1915,
family records

in primary schools and the closing 49 Lutheran primary schools.[68] He maintained that while his constituents had German origins they did not support the current German war effort.

Then there was the nomenclature debate about the suitability of the many German place names in the state, a discussion that took place Australia-wide. As a result, many locations were changed to Aboriginal or British names. Harry requested that Krichauff and Schomburgk be removed from a list of places to have their name changed, stating that both were renowned agricultural scientists and should be regarded as citizens of the world. Sadly, his efforts came to no avail and the rural locality of Krichauff became Beatty, and the Hundred of Schomburgk became the Hundred of Maude.[69]

Harry also spoke out against the federal government's proposal to introduce conscription, a decision that would have a disastrous conclusion.

7

His Final Chapter

Harry was forced to resign from the editorship of the *Daily Herald* in June 1916 having lost the support of the Australian Workers Union and the Trades and Labour Council over his anti-conscription stance.[1]

In mid-December 1916 Harry was nominated for selection as a ULP candidate in the May 1917 Federal Senate election. It was the second time he had been offered this opportunity to move from state to federal level politics. Unlike 1910, he now saw this as an acceptable choice and a way of tackling conscription at a national level.[2] His was one of 12 nominations for the three positions. In the ensuing ballot the ULP members chose Frank Lundie, Thomas Butterfield and Lionel Laughton Hill. The third place had been a very tight competition between Harry and the younger Hill, with the final decision taking until mid-February, much longer than expected. None of the ULP candidates were ultimately successful, the South Australian Senate seats being won by the Labor Nationalists.[3]

This election came in the aftermath of the split in the Australian Labor Party following the narrow win of the 'no' campaign in the November 1916 plebiscite on conscription. Prime Minister Billy Hughes and 24 other pro-conscription Labor politicians left the party to form the National Labor Party and, with the support of the federal Liberal Party under Joseph Cook, formed a minority government. The two parties later merged to form the Nationalist Party, with Hughes as Leader and Cook as Deputy Leader. Prime Minister Hughes and his party were then forced to an election by the Opposition Leader Frank Tudor and his remaining Labor Party. There was a strong sense of betrayal by Hughes' former colleagues and an even stronger sense of dismay among the anti-conscriptionists that the matter would be raised again. Harry, who had taken a particularly active part in opposition to the Hughes conscription proposal, was much in demand. In spite of his pre-selection loss, he willingly hit the campaign trail.

Port Adelaide

On Friday 30 March 1917, with the election just five weeks away, the first campaign meeting for the South Australian United Labor Party was held at the Port Adelaide town hall.[4] Advertised as an address to the voters of Hindmarsh on the current political situation and forthcoming federal election, the evening meeting was convened by John Sweeney, Mayor of Port Adelaide. Joining Harry on stage would be fellow ULP politicians James Jelley, MLC, John Carr, MLC, and the local Member for Port Adelaide, John Lloyd (Jack) Price, MHA, son of the former premier, Tom Price.

Similar meetings were booked at Semaphore on the following Monday night and Rosewater on Tuesday 3 April, with Harry unable to attend the Monday evening due to his attendance at another campaign meeting in Tanunda at the same time. After a break for Easter Harry had committed to speak on Saturday 13 April at the Kapunda Institute to the voters for the seat of Angas, at a meeting to be presided over by Mayor Thomas Jeffs. The next afternoon he was due at meeting at the Mitcham Reserve with Leslie Claude (Les) Hunkin, the Member for East Torrens, together with fellow anti-conscription campaigner and federal Labor candidate, Thomas Grealy. On Monday 15 April he was booked to be at Tanunda with Lionel Laughton Hill supporting the Labor candidate for the Seat of Angas, Sidney O'Flaherty. A frenetic pace![5]

At 8 pm Friday night, the Port Adelaide meeting was opened by Mayor John Sweeney, who explained the purpose of the meeting and then introduced Harry as the first speaker. The press reported that:

> [Coombe] … received a good reception, and after speaking for a few minutes on the Federal political situation, his voice became thick, and he was observed to stagger. He put his right hand to his mouth and his left on the table nearby, apparently to right himself, but no sooner had he done this than he reeled forward, and then backward. Noticing his action, the

> mayor went to his assistance and caught him just in time to prevent him falling to the floor. Mr R.T. Moroney, Secretary of the ULP at Port Adelaide, Mr T. Edwards, and others also assisted the unfortunate member, who was promptly given water and removed to the side of the stage out of view of the audience.[6]

A doctor was telephoned for and the chairman sought the approval of the audience to continue. James Jelley went on to speak.

Dr Covernton arrived and ascertained that Harry had suffered a cerebral haemorrhage, also described as a severe stroke. The meeting was paused to enable the patient to be carried out through the hall on a stretcher to a waiting ambulance. The audience stood while this occurred. Jelley concluded his remarks shortly afterwards and the meeting was abandoned without Carr or Price speaking. The mayor, in closing the meeting, said:

> Owing to to-night's sad event, which I am exceedingly sorry has occurred, the best course is to close the meeting, although in ordinary circumstances I would be better pleased to have seen the meeting brought to a proper conclusion with Mr Coombe leaving us in his former good health. I was speaking with him outside the hall for a few minutes and he seemed to be in his very best mood and quite well ... I sincerely hope the illness is not serious and that he will soon recover.[7]

Semaphore

Harry was taken to the Semaphore Esplanade residence of Thomas Tonkin Edwards with Dr Covernton attending.[8]

Tom Edwards was married to Sarah Coombe's cousin, Florence Heywood, one of the eight children of William Henry Heywood and his wife, Ann. The Heywood and Coombe families were close, with regular holiday visits by train by the Coombes to the Heywood's home at Glanville. They were often accompanied by Sarah Coombe's aunt, Sarah Bright, who was William's sister.

Tom was a member of the Port Adelaide Labor Committee and the Anti-conscription League. As such he had assisted with the election meetings in Port Adelaide.

In a touch of great poignancy, Dr Hugh Selby Covernton was Harry's family doctor back in Gawler. He had emigrated from Lancashire, England to South Australia in 1893 and set up a popular practice at Gawler, working closely with Dr Dawes in his private hospital. In 1913 Dr Covernton left Gawler to enter into a partnership with Dr Frederic St. John Poole (his brother in law) and Dr A.V. Benson at Semaphore. Harry spoke at Dr and Mrs Covernton's farewell at the Gawler Institute describing him as 'skilful, attentive, considerate and kind', and as a friend. Both men and their wives had served together on the board of the Hutchinson Hospital.[9]

Dr Covernton and the ambulance may well have arrived from the nearby Port Adelaide Casualty Hospital where Covernton served as one of the local doctors on a voluntary roster system.[10] The hospital was free and open day and night to anyone with a medical problem, but the decision was made to transfer Harry to his relative's home.

Harry's collapse was a severe shock to all who knew him. The weekend newspapers from as far away as Port Pirie and Mt Gambier reported that he was in a semi-conscious but critical condition the next day.[11] By Monday he was still semi-conscious but showing a slight improvement. Premier Crawford Vaughan sent his deepest sympathies to Sarah with the hope that Harry would recover but by Wednesday his condition declined, and he died in the evening of Thursday 5 April 1917 at the age of 58.[12]

His eldest son, Harry Heywood Coombe, who was an officer in the Marion army camp, was given leave to organise his father's funeral arrangements.[13] He did this in conjunction with Harry's long-time friend Charles George Rebbeck, a funeral director in Gawler, and F.R. Moore, an undertaker and embalmer from Port Adelaide/ Semaphore.

Funeral

Harry was buried on Easter Saturday, 7 April 1917 in the Willaston Cemetery. His body was transported by train from Semaphore to Adelaide, and then, with the attachment of a mortuary car, to Gawler.[14] Many of his relatives travelled on the train with him; Sarah was accompanied by three of their four sons, Harry, James and Ernest (Samuel was still serving overseas), and their two daughters Catherine and Daisy (without her husband George, who was also serving overseas). Harry's body then lay at his brother Thomas's Main North Road, Willaston home until it was loaded on to a hearse for the 3 pm funeral procession.

The funeral was one of the largest ever held in Gawler, with many attendees travelling in from around the neighbouring districts.[15] The cortege spread over half a mile and contained over one hundred vehicles. Five cars collected fellow politicians from the Gawler Railway Station. Among them were Premier Vaughan and his brother, the Attorney-General John Vaughan; the Speaker of the House of Assembly Frederick Coneybeer; Senator James O'Loghlin; and Members of the Legislative Council, including Frederick Wallis, John Bice, James Jelley, John Carr, Walter Hannaford, James Wilson and William Harvey. Also attending were his fellow representatives for the Barossa, Sir Richard Butler and William Hague, and other members of the House of Assembly, including William Ponder, Reginald Blundell, George Yates, Henry Chesson, George Ritchie, Edward Anstey, William Cole and John Price.

Many senior staff of Parliament House also attended. Delegates came from the Gawler Institute, the Gawler Council, the Friendly Societies, the Hutchinson Hospital, and other local organisations. Other familiar names included F.E. Meleng, representing the South Australian Institutes Association; Harry Kneebone, managing editor of the *Daily Herald*; Robert Cheek, son of the 90-year-old Phillip Cheek; and Charles Horne, now councillor for the Port Adelaide Council. Jeanne Forster Young, who represented the Red Cross Ambulance Service and had worked closely with Harry for 20 years as the secretary of the Effective Voting League also attended. Many state union representatives also attended.

At the head of the funeral procession were two hundred men from the United Labor Party, including members from the Gawler and Tanunda Branches and the Barossa electorate committee. Many were workers from Gawler's engineering works, foundries and blacksmith shops. These included John Tulloch, Nelson Greaves, Frederick (Frank) Birrell, Andrew Armstrong, Percy Coxell, Frank Riggs, Ernest Pring and Max Riedel.

Immediately in front of the hearse were the Sons of Temperance with members of the Independent Order of Rechabites following behind together with a stream of vehicles, which were a mixture of horse-drawn and motorised. The five that carried the politicians were motor cars.

When the last of the cortege arrived at the graveside, a large group had already gathered. George Willcocks and Ernest Pring from the local branch of the United Labour Party, Andrew Belton and Percy Coxell from the Sons of Temperance and Theodor Ayling and George McLean from the Rechabite Order stepped forth to be the pallbearers. The service was conducted by Gawler's Methodist Minister Reverend James C. Richmond, who also delivered a short address. Brother George Bright and Brother Evan Gwynne read the burial services of the Rechabite Order and the Sons of Temperance, respectively.

Death notices appeared in numerous local and interstate newspapers paying respect to Harry as a man and a politician who was held in high regard.[16] Regretfully, that week's *Bunyip* circulated on Friday 6 April reported that he was still in a critical state and expressed much sympathy. This error was corrected in the next issue with the addition of a two-page supplement dedicated to Harry that included a tribute from Opposition Leader Peake.[17]

Tributes

Many moving tributes were paid to Harry.[18] On the first anniversary of his death Paul Zimmerman, farmer and vigneron of Lyndoch, wrote in the *Bunyip*:

> In affectionate memory of Ephraim Henry Coombe MP, Journalist, Politician and Christian gentleman who died fighting the Democratic cause of his Country's liberties. Entered into life on the 5th April, 1917, His life was gentle and the elements so mixed in him that Nature might stand up and say to all the world – 'This was a man' Greater love hath no man than this that he lay down his life for his Friends. Inserted by his true friend, a tribute from one of the wide circle of his admirers.[19]

Legacy

The legalities concluded with the winding up of his financial affairs. The Probate reported in the *Advertiser* on Monday 21 May 1917 indicated that Harry left an estate worth £2,300 (today's equivalent of $225,000). He did not grow rich taking up the causes and responsibilities of public life.

The Barossa electorate required a replacement representative and a by-election was called for 2 June 1917. Within days of Harry's death,

Paul Ferdinand Zimmerman was an active member of the Barossa Vinegrowers' Association that negotiated the price of grapes with the large winemaking firms. He was also a member of the Licensed Victuallers' Association, as the licensee of the Barossa Inn in Lyndoch from 1908 to 1910. He was a member of the Tanunda Rifle Club and like Harry, was a singer. In 1908, when the three members for the Barossa, Butler, Coombe and Rudall, addressed a public meeting at Stockwell on the proposed Angaston Railway, Australian born Zimmerman translated the meeting into German.[20]

the topic of who would succeed him in politics was raised. His eldest son, Harry Heywood, who had been the president of the Port Wakefield local committee of the United Labor Party and an elected councillor for that town, was mentioned.[21] Instead, Tom Edwards was nominated on 14 April by the Barossa ULP Committee to be their Anti-conscription candidate, and he immediately took up residence in Willaston.[22] Edwards was unsuccessful in his first attempt at running for parliament. Instead, Henry Burgess Crosby, grocery shop owner of Gawler, was the successful candidate.

A journalist from the *Bunyip* later incorrectly claimed that Harry Heywood Coombe was not selected due to his conscription views, but he, like most soldiers, was in favour of volunteerism. He did not accept nomination because he was in camp awaiting posting overseas and was not able to campaign.[23]

Memorials in Gawler and Tanunda

On 30 April 1917, the Gawler Council agreed to a request by Frank Riggs, as the secretary of the Gawler Trades and Labor Council, for the council to call a public meeting to organise a memorial to the late Ephraim Henry Coombe. A meeting of representatives of the council, the Gawler Institute, and School of Mines, was held on Thursday 10 May, just three years after a similar meeting was held to plan Harry's farewell from Gawler social.[24] Another public meeting was called for 18 June in order to establish a local committee, to discuss what form the memorial would take and to communicate with all public bodies throughout the Barossa District.[25]

It was a time of great emotional turmoil in the town. News of the deaths of local men fighting overseas continued to arrive. Letters of condolence from the council to the Coombe family were sent at the same time as to the families of those killed.[26] There is a sense that some members of council and indeed the community had mixed feelings about a monetary request from the Labor Executive Council and the anti-conscriptionists. On the other hand, Harry was one of their own.

Letters advertising the second meeting were sent out to the surrounding area and advertisements were placed in local newspapers. The Barossa Council resolved to hold its own public meeting regarding a memorial to Harry to be overseen by its chairman, John William Thomas, at Lyndoch. Mudla Wirra South Council nominated councillors John Dawkins and William Leak as delegates to the Gawler meeting.[27] As the *Bunyip* editor Robert Barnet reported:

> On Monday evening the Town Hall Chamber was comfortably filled by citizens of Gawler and the immediate neighbourhood, to discuss the proposed memorial to the late Mr. E.H. Coombe. The Mayor (Mr. W.H. Cox) presided, and the acting secretary (Rev. Thos. Vigis) reported that the preliminary meeting which consisted of delegates representative of societies in Gawler had decided that circulars should be forwarded to the various Institutes and District Councils asking their cooperation. The circulars were sent and in some instances, persons had been appointed to attend the meeting held that evening, but a number of the letters had not yet been replied to.[28]

The preliminary committee had also decided to recommend the form the memorial should take and suggested that one of the following would be most suitable:

> (1.) That a monument should be erected in Gawler;
> (2.) That sufficient money should be raised to endow a scholarship, such as a University Bursary;
> (3.) To raise sufficient money to build an Isolation Ward to the Hutchinson Hospital …

> Messrs. R.H. Barnet, J.K. Tulloch, and C. Porter favored the idea of an Isolation Ward to the Hutchinson Hospital; Mr. J.H. Dawkins ... and Mr. J.H. Garrett favored a scholarship; Mr. H. L Marsh favored a band rotunda; and Messrs. Wrn. Dawkins and others also spoke. Ultimately the following resolution proposed by Mr. J.K. Tulloch and seconded by Mr. Paternoster was carried: — 'That an effort be made to raise the sum of £1,000 to build an 'Isolation Block' in connection with the Hutchinson Hospital, to be called the 'Coombe Memorial Ward.' A further amendment moved by Mr. C.G. Rebbeck and seconded by Mr. Leak ... was carried: — 'Before the proposition to build an Isolation Ward is finalized we ask for an expression of opinion from the various Councils and Institutes upon the proposal.' On the motion of Mr. R.H. Barnet it was resolved that the committee comprise of two members of each of the various societies or bodies interested' in the movement. The Rev. T. Vigis declined to act as Secretary owing to his contemplated removal from Gawler, and Mr. J.F. Rogers was elected as hon. secretary, and Mr. Rogasch hon. treasurer of the movement.[29]

It is poignant that Harry's dedication to lifelong education, health services and cultural pursuits were to be recognised, but perhaps these were ambitious fundraising goals given the privations imposed by the war.

Another meeting was held on 16 July 1917 and again on 13 August.[30] At this second meeting, Michael Lynch occupied the chair in the absence of the mayor. The passage of time had allowed for responses from the wider community. Most of the letters received from the outside districts sympathised with the movement, but people and organisations were not in a financial position to practically support the case for the Isolation Ward proposal, and the idea for it lapsed by a resolution of the meeting. As a spirit of enthusiasm prevailed at the meeting, a subscription list was officially opened that raised a total of £10/10s before the meeting closed. An executive committee was appointed to increase the fund, comprising of Mayor William Cox, Nelson Greaves, Andrew Armstrong, Alfred Rogasch, James Bills, Henry Haydock, and J. Fletcher Rogers.

By the end of August, the *Bunyip* reported subscriptions had been received from Nuriootpa Institute, ULP Gawler Branch, Michael Lynch, Reverend S.T.C. Best, James Beasley, Oswald Cundy, 'A Friend', W. Paternoster, Nelson Greaves and J. Fletcher Rogers, all of whom donated a guinea.[31] Robert Cheek donated ten shillings, Mrs. Hannah Barnet two guineas and William Barnet three guineas.

When Robert Barnet died suddenly in September 1917, much of the enthusiasm for the fundraising was lost. By mid-November Charles Rebbeck had given ten shillings and Harry Crosby, who had replaced Harry as the Member for Barossa, had donated a guinea, bringing the total to ₤17/16s.[32] In early December the new mayor, Hermann Marsh, again suggested that his less ambitious proposal of a Citizens' Band Rotunda memorial was still plausible. By the end of the year more donations were received from Sir Richard Butler, Robert Lavis, Edwards (possibly Tom), the District Council of Angaston, and the Honourable James Jelley, making a total of ₤25/18s.[33]

At a meeting in February 1918, it was reported that fundraising was being affected by other patriotic appeals and suggested that the isolation ward idea would have to be modified. Leslie Duncan, the new editor of the *Bunyip*, replaced Alfred Rogasch as the treasurer. Duncan had previously been the owner of the *Barossa News*.[34]

February 1918 was also the month that Second Lieutenant Harry Heywood Coombe, Harry's eldest son, embarked for overseas duty. His ship arrived in England on ANZAC Day 1918. He was killed in action in France just months later, on 23 August 1918, aged 37.[35]

Meanwhile, possibly frustrated at the slow progress being made in Gawler, Tanunda residents moved to organise their own memorial to Harry. At a meeting held on 1 May 1918, there was a resolution to erect a monument in Tanunda, with the site, design and other details to be decided at a later meeting. There were suggestions that a public park should be the site for a design of a broken column. Contribution lists were opened and circulated throughout the district with promises of support received from residents of Nuriootpa, Tanunda and Lyndoch.[36]

Although the Armistice ended the fighting on the Western Front, marking a victory for the Allies and a defeat for Germany, it was not formally a surrender. The Armistice was prolonged three times until the Treaty of Versailles that was signed on 28 June 1919. For this reason, many Honour Boards, including Gawler's, are marked WWI 1914–1919.

Family and friends at the 1930 opening of E.H. Coombe memorial
Front row: Alma Coombe and her son, Herbert Ernest Coombe, Margaret Coombe, Nell Coombe, Samuel's son, Harry Neville Coombe
Second row: James Coombe, Norman Makin, John Walden, Daisy Coombe, Samuel Coombe, family friend Ern Blutcher
Back row: Tom Edwards, George Ash, possibly Paul Zimmermann, Ernest Coombe

Fundraising events were then overtaken by the anticipation and then the celebration of the Armistice on 11 November 1918.

On 16 December 1918 a ratepayers meeting was called by the Tanunda District Council in response to a request from the Coombe Memorial Committee to discuss a site for the proposed monument. The meeting, held in the Tanunda Institute, had a record attendance and was presided over by the chairman of the council, Moritz Heuzenroeder. No one from the Coombe Memorial Committee attended

Original drawing of the monument.
Presented to the Gawler Institute by T.T. Edwards,
Gawler Heritage Collection

the meeting to address the residents, so it was resolved to leave the matter in the council's hands.[37]

Max Riedel spearheaded the Tanunda project. A prominent main street location was provided on land donated by Albert Julius Henschke, who was more commonly known as Julius. The site on the corner of Julius and Murray streets had been Henschke's home block. Preliminary building work was completed by the end of December 1919, with an expectation that the stone would be sourced and erected in early in the new year, but the inscription took far longer.[38]

Back in Gawler South moves were underway by the Mudla Wirra Council to erect a soldiers' memorial. The E.H. Coombe Memorial Fund was not forgotten in the discussion, with one suggestion that the two memorials be combined in some way. This did not happen, with the Gawler South Soldiers' Memorial finally being erected in 1921.[39] (The Gawler soldiers' memorial, in the form of the Gawler Institute Memorial Balcony, was not finalised until March 1931.)[40]

On 28 May 1919, a meeting of the Coombe Memorial Fund was held in Gawler to finalise the appeal. The committee recognised that owing to the immense pressure put upon the public finances, the ambitious proposal of building a memorial wing to the Hutchinson Hospital could not yet be accomplished. Instead, with the funds in hand, it was proposed that a headstone and railing be erected around Harry's grave in the Willaston Cemetery. 'Now that the war alarms were over it was hoped that the public would turn their attention to home affairs and worthily honour the man who gave of his best freely.'[41]

The plans for the gravestone and railings were submitted to Sarah for her approval. On the afternoon of Sunday 21 September 1919, she performed an unveiling ceremony of the public memorial for her late husband at the Willaston Cemetery. The *Bunyip* reported:

> Fully 500 people gathered around the grave at 4 pm and the Mayor of Gawler and Chairman of the Memorial Committee (Mr H.L. Marsh) assumed control. Riggs' Viceregal Band rendered the music for the hymns, and Mr Coombe's favourites 'Abide With Me', 'Lead Kindly Light' and the 'Song of Australia' were sung. After a prayer by the Rev R. Broadbent, the Mayor made a short address. He said they were gathered together to

> pay honour to a native of Gawler and a citizen who benefited his fellow man being a friend to all and an enemy to none. It was not wanted to be a sad ceremony, for after all the world was a stage wherein people were met and enjoyed, and afterwards parted with the hope of meeting them again elsewhere. Those present had enjoyed the pleasure of Mr Coombe's company, the beam of his smile, and believed to meet him later in another plane. The block of granite that would be unveiled was not erected to remind people of his goodness, but that the warm words spoken that afternoon might resolve into granite to remind future generations of the man who gave so much for his fellow men.
>
> When he thought of Mr Coombe's activities, in their midst, his mind ran riot, for Mr Coombe had been associated with all things, and the momentum of his influence had not ceased today. The History of Gawler was to him a labour of love, and his work in the Institute, Hospital, athletic, and musical bodies would be remembered for all time. In his life he had encountered terrific storms, passing through the frigid zone of indifference right to the torrid zone of political debate, but he had always kept a straight course and maintained a deep interest in his work, and was now enjoying his reward.
>
> Mr Marsh asked Mrs Coombe the widow, to unveil the monument, and afterwards the grave was covered with floral tributes. The stone, a pleasing design, and enclosed with an iron railing, bears the following inscription: — 'Erected by his friends to the memory of E.H. Coombe. MP, dearly loved husband of Sarah F. Coombe. Died April 4 [sic], 1917. Peace fully resting. Also their loved son Lieut H.H. Coombe, of 10th Battalion, who just stepped aside to rest in France, August 23, 1918.[42]

It was not until February 1930, six years after Sarah's death, that the Tanunda memorial to E.H. Coombe was finally unveiled. Harry and Sarah's sons James, Samuel and Ernest, their daughters Catherine and Daisy, and Daisy's recent ex-husband, George Ash, all attended.[43] A souvenir booklet was produced and sold at the ceremony for a one-shilling contribution toward the Memorial Fund.

Tom Edwards, who presided over the occasion, described his cousin by marriage as:

> one of the greatest statesmen we have produced ... and in remembering this man's fine qualities, we are proud he was born in the Barossa district and that he worked so whole heartedly for his district, his people and the State generally. Can you wonder that we gather today on the 13th year of his death to do homage, respect and reverence to so great a man. Is it any wonder that we as a people are prepared to erect, and finish a monument, that will stand for all time to show our gratitude to a man who was cut down in the midst of his work.[44]

He described how Harry had worked tirelessly in the cause of justice and was known to be a strong supporter for 'the welfare of man and the prosperity of all'. He concluded by quoting Harry's favourite words from Longfellow and Wordsworth.

At the time of the unveiling of the memorial, Tom Edwards was standing again as a candidate for the seat of Barossa. The election date, 5 April 1930, would be the exact date of Harry's death. It proved a good omen for Edwards: like Harry, his third election attempt was successful.

As well as stressing his relationship to Harry and his presence with him in his final days, Edwards described his efforts in ensuring that the day's event was taking place after such a lengthy delay. Together with Max Riedel as chairman, Charles Baum and John Walden, he had formed a committee to finalise the monument.

Joel Moses Gabb, who next addressed the crowd, indicated that the delay in unveiling the monument had been caused by a controversy about the use of the word 'crucified' on the memorial's inscription. Many preferred the words 'bitterly persecuted', but Chairman Max Riedel took full responsibility for the wording. He admired Riedel for the fighting spirit he had shown and noted that Riedel had suffered his own bitter experiences of war.

Gabb ended his speech by appealing for all to seek to emulate Harry in fighting and serving 'for the cause that lacks assistance, for the wrongs that need resistance, for the future in the distance, and the good that we can do.' [45] His words also appealed to the 'emotional scars of injustice' held by the Australian German community. Their sense of marginalisation resulting from the anti-German campaigns of both World Wars would last into the 1950s and beyond.[46]

Joel Moses Gabb was the local federal member for Angas. In May 1924 he had made an impassioned speech in the Australian Parliament that proved influential in lifting many of the anti-German restrictions. From 1924 the ban on German immigration and on German newspapers was lifted, and Lutheran schools were allowed to re-open. By the late 1920s church services could again be held in German, the language of the Lutheran faith.[47]

The Tanunda Band played 'Abide with Me' and the Gawler Band played both 'God Save the King' and the 'Song of Australia', the song that owed its existence to the Gawler Institute. John Walden, an elderly gentleman from Lyndoch, then performed the unveiling. He had been a mail contractor as well as chairman of the Tanunda Council, the president of the Tanunda Institute and a vice-president of the Barossa Show. In his speech Walden recalled the happy times when he and Harry were driving the old coach on the Gawler to Tanunda roads, and the possum hunting they indulged in. James Coombe, in his capacity as the eldest surviving son, and supported by his brother Samuel, thanked the committee and all who had assisted in erecting the memorial.

The unveiled monument revealed the inscriptions carved by monumental mason J. Henschke across three of the plinth faces:

Front Inscription

Erected by Friends who honour the memory of Ephraim Henry Coombe, M.P.
He was born in Gawler 26th August, 1858, and served the people faithfully until he died 5th April, 1917.
He saw his duty and did it nobly.

Left Side Inscription

We crowned him in 1901 and all that is evil crucified him in 1917 but truth prevailed, and he died as he lived, an honourable man.

Back Inscription

Let all men draw inspiration from a life well spent. And know that no greater offering can his memory crave, than that which freemen offer to the brave.[48]

Albert Julius Henschke was a stonemason, monumental mason and sculptor who created many gravestones and church fonts throughout the Barossa. He also carved war memorials at Tanunda in 1920 and Freeling in 1923, and carved the Angaston marble reliefs of angels in situ at the National War Memorial in Adelaide. Although a patriotic, third-generation Australian, he was refused the commission for the Gawler South war memorial in 1920 solely because of his German name. He went on to do the carving on the Australian Mutual Provident Society building in 1936, the Art Gallery of South Australia in 1937, the Corinthian capitals and other architectural features on Parliament House, Adelaide, circa 1938, and the emblem of the Savings Bank of South Australia on its King William Street building in 1941. One of his last commissions was to carve the base of the equestrian statue of King George V, in Angas Gardens, Adelaide, which was unveiled in 1956.[49]

It was not just Max Riedel's championing of the word 'crucified' that had delayed the opening of the E.H. Coombe memorial, it was also his fiery temper and strong stance on the continuing anti-German sentiment that made the community nervous. As a chairman of the Tanunda Branch of the ULP he had produced an election leaflet for the campaign for the 13 December 1919 federal election. It included several provocative phrases including, 'Who called you Huns because you honoured your fathers and mother? Who interned Australian citizens without a trial?'.[50]

Not unsurprisingly, there was an immediate outcry and a public meeting was held in Angaston to disparage the publication. Reginald Rudall, son of Samuel and vice-president of the Gawler branch of the Returned Services Association, and Moritz Heuzenroeder were among the many speakers who strongly denounced the wording of the pamphlet and its author. As the *Leader* reported, 'It has opened old sores, stirred up racial feeling and born a bitterness that may lead to serious results'.

The story was widely published and the link was made between the pamphlet and the proposed memorial inscription that had been circulated six months earlier. It too came under heavy criticism, and it took some time before the dust settled.[51]

Back in Gawler, Tom Edwards donated several of Harry's possessions to the Gawler Institute. These included two scrapbooks. One scrapbook that dated from July 1897 contains newspaper articles on general economic, political, religious and social matters as well more Gawler-related entries, such as 'Gawler Economic Class', sports news (cricket, chess, education), and meteorological records. The other scrapbook, inscribed 'Letters written to the *Weekly Herald* commencing July 23, 1897', contains newspaper cuttings entitled 'Open letters to Tom Jones, Working Man' and signed off from 'Uncle Dick'. These are conversational in style on such topics as the inequality of wealth distribution in South Australia and taxation, and provide evidence of Harry's emerging politics. There are also letters written as entries into a 1900 literary competition with a grand prize of a bicycle and a series of letters entitled 'Wireless Telegrams by F.R. Eedom'. Both scrapbooks contain examples of Harry's and his son James' handwriting and remain within the Gawler Cultural Heritage Collection today. Another of the items donated is a sketch by Julius Henschke of what is described as the Tanunda memorial.[52]

There are many lasting memorials to Harry located throughout South Australia and in Canberra:

- the locality of Coombe in the Coorong District Council South Australia was created in 2000 and named for the Coombe railway station;
- the Coombe railway station located on the Adelaide–Wolseley 1887 railway line, the South Australian section of the Melbourne–Adelaide railway. It is one of the 18 crossing loops on the line;[53]
- the Hundred of Coombe in the Murray Mallee region of South Australia, which dates from 1906 when Harry was in parliament;[54]
- his grave marker in the Willaston cemetery in Gawler. Opened in 1919 as a publicly funded memorial, the granite obelisk remains but the railings, unfortunately, have gone;
- Coombe Street in Bonython, ACT. The suburb was named in 1986 for Sir John Langdon Bonython, politician and philanthropist and the sole proprietor of the Adelaide *Advertiser* from 1893 to 1929, and contains streets named after famous South Australians, particularly journalists, and South Australian districts; [55]
- In December 1926, an ornamental fountain and fishpond was built in memory of the Hutchinson Hospital's first chairman, E.H.

Coombe. It was opened as part of the launch of the new eight-bed Maternity Wing. Erected at a cost of £50, it was located in front of the new wing. It was later converted into a raised flower bed and today no longer exists;[56]

- In 1993 there was a Coombe Ward created within the Town of Gawler. It existed until November 1999 when the structure of wards was abandoned by the Council;
- Coombe Street, Gawler East incorrectly reported as having being named for Coombe. There has long been debate as to whether this was named for E.H. Coombe or the earlier Canon W.H. Coomb. Given that the street was named in 1866, it is obviously named in honour of Canon Coomb's 20th anniversary in Gawler, and is simply misspelled;[57]
- Three framed photographic portraits that remain in Gawler. Two were produced by Edwin Walter Marchant of Gawler and were presented to Harry at his farewell social in June 1917.[58] Originally intended to be displayed in the Gawler Institute reading room and the School of Mines they are now held by the Gawler Cultural Heritage Collection and the Gawler Branch of the National Trust of South Australia. A third framed photographic portrait of Harry was presented to the Board of the Hutchinson Hospital in September 1914, by members of Gawler's Friendly Societies in appreciation of their first Chairman's work in obtaining reduced fees for their members when admitted to the Hutchinson Hospital. This photograph remains with the Gawler Health Service, the successor of the Hutchinson Hospital; [59]
- Another photographic portrait of Harry is displayed in the South Australian Parliament House to commemorate his term as Member for the Barossa.

And, of course, there is Harry's *History of Gawler.*

8

Conclusion

To sum up a life is always difficult, but a review of the key events and choices made by a person along their journey can provide a valuable insight.

In Harry's case we begin with his father's and mother's separate decisions to migrate across the world to a new colony established on the radical theories of colonisation by Edward Gibbon Wakefield. Based on a workable combination of labourers, tradespeople, artisans and capital, the Wakefield scheme centred on the sale of land to the capitalists to finance the assisted migration of the others. This gave agricultural labourers like the Coombe, Lock and Riggs families the opportunity for a new future far from the restrictions of the English regime.

For his mother, the leap into the unknown was somewhat cushioned by her emigration as part of a large, supportive family. For his father, following a path taken by earlier family members, it was a brave adventure to take alone.

The attraction of the Gawler area for these immigrants was its easy access to agricultural land and associated industries. His father, Ephraim, progressed from farm labouring work to shopkeeping, providing a service that catered to passing traffic and the growing local population. Hard work and determination gave his family a firm basis for the future.

An act of benevolence from a great uncle to an 11-year-old boy in the form of a legacy of £100 to be paid on his 21st birthday was a major stimulus, offering hope for a future that might grow beyond his father's world of labouring and shopkeeping.

It gave him the determination to continue to educate himself while still working. And here we see the influence of his first mentors, headmaster L.S. Burton and businessman Edward Potter, with their connections to the Gawler Institute. Its affiliated program of adult education classes provided Harry with shorthand, typing, bookkeeping, writing, public speaking and debating; all skills that enabled him to move, step by step, toward a new career.[1]

Harry was part of South Australia's first 'native born' generation – those whose parents migrated here and then had children. This group came of age in the last three decades of the nineteenth century. They were keen to build on the progress of their pioneering parents and reap the rewards of their own efforts.

His religion of Wesleyan Methodism had a tradition of rich associational activities and dynamic, sometimes radical, community organisations.[2] This became instrumental to his belief that the best way to get things done was to form such a group. It also influenced his views on temperance, recognising that excessive drinking often resulted from unsatisfactory social conditions. Alcohol abuse that led to family violence and other crimes would only be permanently reformed by the improvement of those conditions.[3]

Harry's role as journalist and later as an editor allowed him to influence how his readers imagined their community. He gathered and disseminated a wide scope of information from across the state, the nation and overseas, presenting news on such emerging issues as women's suffrage, federation and labour disputes.[4]

His social activism took up a great deal of his time; he attended meetings, offered his organisational skills and took on the responsibility of completing the many resultant tasks. Together with his sporting interests, these responsibilities saw him travel extensively, generally by train. He mixed with many people from across all levels of society and formed friendships and alliances that would prove useful in his roles of shopkeeper, journalist, editor, and politician. With very few exceptions, he remained with the organisations that he joined for many years, only resigning when the time came to leave Gawler.

Many of the cultural, sporting and benevolent societies with which he was involved continue today, a testament to the roles he took on with their associated responsibilities. Under his watch meetings were effectively organised, outcomes were achieved and careful records maintained.

After his marriage his own family responsibilities meant that he engaged in multiple employment roles. He built up finance and support before moving on to the next stage of his career. He engaged the same strategies within community organisations. He was once described as a 'plodder', which quite correctly describes his method of planned advancement; strategic, considered and minimising risk.[5] His slow and steady approach mirrored the methodical approach of his religion.

He championed the labouring classes – the small farmers, farm workers, the shopkeepers and the foundry workers – from which his family had arisen and with whom he rubbed shoulders and did business. His philosophy was an overlap between the Methodist radical social gospel and the aspirational disciplines of small commerce.

Archibald Peake described him better as a 'very able and indefatigable worker who gave his life to the study and practice of public affairs'.[6]

The label of socialist was often attached to him, but it was his faith that produced the tenets of his political beliefs rather than the revolutionary socialism of Karl Marx. He saw politics as the practical implementation of Christianity.

When he first entered parliament, Harry was viewed as a progressive liberal. He described himself as a democratic liberal and today is sometimes referred to as a radical liberal. Whatever flavour, the word liberal differentiated him from the conservatives. Over time, his politics evolved. He was greatly influenced by the political and economic writings of American journalist Henry George.[7] George's 'single tax' system as well as the democratic need for the universal vote would remain constant goals in Harry's political life. This put him at odds with some pastoralists and other wealthy landowners who sought to control the legislation passed by parliament through control of the Upper House of South Australia's bicameral parliament.

Harry came to oppose the long-standing incumbency of Sir John Downer, particularly once the elder statesman devoted more and more of his time away from the electorate. Harry created the Barossa Political Reform League with his brother Thomas and others in the Gawler and Districts Trades and Labor Council. Their aim was to reduce the concentration of capital in the hands the wealthy few, and the domination of conservatives in the Barossa. This provided an early connection with the trade union movement and a willingness to work closely with its members in order to achieve mutual goals.

Both he and William Henry Carpenter were identified as potential candidates for the 1896 election by the Barossa Political Reform League. The members of the Gawler and Districts Trades and Labor Council choose to support Harry for Barossa. Carpenter ran as a Labor candidate for the southern seat of Encounter, an electorate that had far fewer voters than Barossa. And it was Carpenter, not Coombe who was successful in being elected to parliament.

Ironic then that the departure of Sir John Downer to sit in the new federal parliament gave Harry the opportunity to win the 1901 Barossa by-election – a case of third time lucky for our slow and steady 'plodder'.

Harry entered the parliament at a pivotal time in the formation of the party political system. Political alignment had settled into a shifting triangular pattern between the conservatives, the independent liberals and the labour group, with two regularly combining against the third to achieve government.

In Harry's second full term he allied himself with the liberal, Archibald Peake, finding alignment on several matters including the reform of the Upper House. Harry took on leadership positions under him while both in opposition and in government. He was part of a bloc of six liberals supporting the 1905 Peake-Price Liberal-Labor alliance.

With his usual commitment to hard work and meticulous detail, Harry helped Peake form the middle ground Liberal and Democratic Union that combined with the independent liberals. It was created as a party for the wheat-growing areas and deliberately appealed to the wide cross-section of people who occupied these regions.

> Farmers, graziers, miners, other workers, and all who are interested in the progress and welfare of the State shall be eligible as members of the [Liberal Democratic] Union. Objects ... an economic, liberal and progressive policy. Vigorous policy of land settlement to bring into occupation all Crown land ... by repurchase, if necessary compulsory ... Progressive land tax ... Franchise reduction to £15 ... Public ownership of all railways tramways and wharves.[8]

The Liberal and Democratic Union agreed to cooperate closely with the Labor Party, especially on the question of the franchise in the Upper House. This cooperation was relatively short-lived and Peake, in order to remain as premier after Price's death in 1909, commenced negotiations with the conservatives. As a result, Harry, one of Peake's 'nimble nine' ministers, watched as sections of their policy, including the non-alienation of Crown lands, the reform of the franchise and progressive land tax, disappeared from the government program. In December 1909 he was one of the three Liberal and Democratic Union ministers who stepped down to allow three conservative members, including Sir Richard Butler, Leader of the Opposition and fellow Member for Barossa, to join the Peake ministry.[9] Whether Harry was pushed or whether he volunteered, we shall never know, but it was a serious blow and things grew even more problematic for him.

Peake sought to strengthen his position by amalgamating the Liberal and Democratic Union with the two conservative parties to form a Liberal Union. The conservatives readily approved the merger. However, the party for whom Harry had been president salvaged only a few of their principles from the merger, and he was opposed to the alliance.

The embryonic Liberal Union lost the April 1910 election, and Verran's Labor Party took power to form the first Labor government in the world. Harry witnessed Verran moving hard on the platform of adult suffrage for the Legislative Council.

In September 1910 Peake persuaded the Liberal and Democratic Union party conference that 'the day of the middle party is passed' and approved the merger by one vote. In October 1910 Harry refused to sign the pledge of the new party that read: 'I am a member of the Union, and if selected I will support the principles of the Union and its platform. I will not contest the election if not selected by the Union.'

Instead, he ran as an independent democratic liberal and won. When the parliament formed, he gave his support to John Verran and South Australia's first Labor government.

With the support of the Northern Democratic Association, Harry re-formed the Liberal and Democratic Union and under its banner ran as its candidate in the 1912 state election. The two-party system was now entrenched, and he was one of only six of the 78 candidates who ran independently of the two major parties. None of the six won, and the Liberal Union led by Peake was successful.

After six tumultuous years interacting with Peake and his bid to retain power, Harry now found himself in the political wilderness. It was a pivotal point in his life and he reflected on what his next step should be. His unsuccessful attempt to move into local government administration proved damaging and led to his decision to leave Gawler to take up employment with the *Daily Herald*. It also confirmed the inevitable and final move in his political allegiance. Given the polarisation of a two-party system, he accepted he had more in common politically with the Labor Party than the conservative Liberal Union. Gone were the days when he could retain his independent stance and negotiate his allegiances to bring the best for his electorate. To return to parliament he needed to commit to a party. He chose the party of his brother and his eldest son.

His move was decried as a betrayal by his former colleagues, but the last laugh was with him. The electorate voted for him in as the Barossa's United Labor Party candidate for 1915 election. The United Labor Party won the election and Harry served under Premier Crawford Vaughan.

None of the independents that offered themselves for the 1915 election were successful, so his decision to join a party had proved to be a good one.

His determination to walk his own path continued. Joining the anti-conscription council, formed by the United Labor Party opponents of conscription, he found himself pitched against many of his colleagues. Never more so than when Premier Vaughan, Leader of the Opposition Peake, and Senator for South Australia Robert Guthrie signed up the support of South Australia to Billy Hughes' final appeal before the referendum. Instead, he found himself naturally in league with the international socialists, religious pacifists, other single-taxers, Roman Catholics and trade unionists that belonged to the Anti-conscription Council and its partner organisation the Anti-conscription League.

His hard work and attention to detail led to his undoing. The stress of campaigning, an increasing number of verbal attacks on Harry, the demands of constant travel and the trauma of being taken to court took its toll. Minutes into an impassioned anti-conscription speech, he collapsed. He lingered in and out of consciousness for a week before dying aged 58.

His legacy was complex. The second referendum and the continuing spectre of community mistrust clashed with a genuine feeling of loss felt by so many at his death. It took many years for a fulsome and lasting memorial to be raised, and then not in his hometown of Gawler. Regardless, his gifts to his birthplace remain and his name has become synonymous with continuing education, community organisation, political achievement, principles in public life, powerful writing and placing Gawler firmly upon the public stage.

Vale Ephraim Henry Coombe.

Appendix A
Timeline of His Adult Life

Harry turned 21 on 26 August 1879. By looking at the years before and after he reached adulthood, we can view the world he lived in and its impact on his development.

1873 – A period of great activity and considerable achievement for the Eight Hours Movement in South Australia. Against the background of a stronger economy, shortages of labour and a degree of empathy among some employers, successful campaigns were undertaken to reduce the hours of work in some, but not all, trades. Organised labour in Gawler's factories was quick to join with other trade organisations in negotiating better outcomes.

Recreation was a key symbol in the campaign, and with the achievement of shorter working days, included with that was a block of hours free on a Saturday afternoon, when team games and social activities blossomed.[1] A plethora of technical, scientific, musical, dramatic and literary societies were established, many under the auspices of the Gawler Institute. Local 'continuation' classes were also offered.[2] Fourteen-year-old Harry, who worked directly opposite the Institute, was able to access its services.

1874 – In December, 16-year-old Harry played with his father in the Wesleyan Sunday School v. St George's Sunday School cricket match. Harry top scored with 27 not out in the second innings.[3]

1877 – Aged 19, Harry became a charter member and financial secretary of the Sons of Temperance, Perseverance Division No. 17.[4] While based on the promotion of the temperance movement, this organisation also acted as a friendly society, providing mutual support in times of sickness or bereavement, during a time when there was no welfare state, trade unions or universal health care. An earlier temperance society, a branch of the South Australian Total Abstinence Society, was founded in 1856 by a group that included his maternal grandfather, Henry Lock.

1878 – Harry became a member of the Rose of Gawler Tent of the Independent Order of Rechabites, another temperance and friendly society.[5] His father belonged to another friendly society, the Loyal Gawler Lodge of Oddfellows, having been a member since 1859.[6] In March, Harry captained Willaston in a cricket match against Gawler River, topping the score in his team's second innings with 20 out of the team's total of 96.[7]

1879 – An association was formed to represent and unite Gawler's nine friendly societies. Aged 21, Harry represented yet another temperance society, the Good Templars, in the Friendly Societies Association.[8] This was the year he came into his £100 inheritance from his great-uncle Ephraim giving him the opportunity to make some important decisions about his future enterprises.

1880 – The newly married Harry became the secretary of the new Gawler Temperance League, a union of the three temperance societies in Gawler: the Rechabites, the Sons of Temperance and the Good Templars. The League was formed to admit men of influence who agreed with their object, although not total abstainers, and who would work with them.[9] He remained a member of the Sons of Temperance and acted as their secretary from 1883–1890.

This year also saw the furthering of Harry's cricketing career when, together with his brother Thomas, he became a founder of the Union Cricket Club. Harry was the club's first secretary, serving until 1890. He remained a playing member of the Gawler Union Cricket Club for 25 years and was then made patron in 1907–1908, by which time the club needed to appoint two secretaries.[10]

1887 – Having played cricket for South Adelaide, he became a state representative for an intercolonial cricket game against Victoria. Harry's extraordinarily successful cricket career, particularly as an underarm bowler, has been highlighted by cricket historian Geoff Sando.[11]

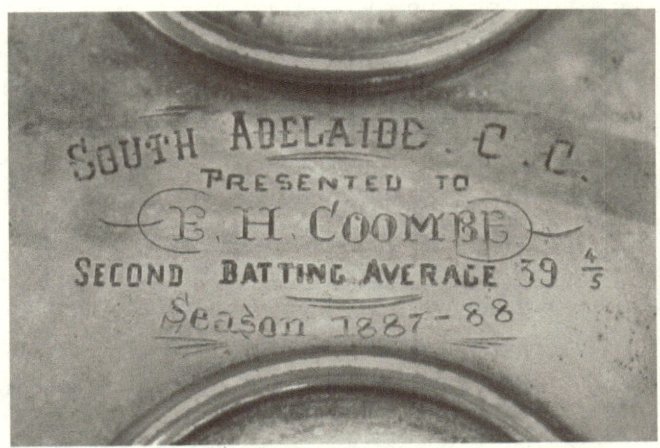

Gawler Branch National Trust

Harry helped revive the Gawler Chess Club, which then affiliated with the Gawler Institute. Both he and the club had considerable success at inter-town and state championships. Adelaide clubs became reluctant to travel up to Gawler, so in the early 1890s games held by telephone were introduced. The club also participated in interstate competitions, leading Harry to later say that he played in more interstate matches than any other 'Gawlerite'. This involved travel, presumably by sea, to New South Wales and Western Australia, and by rail Victoria in the 1890s.

He was active in local dramatics with walk on roles with the Gawler Amateur Comedy Company in 1887, 1888 and 1889.[12] His public performance skills were now finely honed.

1888 – In the year that he turned 30, Harry began his journalistic career by becoming the corresponding literary representative for the *Register* newspaper. He also became the founding secretary of the Gawler Cricket Association that comprised four clubs: Union, Gawler, Prince Albert and One Tree Hill. The association fielded combined teams to play against other areas. Harry would remain a committee member for many years.[13]

Signalling his growing interest in politics, Harry founded the first iteration of the Barossa Political Reform League. This was a progressive political association whose aim was to progress the cause of liberal candidates in an area that had been dominated by conservatives.

1889 – Harry became the honorary secretary of the Gawler Geological and Mineral Class, which had formed the year before as the Amateur Assaying Club.[14] The class would become associated with the Adelaide School of Mines, allowing it to be guided by a paid lecturer. From September 1890 its members were able to take examinations for certificates, and Harry became one of four successful candidates for the first Gawler branch of the Adelaide School of Mines' examination in Geology. There had been eight exam candidates from a class of 22 students.

In 1892 the class changed its name to the Gawler Geological and Mineral Society, and when the Adelaide School of Mines withdrew its support, secretary Harry, together with Sir John Downer, formed a successful deputation to the Minister of Education to seek alternative funding. This resulted in the group's 1893 evolution into the Gawler

1890 Gawler Amateur Geological & Mineralogical Club at Mt Crawford.
E.H. Coombe far left. Gawler Heritage Collection

School of Mines, and a move from its Institute rooms to the Murray Street premises provided by James Martin. Overflow classes continued at the Institute until 1898, when there was a final move of the Gawler School of Mines to larger premises at the former Telegraph Office. Regular lectures in chemistry, physics and maths were progressively introduced, providing further education opportunities for young men, and with the introduction of dressmaking classes in 1898, young women. At Harry's instigation, townspeople donated money to provide scholarships for the students.[15] He would remain the secretary of the Gawler School of Mines until 1914.[16]

This was just the start of Harry's long association with the technical education that would include his involvement in the 1905 building of the Gawler Technical and High School on Lyndoch Road, Gawler East (now Immanuel Lutheran School).[17]

1885 – Aged 27, Harry joined the Gawler Methodist Choir that was associated with the Tod Street Church. He had earlier been a member of the Willaston Methodist Choir under the leadership of his brother Thomas.[18]

1890 – Harry became a committee member of the Gawler Institute, the start of a very long association that would include Harry serving as its president in 1898 and 1899. A subscription library was immediately established, with nearly half of the books donated. At a time when the cost of a book could equal a workman's weekly wages, this was a valuable community resource.

Harry undertook jury duty in 1890 for the coronial inquests into the deaths of Mr F.C. Schumaker of Gawler, Mrs Robert Fotheringham of Gawler West and Mr Richard Tancock of Kangaroo Flat Road. He also took on the role of auditor for the Gawler Agricultural, Floricultural and Horticultural Society, having won a prize for the entry of his dog in that year's Gawler Show.[19]

The most important event of the year was Harry's appointment, in July 1890, as editor of the *Bunyip* newspaper.

1890 was a hard year economically, as the state entered a downturn after two decades of strong growth. The effects of the general depression were obvious locally, with relief operations being set up by government and private groups. Many of the organisations Harry belonged to provided practical support by such means as housing for the needy, and cooperative loan schemes.

1894 – Harry became auditor for the newly formed Gawler Starr-Bowkett Society, whose aims were to apply the principles of cooperation for the purpose of providing homes free of rent or interest to its members.

In the same year, Harry became the inaugural president of Gawler's Institute Literary and Sociological Society. This sponsorship of cultural societies saw the Gawler Institute sometimes referred to as the Gawler Literary Institute.[20] From 1894–1902 Harry taught shorthand, bookkeeping and typewriting at the Gawler School of Design, another offshoot of the Gawler Institute created in 1889 for the purpose of providing further technical education.

Unions of literary societies soon formed, generally based on a regional area. The Gawler Institute Literary Societies' Union formed in 1898, with 12 member societies from as far away as Tarlee, Kapunda, Lyndoch, Salisbury and Gawler River. Harry was one of the union's early presidents.[21]

By uniting, the literary societies were able to broaden the scope of their activities and were soon holding conferences; publishing the monthly *Literary Societies' Journal*; pioneering educational reforms such as the introduction of evening classes at the University of Adelaide; organising literary competitions, debating tournaments, and reading clubs for members of the associated societies; and presiding over one of its earliest and most influential innovations, the Union Parliament.

Also known as Model or Mock Parliaments, Union Parliaments were held to promote understanding of the working of government and sometimes to advocate social or political change. They continue today in South Australia in the form of an annual Youth Parliament hosted by the YMCA.

The Gawler Institute Literary Societies' Union established its own Model Parliament in 1901 with Harry elected as the first Speaker.

Also in 1894, and with Harry's assistance, the Barossa Political Reform League was re-established at the instigation of the Gawler Institute Sociological Class and the Gawler Trades and Labor Council. It would have branches at Gawler and Williamstown and became a vehicle for the selection of candidates for the next election.

1896 – Harry was nominated by the Barossa Political Reform League to stand as a liberal candidate for the Barossa electorate in the House of Assembly. He was unsuccessful in this, his first bid to enter parliament.

1897 – He was appointed as the only country journalist on the Hansard staff for the Federal Convention in Adelaide. This opportunity was won through the high regard for his stenography skills, honed from many years of state Hansard reporting for the *Register.*[22]

1898 – As the President of the Gawler Institute, Harry became the founding chair and secretary of the Gawler Institute Technical Education Vigilance Committee. As a member of both the Gawler School of Mines and the Institute's School of Design, he created this committee to induce young people of Gawler to join the existing classes; to ascertain the demand for new classes; to encourage the School of Mines Council or the Institute Committee to form them; and generally, to promote interest in and desire for technical training often through the means of his newspaper.

Several new classes were formed at the suggestion of the Gawler Institute Technical Education Vigilance committee.

During the same year, and again as the president of the Gawler Institute, Harry became a founding committee member of the South Australian Institutes Association. Initially he served as its vice-president and then, in 1911–1913, as its president. The Institutes Association was formed to protect the Institutes' government subsidy grant after the *Free Libraries Act* 1899 empowered municipal councils to raise a levy for the provision of free libraries. This fear was short-lived, as the depressed economic climate meant that no councils took up the levy. This stand-off would continue for nearly 60 years.[23]

In 1898 Harry joined the committee of the Gawler District Trained Nursing Society. His wife, Sarah, was also a member of this committee, and the Adelaide Children's Hospital Gawler Committee, perhaps with the memory of the loss of their baby daughter in 1893 to whooping cough.[24]

Both committees raised funds by recruiting local subscribers and organising special events. The District Trained Nursing Society saw its role as 'bringing order and assistance to homes under stress of poverty and sickness', an example of how community members could enact their Christian Socialism by the cooperative provision health and social care.[25] Sickness, injury, destitution and premature death were very much part of life for many living in Gawler. The economic depression of the 1880s and 1890s severely affected the quality of housing, public sanitation and health of its citizens. The passing of the *South Australian Public Health Amendment Bill* in 1884 had tried to address the worst conditions but the local health board often struggled with the effects of systemic poverty.

1899 – Harry made his second unsuccessful attempt as a liberal candidate for Barossa.

1900 – Harry, as the president of the Gawler Theatrical Club, presented the Institute, of which he was the immediate past president, with a new drop scene for its stage. The two-year-old amateur dramatic club had just completed a second performance of *Octoroon*, an American play about race and slavery, to raise funds for the painted cloth background. Another play performed in April raised funds for the District Trained Nursing Society. A month later they would tour another play to Kapunda.[26]

1901 – The transfer of his long-term rival, Sir John Downer, into federal politics, created a by-election for Barossa. Harry was successful in his third attempt for the House of Assembly. He would win re-election at the 1902, 1905, 1906, 1910 and 1915 elections.

1902 – Harry began a four-year term as a Governor of the Public Library, Museum and Art Gallery. He represented the Institutes Association of South Australia as one of the five institute representatives on a fourteen member Public Library, Museum and Art Gallery Board. Often referred to as the Library Board, this body was formed in 1883 to govern the three departments that had grown from the 1856 South Australian Institute. It had responsibility for the network of country and suburban institutes and a new and independent body, the Adelaide Circulating Library, that took over the business of circulating books on a subscription basis to the institutes. The board reported to the Minister of Education.

There were considerable tensions between the board, the Institutes Association and the Library's administration. Harry knew several board members from his journalistic and community work. These included William Sowden, editor-in-chief and joint proprietor of the *Register* and the Board President, Sir Samuel James Way. Their rivalry eventually resulted in Way's 1908 resignation and new legislation in 1910 that vested full responsibility for the institutes and their grant in the Institutes Association. Harry became its president the following year.[27]

1904 – Harry took on the editorship of the *South Australian Institutes' Journal*, the monthly publication for institute subscribers that provided lists of new books, literary essays and advertisements. He had already been a contributor, submitting a lengthy article on the Gawler Institute for the 12th edition of the *Journal* in July 1901. After Harry's departure as editor in 1910, the publication became bi-monthly. It continued to be produced until 1964.[28]

As a parliamentarian, Harry took on additional responsibilities. In 1904, he became the Opposition Whip.

1905 – Harry began a four-year term as the parliamentary Chairman of Committees. This administrative role oversaw the chairs of each committee to ensure that they set their committee's agenda; determined when or if Bills would be considered; presided over meetings; supervised the staff and the preparation of the report of the committee; and ensured that the report and all papers referred to the committee were transmitted to the Clerk of the Chamber.

Harry was the chair of a committee enquiring into the handling and marketing of wheat; an obvious role given the agricultural interests throughout his electorate of Barossa.

Back in Gawler Harry became a representative of the Sons of Temperance on the Gawler Cottage Homes Committee.[29] Using funds raised from Gawler's 1897 Queen Victoria Diamond Jubilee celebrations, in 1907 the committee purchased and opened two cottages in Tod Street for use, rent free, by deserving families. Another two homes were opened in 1915.

Finally, at the age of 46, Harry retired from active cricket playing. His 25 years of contributions were celebrated by a community gathering at the Gawler Arms Hotel. Eight years later he was presented with an engraved gold medallion commemorating this achievement.[30]

1906 – Harry joined the committee of the Adelaide University – Gawler Centre, another further education facility. He helped Archibald Peake form the new South Australian political party, the Liberal and Democratic Union. With his brother, Thomas, taking on the role of secretary, he formed a branch in Gawler.

1907 – Harry took on the state presidency of the Liberal and Democratic Union. In Adelaide Harry played in, and likely organised, a Parliament v. Press cricket match that was held again the following year. In Gawler he was invited to become the Patron of Union Cricket Club, the Willaston Football Club, where his brother Thomas was Gawler Football Association delegate, and the Willaston Athletic and Sports Club.

Willaston Football Club, 1907, E.H. Coombe centre third row, Gawler Heritage Collection

A group of cricket players photographed during a Parliament versus the Press match; Tom Price, Premier of South Australia 1905-1909, is sitting centre holding a hat in his hands. Harry sits to his left. c. 1907. PRG 280/1/7/407

1908 – In his 50th year, Harry became the vice-president of the Australian Proportional Representation Society that Catherine Helen Spence founded. The society, which still exists today, now advocates the use of Hare-Clark proportional voting.

In Gawler, Harry became a committee member of the newly formed Gawler Tourists' Association. Chaired by Mayor William Dawkins, this body promoted the many beauty spots around Gawler and organised the printing of a promotional pamphlet. He was also made president of the Gawler Chess Club.[31]

Harry was elected, together with fellow chess player Theodor Ey, as joint auditors for the Gawler Agricultural, Horticultural and Floricultural Society. He became a committee member of the Gawler Branch of the British and Foreign Bible Society, an interdenominational organisation that had been in Gawler since 1860, whose aim was to distribute copies of Holy Scripture (Bibles and Testaments) around the world.[32]

He also became one of eight vice-presidents of the Gawler Methodist Tennis Club where his son, Samuel Walter, was secretary.

1909 – Harry was appointed the Commissioner of Crown Lands and Immigration and Minister of Agriculture in the Peake Ministry.[33] He was made patron of the newly formed Gawler Angling Club.[34]

1911 – Harry became a trustee and chairman of the Hutchinson Hospital Board, replacing the inaugural trustee and chairman, John Felix Martin, who had died. Sarah Coombe joined the board at the same time.[35]

Following Mrs Hutchinson's death in April 1911, a generous bequest from the 1901 will of her late husband became available. The trustees appointed a board of management and land was sought for the building of a hospital. A site was chosen in East Terrace adjoining the Gulf View area where Harry and Sarah had earlier lived. The hospital was opened in 1913. Both Harry and Sarah resigned in 1914. The following year Thomas Coombe joined the board.

1914 – Together with Thomas, Harry became a founding member of the Willaston Quoits Club. taking on the role of vice-president of the club. He played bowls for Gawler against Lockleys and Grange Clubs and became patron of the Willaston Coursing Club and the Gawler Fishing Club, which he had helped establish.[36]

In May he was appointed editor of the *Daily Herald* and the family made the move to Adelaide. In August, war was declared and his third son, 25-year-old Samuel, enlisted.

1915 – In January his youngest son, 20-year-old Ernest, enlisted, followed in December by his eldest son, 34-year-old Harry Heywood, and son-in-law George Ash. In March he was re-elected as a Member of Parliament for Barossa. He was immediately caught up in the heated debates concerning the restrictions on Lutheran Schools.

1916 – By June Harry had resigned from the editorship of the *Daily Herald.* He was replaced by the returning Henry Kneebone who reported almost daily on Harry's frenetic anti-conscription campaign. Harry was able to redirect his time to travelling to country and suburban areas to speak.[37] In August he was appointed to the Advisory Council of Education under the *1915 Education Act* as the representative for country technical schools.[38] After the October referendum vote he continued to lobby for Lutherans, returned soldiers and the release of farmers from military camps. He became the target of many personal attacks from the floor of parliament and in the press.[39]

In late December he was approached to be a ULP candidate for the Federal Senate election. This time he accepted the nomination; a sign that he was looking to take the anti-conscription fight up at the national level.[40]

1917 – He was unsuccessful in his nomination, with the ULP members choosing Frank Lundie, Thomas Butterfield and Lionel Laughton Hill. The third place had been a very tight competition between Harry and the younger Hill with the final decision taking until mid-February, much longer than planned.[41] By April he was on the hustings, supporting ULP federal election candidates until his collapse and death, a week later, on 5 April 1916.

Appendix B

Where the Coombe Family Lived

Despite the promotion of South Australia as a colony where land could be afforded by the working man, neither Harry nor his father owned extensive property. They lived in rented accommodation most of their lives, preferring to channel their earnings into raising their families and their businesses. One exception occurred when, in anticipation of an inheritance to be bestowed on his 21st birthday, Harry purchased a block of farming land in Bertha, now part of Willaston. This investment was sold two years later to clear a family business debt. Twenty-five years later Harry bought another block of land and in 1905, aged 47, he bought his first house. His father did not own the premises of his business, the Willaston General Store, until he was 61. Four years later, he bought his retirement property, a block of farming land that adjoined the North Para River at the corner of Burrows and Barber Street, in Willaston.

Like most people, they purchased their property through a mortgage and continued to take out further mortgages against their asset. In the early days of the colony most mortgages were raised via private arrangements rather than through banks. In 1909 Harry made use of the Gawler branch of the Starr-Bowkett Society. This was a co-operative, non-profit financial institution that provided interest-free loans to its members and operated on the principle of mutual self-help. Members made weekly payments to the fund. When enough money was raised, a random number was drawn from a barrel. The Society member assigned that number would receive a loan to build or buy their home or, as in Harry's case, discharge an earlier, private mortgage and subdivide his land. Draws continued until all members had received their loan.[1]

The homes that the Coombe family occupied in Willaston and Gawler were not large, between two and six rooms in size. They had verandahs and cellars to cope with the summer heat. There was no electricity or reticulated water in Willaston until after 1918, and no sewerage systems until 1970. This meant that wood stoves, deep wells and external toilets were standard features of the day.

They also walked a great deal. The shop's delivery business made use of work horses but mostly the family relied upon 'shank's pony' or public transport. As a child, Harry attended L.S. Burton's school in the Gawler Church Hill area, a walk of just over half a mile. Later, as an 11-year-old, he worked for James Harris in Murray Street, entailing a walk of three-quarters of a mile. Today, a child might ride a bicycle for these journeys. However, although this mode of transport arrived in Australia in the 1860s, it was not taken up by the working classes until the 1890s. Throughout his parliamentary career Harry was a strong supporter of the railway. We have no evidence that he ever owned or drove a car.

Gawler South 1858–1866

Up to the age of five, Harry, his parents and his younger brother, Thomas, lived in a rented cottage in Elizabeth Street, Bassett Town. This street is now known as 21st Street, Gawler South.

The location was a short walk to his father's work as a porter at the Gawler Railway Station. At the time of the station's establishment in October 1856, much of the land immediately to its east was owned and farmed by William Bassett. In 1857, Bassett commissioned prominent local surveyor George Warren to survey his land, and on 24 March 1858 the subdivision of Bassett Town was officially created.[2] Bassett had his own house built at 13 Elizabeth Street, and the Coombe's cottage, where Harry was born in August 1858, was one of the workers' cottages built nearby.

Just months before the formation of Basset Town, an adjacent area, Gawler South, was created. This subdivision was on the other side of Adelaide Road and south of Dead Man's Pass. Both townships were affordable areas for workers involved with the railway and the nearby agricultural industrial manufacturing businesses. Neither Bassett Town,

Gawler South nor the adjacent Gawler West area were originally part of the Gawler Town Council. Originally the three areas stood within the District Council of Munno Para West that was administered from Penfield, ten miles to the south. In 1899 the three areas were combined to form the District Council of Gawler South, and in 1933 this council was amalgamated, together with other areas, into the greater Gawler Council.

During the 19th century nearly every settled Hundred in South Australia gained and retained its own District Council. By 1858 there were already 45 councils in South Australia. The amalgamation of many local government areas in the 1930s reduced the number considerably.[3]

It was from Elizabeth Street that Harry's father walked into Murray Street when he worked for James Harris at the Gawler Stores. Interestingly there is a record in 1868 of a lean-to structure being owned by E. Coombe on the land at Lot 208 fronting Murray Street, where the Gawler Cinema is located today.[4]

As the land slopes steeply, this lean-to may have rested against the hill. Could this have been a stable, perhaps, or a storage shed? And was it owned by Harry's father? More likely, it belonged to his great-uncle Ephraim, who was providing mortgages to people in the Gawler area. The structure could have come his way through a mortgage arrangement.

Willaston 1866–1884

Soon after Ephraim's second marriage in February 1866, the family relocated to Willaston. This move was to be near to Ephraim Senior's new place of employment as a storeman at the Willaston General Store. Next to the store, at number 7, now stands a six-roomed cottage, and behind this house there is an earlier two-room colonial cottage. Both the front and back cottages became homes for the Coombe family. It is likely that the family also occupied a cottage immediately behind the General Store that was later destroyed by the 1889 flood.

After his marriage, Harry became a partner in the family business of E. Coombe & Son. Although multi-generational family living was not uncommon at this time, the limited size of the cottage and the arrival of

The Coombe Willaston residence, at 7 North Road
Photo J. Menhennet

baby Harry Heywood meant that relocation for the young family, possibly into accommodation associated with the confectionery business premises across the road, was necessary.

Gawler 1884–1905

Harry moved away from Willaston when he was 25 to set up in his own business in the main street of Gawler. The family would live in the residence located at the rear of their confectionary shop, located at 296c Murray Street, the southernmost of a group of five shops.[5] They were soon joined by baby James in September 1884, and Samuel in January 1889. This rented property may have been their home when he was appointed as the editor of the *Bunyip* in July 1889, however their fourth child, Daisy, who joined the family in November 1890, was born at Willaston.[6]

By 1892 they had moved to a four-roomed colonial cottage at 49 Finniss Street, Gawler.[7] This location was close to the older children's school and a short walk away from his work. With the arrival of baby Mary in September 1892, this rented accommodation would house seven family members.[8]

Harry's circumstances continued to improve, and in 1897 the family moved into a cottage in Bishop Street, Gulf View, Gawler, one of a cluster of houses that still exist at the Lyndoch Road end of the street. This was a greater walking distance to his employment but was considered a more desirable and healthy area to live in. Baby Mary's death in October 1893 may well have contributed to the move.[9]

In January 1904 Harry purchased a block of land in Gulf View at what is now 1 East Terrace, Gawler East. Perhaps they had thoughts of building their own home, however the family moved to Willaston a year later, and the undeveloped land was sold in 1911. At about the same time the Thomas Hutchinson Trustees, of whom Harry was a member, purchased a large block further along the road at 6 East Terrace with the intention of building the Hutchinson Hospital.[10] His knowledge of the area may well have influenced the choice of location.

Willaston 1905–1914

In August 1905, Harry purchased his first home, later described as a 'Gentleman's Residence', at 8 Burrows Street, Willaston. The house is perched on the hill with spectacular views across Murray Street and Willaston. It was built by Job Freak, a blacksmith.[11] This 1890s symmetrical cottage was not unlike the home adjacent to the Willaston General Store. There is a possibility that the acquisition of this house was aided by a legacy left to his wife by Sarah's childless aunt, Sarah Bright, who had lived with them at Gulf View until her death in November 1904.

The house at 8 Burrows Street. Photo Church Hill Photography

The property was diagonally opposite the farming land that his father had bought in 1890. Perhaps their return to Willaston was to help support his widowed father? Elizabeth had died aged 82 in 1901, having been blind for the last five years of her life and cared for by Thomas's wife, Lucy.[12]

The larger Burrows Street property housed fewer of the family. Only four children, ranging in age from seven to sixteen, lived at this home, Harry and James having left to pursue their own independence. Samuel and then Daisy would soon follow.

It was from this house that Harry campaigned and lost the 1912 election. He continued with his role as editor of the *Bunyip*, while looking for other work opportunities.

Adelaide 1914–1917

In May 1914, the family moved to Adelaide into rented accommodation at 10 Morcomb Street, Stepney. This was a property owned by George Penhall, a grocer and mining director from Broken Hill.[13] The newly built return verandah villa would provide accommodation for Harry, Sarah, their 19-year-old son Ernest and 16-year-old daughter Catherine.

Stepney was a residential village with a strong German component, where artisans, carters and gardeners worked from home. Many of the cottages were small, dating back as far as 1849. The location had the advantage of being a two-mile walk or a tram ride to the *Daily Herald* Offices in Grenfell Street. The Coombe family remained at Morcomb Street throughout 1915.

Meanwhile, Harry divided the Willaston Burrows Street property into two, selling the spare land. The house was then rented out, and it was likely that Daisy and her husband, George Ash, lived there when he found employment with the *Bunyip* and as an auditor with the local council.[14]

At the end of November 1915, less than a year after his successful return to parliament, Harry purchased 57 (now 96) Kingston Terrace, North Adelaide. The move to their own, larger property in a prestigious area would provide a refuge from the impact of the war on their family. Kingston Terrace, North Adelaide was described by Sarah's granddaughter as being a 'typical middle class home' with 'a cook, housemaid, a woman to do the washing, and a sewing woman who came in one day a week to do the mending, make sheets etc. as well as other duties'.[15]

96 Kingston Terrace, North Adelaide 2020

Their 25-year-old son Samuel enlisted into the Australian Imperial Force on 25 August 1914, just three weeks after the declaration of war. He embarked two months later. Like the thousands of Australians who rushed to volunteer he was sent first to Egypt, to meet the threat that the Ottoman Empire posed to British interests in the Middle East and the Suez Canal. After months of training, the Australians, along with troops from New Zealand, the United Kingdom and France, then departed by ship for the Gallipoli peninsula.

Samuel had earlier military training. The compulsory 1911 Universal Military Training Scheme required all young men between 18 and 25 to register with the home defence militia and he had been an enthusiastic participant reaching the level of Captain in the senior army cadets.

Nine months after Samuel's embarkation, in July 1915, Samuel's unmarried colleague Olive Pellew Pearce gave birth to their daughter, Dorothy Fraser. Olive and baby Dorothy lived with the Coombe family at Kingston Terrace until late 1916. Mother and daughter then sailed to England to be reunited with Samuel, who had been repatriated to England after suffering wounds at Gallipoli in May 1915. He subsequently returned to duty and suffered shellshock in France. He returned to England where he obtained staff work.[16] The couple married in England when they reunited in 1916. The family did not return to Australia until April 1918.

In January 1915, on his 20th birthday, youngest son Ernest enlisted.

His occupation was recorded as a grocer. In August he was sent overseas. Eighteen months later he received bomb and shrapnel wounds to his lower back at the Suez Canal. Ernest's injuries were so serious that he was repatriated, as an invalid, back to Australia in July 1916. Following his return to Australia, he required ongoing medical treatment at the Keswick Military Hospital and was not officially discharged from the army until the end of May 1917.[17]

When their son-in-law George Arthur Ash enlisted in December 1915, the address he gave on his enlistment form for himself and his wife was Willaston, but this was soon changed to the Kingston Terrace house. With George at the Front, Daisy too joined the family. In 1916 the North Adelaide house contained three generations of the Coombe family – Harry, Sarah, Daisy, Catherine, Olive, baby Dorothy, and possibly the injured Ernest. A very full house may explain the departure of Daisy, Olive and Dorothy later in the year. It would not have helped that Sarah, aged 54, underwent an operation in June 1916 following a severe illness. She recovered and travelled for a few weeks' visit to Mt Gambier in November.[18]

In December 1915 their eldest son, Harry Heywood, enlisted, and his wife Margaret Florence (née McLeod) and their two sons, Alick Ephraim and Stuart John Fraser, moved from Port Wakefield to Howard Street, Norwood Park, now known as Beulah Park. Their new home, located less than a mile from their parents, was named *Honiton*, presumably after a town in East Devon. Harry spent most of 1916 in base training at the Mitcham Army Camp with a period at the Royal Military College at Duntroon in Canberra from which he was commissioned as a second lieutenant.

He was released from duty to assist with his father's funeral in April 1917. The Kingston Terrace and Burrows Street properties transferred to Sarah's ownership and she, Catherine and Ernest continued living in Kingston Terrace. They were possibly joined by Samuel, Olive and Dorothy on their return from England in mid-1918.

In February 1918, Harry Heywood embarked for overseas service and Margaret and their sons moved south of the city to Goodwood Park. Harry Heywood was killed just six months later, and his widow and sons relocated to Kensington Park.

Renmark

In 1919 Ernest, Samuel, Olive and Dorothy moved to Renmark, where the men became orchardists rather than returning to their pre-war occupations. Samuel had applied, late in 1918, for the surrender value of his Teacher Superannuation Fund policy, presumably to help fund this new venture. He also sold a block of land in Berri that he had purchased just before his 1914 enlistment, and was now able to take advantage of a training scheme for soldiers.[19]

Sarah sold the Burrows Street, Willaston property in August 1919, and these funds may also have helped to relocate and re-establish her two sons. The purchaser was Ernest Albert Smith, the Gawler Town Clerk, who had been selected in preference to her husband. The house was quickly sold on to Norman Thomas Coombe, son of Thomas, with the Gawler & Barossa Starr-Bowkett Building Society providing a mortgage.

Renmark was already well known to the family. During his parliamentary career Harry visited the area several times, including a 1909 visit as the Commissioner of Lands. In supporting the passing of the 1910 *Vine, Fruit and Vegetable Protection Amendment Bill*, he formed strong connections with growers in the area and his name appeared favorably in the local press, the *Murray Pioneer and Australian River Record*, edited by Henry S. Taylor.

Daisy had moved to Renmark in 1916 to work as a 'typiste' and later as a shorthand teacher at Messrs. R.P. James & Co while her husband, George Arthur Ash, was serving overseas.[20] Her father visited her in January 1917, travelling by train to Paringa, three miles from Renmark. Her move to Renmark for work may have been a result of a friendship between her father and Henry S. Taylor.

Whilst serving in France, George Ash contracted trench fever; a disease caused by bacterium spread by body lice common among the soldiers. Although serious, trench fever was generally not lethal, however the persistent fever could lead to nerve damage, muscle pain and heart failure. George was admitted to a hospital in England in September 1917, and two months later he was medically repatriated to Australia suffering from severe rheumatism. Daisy returned to Gawler in October 1917 to wait for him.[21]

But they were not to remain in Gawler for long. Speaking to a *Bunyip* reporter in January 1918, George described the benefits of living in sunnier climes and contemplated a move to Renmark to work as a horticulturalist. This he did after being discharged as medically unfit in March 1918.[22] He suffered ongoing health problems that necessitated him regularly returning to hospital in Adelaide. He worked as a journalist for the *Murray Pioneer and Australian River Record* and welcomed the arrival his two brothers-in-law, Ernest and Samuel, to the area. A year later George bought a block in the Block É section of Renmark, an area opened in response to the returning soldiers' need for land.

Renmark was a young town. Established in 1887 by the Chaffey Brothers, it was the first irrigation colony in Australia. Like the Chaffey's settlements in California and Canada, and to 'attract the right sort of people', the colony would be 'dry'. The bank crash and depression of the 1890s stymied the town's development but by the outbreak of war Renmark was thriving and growing fresh produce that was delivered by boat up and down the Murray River.

As the war casualties were sent home the military authorities in South Australia issued orders prohibiting the supply of alcohol to all military personnel who were patients of military hospitals or convalescent camps or undergoing medical treatment. This restriction, their family background of temperance and Samuel's wartime drunkenness, no doubt a PTSD symptom, may have also made the community of Renmark attractive. It certainly wasn't to outrun the spread of the devastating world flu epidemic, which arrived in Adelaide in February 1919 and soon reached Renmark, brought back by the returning military.

Renmark had the highest proportion of its population enlist than any other town in South Australia; perhaps explaining why the town went against the national trend and voted in favour of conscription. When the men returned to re-establish their lives, they formed a Returned Soldiers Association. (The returning nurses were overlooked for a long time.) In October 1918 George Ash helped establish this association and served as its secretary for several years.[23] He also helped establish the Block E Primary School in 1924 despite he and Daisy never having children.[24]

That Renmark offered a strong, cohesive community where neighbours and fellow farmers helped each other in times of need was highlighted when George's regular absences in Adelaide for medical attention prevented him from pruning his grapevines. A group of community members including his two brothers-in-law undertook to do the work for him.[25]

There was yet another family connection to Renmark. In August 1919 Catherine, still living with her mother at Kingston Terrace, became engaged.[26] Her fiancé, Wilfred George Lord (known as Wilf) was a horticulturalist who served in the AIF Hospital Transport Corps. His grew up in a farming family from Berri. They married in Renmark in September 1920.[27] Perhaps it was Wilf's local knowledge that assisted his brothers-in-law to gain work in the blocks specialising in dairy, grapes, vegetables, grains and grazing that developed along the Murray River.

The four men would all go on to purchase land, yet no record can be found of them taking up land offered under the soldier settlement scheme. Like most returned service personnel, they were shattered by their wartime experiences. Samuel, who had had a stellar military career and was wounded in action twice, had been court martialled twice. In March 1918 he was dismissed from the army and made ineligible for war medals. This long, sad affair is detailed by records now available from the National Archives of Australia but suffice to say he clashed strongly with his superiors about the dreadful effects of trench foot on the soldiers under his charge.[28] With the wartime loss of both their father and their brother and the treatment of Samuel, is it any wonder that the family wished to start afresh in a new area.

In March 1921, in bad health and with four of her five remaining children now living in Renmark, Sarah sold the Kingston Terrace house. With the proceeds she purchased a small home for herself at the corner of Cowra and Fifteenth streets in Renmark. She died two years later in November 1923, aged 63. Her obituary acknowledged her strong character and keen interest in public affairs.[29]

Sarah's body was transported to Gawler for burial beside her husband in the Willaston Cemetery. Her name and that of their eldest son Harry Heywood were added to the headstone that was raised through public subscription as a tribute to Harry Senior.

The move to Renmark had not severed the links between Harry's family and Gawler. News of their lives regularly appeared in the *Bunyip.*

Thomas Coombe and his family continued running the Willaston General Store and Post Office, and in 1923 his son, Herbert Stanley, built a new grocery shop in Berri, a town not far from his cousins in Renmark.

Three generations of Ephraim Coombe's family in Australia were connected to agricultural work and shopkeeping. All Coombes displayed a strong interest in self-improvement, politics and social issues, something that continues into the following generations.

Acknowledgements

This project is truly the result of the support and encouragement of many people. It is almost impossible to acknowledge them all, but here's an alphabetical attempt:

The late Craig Barnet, journalist, for bringing to Helen's attention the misnaming of Coombe Street

The late John Barnet, former editor of the *Bunyip*, for sharing his article on the history of the Humbug Society and the *Bunyip*;

Paul Barnet, photographer and local historian, for sharing his knowledge of the Bunyip's history;

The late Cynthia Beare, great-granddaughter of Thomas Coombe, for her support and encouragement;

Meredith Blundell, Port Adelaide local history officer, for her assistance in tracing the Port Adelaide and Semaphore links;

Michael Bollen, Director of Wakefield Press, for his informative workshop at the 2019 City of Marion's WordFest;

The late Mark Boon, journalist, who compiled the extremely useful Detailed index to the *History of Gawler by E.H. Coombe* for the Gawler Public Library in April 1993;

Graeme Brookman of the Food Forest, for providing the link between his land and Henry and Hannah Lock;

Andrew Buxton, for providing advice and support for our grant applications;

Anthea Buxton, for checking family tree associations and being a very willing assistant;

John Clift, member of the Gawler Institute Committee and local historian, for providing Helen with a portrait copy of E.H. Coombe's photograph all those years ago;

David Coombe for the *Mainly Coombe* website[1];

Geoff Coombe (great-grandson of Thomas Coombe) for sharing many early family records;

Margaret Crohn, for sharing information on the farm of Samuel and Ann Pope;

Ross Dawkins, for his assistance in providing a photo of his grandfather, A.M. Dawkins

Rebecca Digirolamo, journalist with the *Advertiser*, for her interest in writing the article in the 13–14 July 2019 edition of the *South Australian Weekend Magazine*;

Kelly Dyer, Library Officer: Local History, City of Onkaparinga Libraries for information on the Tall family;

The late Dawn Eastick, for informing Helen, very early on in this project, of her family connection to E.H. Coombe through the Riggs family;

Ingrid Eidam, local historian, Williamstown;

Heather Everingham, local historian, Paringa and Renmark;

Dr David Faber, professional historian, for his encouragement and valued feedback;

Helen Ferguson, a great-granddaughter of E.H. Coombe, for her donation of material to the Gawler National Trust and for sharing her mother's reminiscences about the Lord family;

Judy Ferguson, for her valued proofreading and support;

Tom Gara, cricket historian, for providing information on Ernest Hiscock;

Gawler Environment and Heritage Association for supplying details from their Gawler Rates Database, adding the E.H. Coombe Walking Tour map to their Gawler Maps Database, and providing support for our grant applications;

The Gawler History Team for their help in sourcing photographs and providing support for our grant application;

Genevieve Hebart, for confirming the whereabouts of the portraits of Samuel and Ann Pope;

The late Mrs Hilda Heinrich, last of the Gawler Institute Librarians, who so graciously handed on the baton and ensured that Helen was aware of Gawler's significant history;

Dr David Hilliard, OAM, for alerting us to information in SA Methodist weekly paper, the *Australian Christian Commonwealth*;

The History Council of South Australia, for their presentation to Helen of the 2019 Regional Historian of the Year Award;

The Historical Society of South Australia, for their 2015 grant and the opportunity to present the E.H. Coombe project lecture in October 2020;

The History Trust of South Australia, for their coordination of the History Month in May. We presented the E.H. Coombe Walking Tour as a May 2017 event, and we were supported by a grant from the South Australian History Fund 2021 to publish this book;

Margaret Howse, local historian and genealogist, Gawler;

Chris Illman, for providing details of the Lock family tree;

The late Kingsley Ireland, historian and genealogist, for his assistance in tracing Barossa identities;

Neil Jacobs of Church Hill Photography, for his assistance in enhancing old images;

Marie Kibble of the Gawler Visitor Information Centre, for her adaptation and continuing delivery of the E.H. Coombe Walking Tour;

Graeme Lange, author of *The Lange Rainbow*, for information on Jim and Alma Coombe;

Janette Menhennet, photographer, Gawler;

Barry Neylon and David Ward of the Gawler Oral History Society, for facilitating our interview on the E.H. Coombe Project and for bringing useful sources to our attention;

Lyn O'Grady, local historian, Walkerville, for assistance with researching Uncle Ephraim Coombe;

Raffaele Piccolo, for bringing to our attention an article on the Gawler Institute's role in South Australian legal history;

Tony Piccolo, Member for Light, for his continuing support throughout our journey and supplying information regarding E. H. Coombe and his involvement with the Australian Labor Party. We were proud to be able to make a presentation based on the E.H. Coombe Walking Tour to the Gawler branch of the ALP in May 2019 & 2022;

The late Bob Purdam, married to Jennifer Anne (née Coombe), granddaughter of E.H. Coombe, who in 1989 shared details of the family tree with Helen;

Craig, Margaret, Philip and Andrew Purdam, children of Bob and Jennifer, who, after their mother's death in February 2021, were extremely helpful in identifying and sharing family items;

Karen Redman, Mayor of Gawler, for being the catalyst who introduced Helen to Patricia and for later launching the E.H. Coombe Walking Tour in April 2017. We also acknowledge her support in our grant applications;

Jo-Anna Robinson, photographer;

Stan Roulston, local historian, Gawler, for his assistance in sourcing photographs;

Brian Samuels, professional historian, for his encouragement and assistance;

Geoff Sando, cricket historian, for sharing his research on E.H. Coombe;

Christopher Scott, great-grandson of E.H. Coombe, for providing details of and photographs from the Coombe and Lock families;

Adrian Shackley, local historian, Gawler;

Patricia Sheahan, local historian, Gawler;

Julia Stocker, great, great granddaughter of Ann Pope née Coombe;

Patricia Sumerling, professional historian, for her most valued critique of our work;

The Town of Gawler, for awarding us a 2016/17 Community Grant;

Dr David Tucker and all at the Gawler National Trust with thanks for their collaboration;

Martin Walker, local historian, Gawler;

Jacinta Weiss, Cultural Heritage Centre Coordinator, Town of Gawler;

Tamara Wenham, Team Leader, Archival Services, Archive Team State Records of South Australia, for her assistance with the correction to the Women's Suffrage Petition;

Jacque Zagotsis, local history officer, Berri Public Library;

And of course, to our family and friends without whom we may have never started, continued or completed this project: thank you.

Notes

Preliminary pages

1 'A Tribute To Mr. E.H. Coombe', *Register*, 3 June 1914, p. 9., viewed 19 October 2020, http://nla.gov.au/nla.news-article59397721

2 'Memorial to the Late Mr. E.H. Coombe, M.P.', *Chronicle*, 27 September 1919, p. 11., viewed 19 October 2020, http://nla.gov.au/nla.news-article89162621

3 'Farewell Social', *Bunyip*, 5 June 1914, p. 6, viewed 30 June 2021, http://nla.gov.au/nla.news-article97731317 1907; 'Local Mems', *Bunyip*, 8 February, p. 4, viewed 30 June 2021, http://nla.gov.au/nla.news-article97601051

4 *Ephraim Coombe* n.d., Monument Australia, viewed 17 July 2015 http://monumentaustralia.org.au/themes/government/dissent/display/51767-ephraim-coombe

Preface

1 Hennessy, H. (1991) 'Willaston – the beginning', Paper submitted as part of Graduate Diploma in Local & Applied History, UNE

Chapter 1 - Anti-conscription

1 Kearney, R., & Cleary, S., 2018, *Valour and Violets,* Wakefield Press, p. 204; *Conscription During the First World* War, n.d., Museum of Australian Democracy at Old Parliament House, viewed 18 January 2022, https://billyhughes.moadoph.gov.au/conscription/index.html

2 *Defining moments: Conscription referendums,* n.d., National Museum of Australia., viewed 25 November 2019, https://www.nma.gov.au/defining-moments/resources/conscription-referendums

3 Prest, W., Round, K., & Fort, C.S., 2001, *The Wakefield Companion to South Australian History,* Wakefield Press, p. 120

4 Horne, D., 1979, *In search of Billy Hughes*, Macmillan Melbourne; McKinlay, B., 1988, *A century of struggle: the A.L.P. a centenary history,* 2nd ed, Collins Dove, Blackburn, Vic; Kelly, P.,, 'A nation divided', from 'The Great War Part Two: The Western Front', *Weekend Australian*, July 23–24, 2016, pp. 22–27

5 Church, Dr N., 'Political attitudes to conscription: 1914–1918', Parliamentary Library Research Paper, October 2016, viewed 25 November 2019, https://

www.aph.gov.au/About_Parliament/Parliamentary_Departments/Parliamentary_Library/pubs/rp/rp1617/PoliticalAttitudesConscription

6 Jauncey, L.C., 1935, *The story of conscription in Australia*. G. Allen & Unwin, London,1914, pp. 196–197; Broomhill, R., 'Hill, Lionel Laughton (1881–1963)', , National Centre of Biography, Australian National University, first published 1983, accessed online 28 July 2021, https://adb.anu.edu.au/biography/hill-lionel-laughton-6671/text11485; 1916, 'Local 'Anti' Manifesto', *Register*, 2 October 1916, , p. 6, viewed 9 January 2022, http://nla.gov.au/nla.news-article59920842

7 'Big Meeting at the Exhibition', *Advertiser*, 9 October 1917, p. 9, viewed 9 January 2022, http://nla.gov.au/nla.news-article6455129

8 Kearney, R., & Cleary, S., 2018, *Valour and Violets,* Wakefield Press, pp. 207–208

9 'Mr. Coombe's Trip', *Daily Herald,* 3 October 1916, p. 5, viewed 9 January 2022, http://nla.gov.au/nla.news-article124838086; 'An Opposition Address', *The Journal*, 2 October 1916, p. 1, viewed 9 January 2022, http://nla.gov.au/nla.news-article204676054; 'The Great Crisis in Our History – Shall We Quit Ourselves Like Men?', *Narracoorte Herald*, 20 October 1916, p. 2, viewed 9 January 2022, http://nla.gov.au/nla.news-article147265896; 'Country Meetings', *Chronicle*, 28 October,1916, p. 16, viewed 9 January 2022, http://nla.gov.au/nla.news-article87525679

10 'Mr. Goode Replies to Mr. Coombe', *Advertiser*,, 20 October 1916, p. 9, viewed 21 October 2020, http://nla.gov.au/nla.news-article6457021; Moss, J., 1985, *Sound of Trumpets: History of the Labour movement in South Australia*, Wakefield Press, p. 241

11 Kearney, R., & Cleary, S., 2018, *Valour and Violets,* Wakefield Press, p. 208

12 Fitzhardinge, L.F., 'Hughes, William Morris (Billy) (1862–1952)', *Australian Dictionary of Biography*, National Centre of Biography, Australian National University, first published 1983, accessed online 18 January 2022, https://adb.anu.edu.au/biography/hughes-william-morris-billy-6761/text11689

13 Payton, P., 2016, *One and All: Labor and the radical tradition in South Australia*, Wakefield Press, pp. 209–210

14 'Hot Words in the Assembly', *Chronicle*, 4 November 1916, p. 15, viewed 25 November 2019, http://nla.gov.au/nla.news-article87526594; 'A Storm in Parliament', *Chronicle*, 11 November 1916, p. 36, viewed 25 November 2019, http://nla.gov.au/nla.news-article87530323; 1916, 'A Parliamentary Breeze', *Chronicle*, 11 November 1916, p. 14, viewed 25 November 2019, http://nla.gov.au/nla.news-article87530063; 'Mr. Coombe and National Service', *Register*, 10 November 1916, p. 6, viewed 27 Jul 2021, http://nla.gov.au/nla.news-article59913742

15 Homburg, H., 1947, *South Australian Lutherans and wartime rumours,* Adelaide, p. 66

16 'Lutheran Schools', *Advertiser*, 6 October 1915, p. 11, viewed 24 July 2021, http://nla.gov.au/nla.news-article5482925

17 'Teachings in German', *Advertiser*, 8 November 1916, p. 9, viewed 1 July 2022, http://nla.gov.au/nla.news-article5533212; 'German Schools and Language', *Register*, 8 November 1916, p. 6, viewed 21 December 2021, http://nla.gov.au/nla.news-article59904149; 'Closing of German Schools', *Bunyip*, 17 November 1916, p. 2, viewed 21 December 2021, http://nla.gov.au/nla.news-article97733148

18 Klassen, N., n.d., *South Australian attitudes toward Lutheran Schooling during World War I*, Flinders Ranges Research, viewed 25 November 2019, http://www.southaustralianhistory.com.au/lutheran.htm; *Children and World War 1: Lutheran Schools*, n.d., State Library of South Australia, viewed 25 November 2019, https://

guides.slsa.sa.gov.au/c.php?g=410371&p=2794577; 'Shut Them Up', *Register*, 27 October 1915, p. 7, viewed 24 July 2021, http://nla.gov.au/nla.news-article59622084

19 'Mr. Coombe and National Service', *Register*, 10 November 1916, p. 6, viewed 23 September 2022, http://nla.gov.au/nla.news-article59913742; Victorian Allotments', *Pinnaroo and Border Times*, 10 November 1916, p. 3., viewed 23 September 2022, http://nla.gov.au/nla.news-article189163116

20 'Advertising', *Bunyip*, 9 February 1917, p. 4, viewed 18 December 2018, http://nla.gov.au/nla.news-article100419419; 'Mr. Coombe Arraigned', *Bunyip*, 9 February 1917, p. 2, viewed 18 December 2018, http://nla.gov.au/nla.news-article100419433

21 'A Federal Prosecution', *Barrier Miner*, 8 February 1917, p. 4, viewed 9 January 2022, http://nla.gov.au/nla.news-article45432121; 'Coombe-McIntyre Defence Fund', *Daily Herald*, 15 February 1917, p. 4, viewed 9 January 2022, http://nla.gov.au/nla.news-article105391869; 'Coombe-Mcintyre Fund', *Daily Herald*, 6 March 1917, p. 4, viewed 9 January 2022, http://nla.gov.au/nla.news-article105394892

22 'Anti-Conscription', *Daily Examiner*, 26 February 1917, p. 2, viewed 9 January 2022, http://nla.gov.au/nla.news-article195769823

23 1928, 'Prominent Persons', *Mail*, 14 January 1928, p. 2, viewed 2 September 2020, http://nla.gov.au/nla.news-article58551229

24 Playford, J., 'Smith, Francis Villeneuve (1883–1956)', *Australian Dictionary of Biography*, National Centre of Biography, Australian National University, first published 1988, accessed online 2 September 2020, http://adb.anu.edu.au/biography/smith-francis-villeneuve-8467/text14889; 'A New King's Counsel', *Register*, 26 September 1919, p. 7, viewed 25 July 2021, http://nla.gov.au/nla.news-article62400666; Peter, M., 2014, 'Paris Nesbit, KC' in *S.A.'s Greats: The men and women of the North Terrace plaques*, ed. Healey, J., Historical Society of South Australia, viewed 2 September 2020, http://adelaidia.sa.gov.au/people/paris-nesbit-kc; George, D., 2018, *Mary Lee: The life and times of a 'turbulent anarchist' and her battle for women's rights*, Wakefield Press, p. 209

25 'Personal', *Advertiser*, 22 March 1918, p. 6, viewed 26 July 2021, http://nla.gov.au/nla.news-article5537762

26 'Anti-Conscription Cases', *Chronicle*, 3 March 1917, p. 16, viewed 25 November 2019, http://nla.gov.au/nla.news-article87438740

27 'Anti-Conscription Cases', *Advertiser*, 27 February 1917, p. 8, viewed 21 October 2020, http://nla.gov.au/nla.news-article5565406

28 'The Tanunda Trials', *Advertiser*, 28 February 1917, p. 6, viewed 21 October 2020, http://nla.gov.au/nla.news-article5565690

29 'Second Case Against Mr. Coombe', *Chronicle*, 3 March 1917, p. 16, viewed 25 November 2019, http://nla.gov.au/nla.news-article87438775

30 'The Coombe Case', *Register*, 3 March 1917, p. 12, viewed 9 January 2022, http://nla.gov.au/nla.news-article59975479

31 'Mr. Coombe's Seat', *Register*,, 3 March 1917, p. 8, viewed 10 December 2021, http://nla.gov.au/nla.news-article59975368

32 Wohltmann, M., 2016, *A future Unlived: A forgotten chapter in South Australia's history*, Michael Wohltmann, p. 14; 'The War Precautions Regulations', *Bunyip*, 16 March 1917, p. 4, viewed 25 November 2019, http://nla.gov.au/nla.news-article100417534

Chapter 2 - Family Background

1 Brown, R., 2011, *Literacy: revised version*, Looking at History, viewed 18 August 2016, http://richardjohnbr.blogspot.com.au/2011/01/literacy-revised-version.html
2 'At Home with God', *Australian Christian Commonwealth,* 6 November 1908, p. 13, viewed 4 August 2021, http://nla.gov.au/nla.news-article213589698
3 Barnes, A., 'Australia's Early Immigration Schemes', reprinted from *Tulle*, vol 17, no. 2, viewed 10 July 2015 http://www.angelfire.com/al/aslc/immigration.html
4 Smith, R., 1973, 1850, *A Very Good Year in the State of South Australia: Selected items of historical interest*, Shakespeare Head Press, pp. 82–83
5 Mulcahy, L. (transcriber), 2004, *Ebba Brahe – Mariners and Ships in Australian Waters,* Mariners and Ships, viewed 12 July 2015, http://marinersandships.com.au/1855/01/065ebb.htm; *Coombe, Ephraim: Assisted Immigrants Index*, n.d., NSW State Archives and Records, https://records-primo.hosted.exlibrisgroup.com/primoexplore/fulldisplay?context=L&vid=61SRA&lang=en_US&docid=INDEX849084
6 'Sydney Shipping', Adelaide Observer, 13 October 1855, p. 5, viewed 5 July 2016, http://nla.gov.au/nla.news-article158105953; 'Shipping Intelligence', *Adelaide Times*, 13 October 1855, p. 2, viewed 5 July 2016, http://nla.gov.au/nla.news-article207074319
7 Peters, A., 1998, *Recollections: Nathaniel Hailes' adventurous life in colonial South Australia*, Wakefield Press, p. 34; 'Sixty-Four Years Ago', *Bunyip*, 29 January 1915, p. 3, viewed 23 August 2021, http://nla.gov.au/nla.news-article97732295
8 Cummings, D., n.d., *Lloyds from London* 1838, Bound for South Australia, viewed 16 July 2015 https://bound-for-south-australia.collections.slsa.sa.gov.au/1838Lloyds.htm
9 *The Bounty System*, n.d., extracted from the 'Concise Guide to State Archives of New South Wales', viewed 10 July, 2015 http://www.roosen.com.au/RoosenComAuWeb/Genealogy/Background/Bounty_System.html
10 'The Agricultural Return', *Adelaide Observer*, 10 February 1849, p. 2, viewed 14 July, 2015, http://nla.gov.au/nla.news-article158927129
11 'Local Intelligence', *South Australian Register*, 10 January 1849, p. 3, viewed 14 July, 2015, http://nla.gov.au/nla.news-article50247116
12 'Memorial by the Colonists of South Australia Against the Introduction of Convicts', *South Australian*, 14 February 1845, p. 3, viewed 9 January 2022, http://nla.gov.au/nla.news-article71600655
13 Brown, J.M., 1970, *The Almonds of Walkerville*, Forlib Books, p. 37
14 'Walkerville', *South Australian Weekly Chronicle*, 2 August 1862, p. 7, viewed 9 January 2022, http://nla.gov.au/nla.news-article90257090
15 *Architects of South Australia*, Copyright 2008, Architecture Museum, University of South Australia, viewed 7 September 2016, http://www.architectsdatabase.unisa.edu.au/arch_full.asp?Arch_ID=42
16 'Family Notices', *South Australian Register*, 4 November1876, p. 7, viewed 16 August 2015, http://nla.gov.au/nla.news-article43010744
17 'Family Notices', *South Australian Advertiser*, 26 April 1871, p. 2, viewed 27 July, 2015, http://trove.nla.gov.au/newspaper/article/28600973
18 'Shipping Intelligence', *Adelaide Observer*, 24 March 1849, p. 2, viewed 14 July, 2015, http://nla.gov.au/nla.news-article158927335; Cummings, D., n.d., *The Pakenham*

1849, Bound for South Australia, viewed 16 July 2015, https://bound-for-south-australia.collections.slsa.sa.gov.au/1849Pakenham.htm; ibid. *South Australian passenger lists* 1849, viewed 16 July 2015, https://bound-for-south-australia.collections.slsa.sa.gov.au/ShipLists%20Alpha%20by%20Year/1849Chamberlain-Davies.htm; Janmaat, R., 2007, *The passenger list for the ship Pakenham,* 660 *tons, Captain F. Boyce, from Liverpool & Plymouth* 16 *December* 1848, *arrived at Port Adelaide, South Australia* 21 *March* 1849, The Ships List, viewed 15 July 2015, http://www.theshipslist.com/ships/australia/pakenham1849.shtml

19 Richards, S., 1848–1849, (transcribed by Seifert, J., 2007), *Journal of Stephen Richards aboard the Pakenham*, 1848–49, State Library of South Australia, viewed 18 August 2016, http://www.slsa.sa.gov.au/archivaldocs/d/D7776_Richards_journal_transcript.pdf

20 Barnet, W., 1860, *A general and commercial directory for Gawler & surrounding districts: comprising correct lists of the corporation and public offices in Gawler; also the district councils of Barossa East & West, Mudla Wirra, Muno Para East & West, and Mount Crawford: to which is added a short sketch of the rise and progress of Gawler, and a mass of general & statistical information collected from the census returns of the present year*, p. 10, viewed 16 July, 2015 http://handle.slv.vic.gov.au/10381/187642

21 Gawler History, n.d., *St Georges Gawler Marriages* 1851 (5) Ure (6) Pope, viewed 20 July, 2015 https://www.flickr.com/photos/gawler_history/19844114372/in/album-72157656090580512/

22 McConnell, B.E. 1996, *Looking back: recollections of the 'Church of England' in Gawler 1846–1996*. privately published, p. 5

23 Cummings, D., *South Australian Passenger lists* 1845, Bound for South Australia, viewed 16 July 2015, https://boundforsouthaustralia.collections.slsa.sa.gov.au/ShipLists%20Alpha%20by%20Year/1845PassengersN-Y.htm

24 no title, *Bunyip*, 9 December 1892, p. 2, viewed 28 July 2016, http://nla.gov.au/nla.news-article97237241; Huxley, M., 'Duffield, Walter (1816–1882)', *Australian Dictionary of Biography*, National Centre of Biography, Australian National University, first published 1972, viewed online 25 April 2018, http://adb.anu.edu.au/biography/duffield-walter-3449/text5239

25 'Gawler, from Girlhood Recollections', *Bunyip*, 5 August 1932, p. 7, viewed 27 July, 2015, http://nla.gov.au/nla.news-article96680458

26 Crohn, M., 2004, The story of Sunnydale Farm, Gawler East, 1860. A general and commercial directory private paper, p. 14

27 Hoad, J. L, 1986, *Hotels and Publicans in South Australia 1836–1984*, Gould Books, p. 507

28 'Local Court.—Gawler', *South Australian Advertiser*, 4 May 1864, p. 3, viewed 20 July, 2015, http://nla.gov.au/nla.news-article31836192

29 Auhl, I., & Perry, M., 1973, *Gawler Sketchbook*, Rigby, p. 36

30 1892, 'The Country', *Advertiser*, 6 December, p. 6, viewed 7 July 2016, http://nla.gov.au/nla.news-article25343657; no title, *Bunyip*, 9 December 1892, p. 2, viewed 28 July 2016, http://nla.gov.au/nla.news-article97237241

31 'Family Notices', *Bunyip*, 24 February 1939, p. 3, viewed 9 January 2022, http://nla.gov.au/nla.news-article96704723

32 'The Open Column', *Bunyip*, 1 December 1950, p. 1, viewed 30 December 2020, http://nla.gov.au/nla.news-article96852235; 'The Old Old-Cemetery', *Bunyip*,

22 December 1950, p. 8, viewed 30 December 2020, http://nla.gov.au/nla.news-article96851996

33 Donovan, P., 1986, *Between the City and the Sea: A History of West Torrens from Settlement in 1836 to the Present Day*, Wakefield Press, p. 37

34 Fort, C., 2008, *Keeping a Trust: South Australia's Wyatt Benevolent Institution and its founder*, Wakefield Press, p. 30; Main, J.M., 'The Foundation of South Australia', in Jaensch, D., Richards, E. & Sinclair, W.A., 1986, *The Flinders History of South Australia,* Wakefield Press, pp. 1–25

35 'Advertising', *Adelaide Observer*, 26 March 1859, p. 8, viewed 30 October 2018, http://nla.gov.au/nla.news-article158126603

36 'At Home with God', *Australian Christian Commonwealth*, 6 November 1908, p. 13, viewed 4 August 2021, http://nla.gov.au/nla.news-article213589698

37 Curnow, E.A.,. 2015, *Bible Christian Methodists in South Australia, 1850–1900 : a biography of chapels and their people*, Uniting Church SA Historical Society, chapters 10 & 11

38 'Notes', *Bunyip*, 13 April 1900, p. 2, viewed 10 December 2021, http://nla.gov.au/nla.news-article100579874

39 *Food Forest, The,* n.d., Gawler History, viewed 22 December 2021, https://gawlerhistory.com/index.php/Food_Forest_The

40 Anderson, D., 1993 *The story of John Riggs, the gaffer: from Osmington, Dorset, United Kingdom, and Gawler, South Australia and his descendants*, Riggs family

41 'Family Notices', *Adelaide Observer*, 31 October 1857, p. 5, viewed 9 January 2022, http://nla.gov.au/nla.news-article158118738

42 Corporation of the Town of Gawler & Danver Architects, 1998, *Gawler Heritage Survey*, Danver Architects, pp. 213–214, viewed 10 August 2016, https://data.environment.sa.gov.au/Content/heritage-surveys/2-Gawler-Heritage-Survey-1998.pdf

43 Hignett & Company, South Australia Heritage Unit, & Gawler Corporation, 1981, *Gawler Heritage Study: Stage 1*, Hignett & Company, p. 4, viewed 4 December 2018, https://data.environment.sa.gov.au/Content/heritage-surveys/2-Gawler-Heritage-Study-Stage-One-1981.pdf

44 Barnet, W., 1860, *A general and commercial directory for Gawler & surrounding districts: comprising correct lists of the corporation and public offices in Gawler; also the district councils of Barossa East & West, Mudla Wirra, Muno Para East & West, and Mount Crawford: to which is added a short sketch of the rise and progress of Gawler, and a mass of general & statistical information collected from the census returns of the present year*, p. 13,

45 Farrant, R.W., 1995, *Staff registers – South Australian Railways, 1853–1913*, State Records, viewed 21 Dec 2021

46 Anderson, D., 1993 *The story of John Riggs, the gaffer: from Osmington, Dorset, United Kingdom, and Gawler, South Australia and his descendants,* Riggs family pp. 4–6

47 'Family Notices', *Register*, 23 February 1866, p. 2, viewed 9 January 2022, http://nla.gov.au/nla.news-article41018107

48 'Family Notices', *Observer*, 24 May 1862, p. 5, viewed 15 February 2018, http://nla.gov.au/nla.news-article158186943

49 'Editor's Notes', *Bunyip*, 8 November 1901, p. 2, viewed 16 August 2015, http://nla.gov.au/nla.news-article100579570

50 Coombe, E.H., 1908, *History of Gawler*, Gawler Institute, p. 267

51 'New Wesleyan Church at Gawler', *South Australian Chronicle and Weekly Mail*, 3 April 1869, p. 5, viewed 26 February 2017, http://nla.gov.au/nla.news-article91269941

52 Wegener, M., 1998, *Willaston – the first* 60 *years*, self-published; Hennessy, H., 1991, *Willaston – the beginning*, paper submitted as part of Graduate Diploma in Local & Applied History, UNE; 'Early history of Gawler Methodism', *Bunyip*, 15 February 1946, p. 2, viewed 24 July 2021, http://nla.gov.au/nla.news-article96845947

53 1858, 'Advertising', *South Australian Register*, 16 June 1858, p. 4, viewed 10 January 2022, http://nla.gov.au/nla.news-article49773714; 'Gawler', *South Australian Register*, 18 November 1859, p. 3, viewed 9 July 2016, http://nla.gov.au/nla.news-article49825951

54 'Advertising', *Adelaide Observer*, 26 April 1862, p. 2, viewed 10 January 2022, http://nla.gov.au/nla.news-article158186427; Hennessy, H., 1991, 'Willaston – the beginning', paper submitted as part of Graduate Diploma in Local & Applied History, UNE; 'Advertising', *Adelaide Observer*, 26 April 1862, p. 2, viewed 9 July 2016, http://nla.gov.au/nla.news-article158186427

55 Hoad, J.L., 1986, *Hotels and Publicans in South Australia 1836–1984*, Gould Books, p. 405; Job Harris, n.d., Wikipedia, viewed 27 October 2020, https://en.wikipedia.org/wiki/Job_Harris#cite_note-8

56 'Agents for the 'Register', 'Observer,' and 'Evening Journal', *Register*, 5 February 1869, p. 4, viewed 1 August 2015, http://nla.gov.au/nla.news-article41400682; 1869, 'Agents for the 'Observer,' 'Register', and 'Evening Journal', *Register*, 27 July, p. 4, viewed 1 August, 2015, http://nla.gov.au/nla.news-article41397518; 'Agents for the 'Observer,' 'Register,' and 'Evening Journal', *Register*, 14 September, p. 4, viewed 1 August, 2015, http://nla.gov.au/nla.news-article41405815

57 Loyau, G.E., 1880, *The Gawler handbook: a record of the rise and progress of that important town, to which are added memoirs of McKinlay the explorer and Dr. Nott*, Goodfellow & Hele, p. 110; Coombe, E.H., 1908, *History of Gawler*, Gawler Institute, p. 110; *SA Memory: Job Harris*, 2016, State Library of South Australia, viewed 17 July 2015, https://www.samemory.sa.gov.au/site/page.cfm?u=1086&c=9359; Walker, M., 2004, *The post, telegraph and telephone offices of South Australia and the Northern Territory*, p. 334; 'Family Notices', *Gawler Times*, 3 February 1871, p. 2, viewed 14 June 2021, http://nla.gov.au/nla.news-article245000292

58 'Advertising', *Observer*, 12 December 1874, p. 2, viewed 14 June 2021, http://nla.gov.au/nla.news-article159480820

59 Lands Title Certificate 526/165 sourced from SAILIS – South Australian Integrated Land Information Service Historical Search https://sailis.lssa.com.au/

60 'Advertising', *South Australian Weekly Chronicle*, 6 December 1862, p. 8, viewed 14 JunE 2021, http://nla.gov.au/nla.news-article90257662; 'Advertising', *The Express and Telegraph*, 14 January 1868, p. 1, viewed 22 December 2021, http://nla.gov.au/nla.news-article207739433; 'Advertising', *Evening Journal*, 8 February 1869, p. 4, viewed 14 June 2021, http://nla.gov.au/nla.news-article196724705

61 'Advertising', *South Australian Register*, 14 July 1870, p. 8, viewed 29 July, 2015, http://nla.gov.au/nla.news-article39205311; 'Advertising', *Bunyip*, 26 June 1869, p. 1, viewed 15 June 2021, http://nla.gov.au/nla.news-article97215069

62 Cassidy, R.B., 2015, *Convict ancestors of Marion Lillian Barnes: Thomas Humphstone Willington*, viewed 17 July, 2015, http://cassidyfamilyqueensland.com/Thomas%20Humphstone%20Willington%20-%20Clyde%201830.html; Flynn, R., n.d., *Immigration Place Australia: Thomas Willington,* Immigration Place Australia, viewed 17 July 2015, https://immigrationplace.com.au/story/thomas-willington/

63 'The Floods At Gawler', *South Australian Register,* 4 April 1889, p. 6, viewed 22 December 2021, http://nla.gov.au/nla.news-article47059053; 'The Late Heavy Rains', *The Express and Telegraph*, 4 April 1889, p. 4., viewed 22 December 2021, http://nla.gov.au/nla.news-article208528159; 'The North Para', *Bunyip*, 5 April 1889, p. 2, viewed 22 December 2021, http://nla.gov.au/nla.news-article97225479; 'Big Floods', *Bunyip*, 19 April 1889, p. 2, viewed 22 December 2021, http://nla.gov.au/nla.news-article97230599; 'The Late Floods', *Evening Journal*, 20 April 1889, p. 7, viewed 24 July 2021, http://nla.gov.au/nla.news-article199864082; 'Floods At Gawler', *South Australian Chronicle*, 20 April 1889, p. 9, viewed 25 July 2021, http://nla.gov.au/nla.news-article95149047; 'Advertising', *Bunyip*, 26 April 1889, p. 3, viewed 22 December 2021, http://nla.gov.au/nla.news-article97227893

64 Lands Title certificate 186/41 sourced from SAILIS – South Australian Integrated Land Information Service Historical Search https://sailis.lssa.com.au/; 'Advertising', *Bunyip*, 19 April, p. 2, viewed 25 July 2021, http://nla.gov.au/nla.news-article97209012

65 Loyau, G.E., 1880, *The Gawler handbook: a record of the rise and progress of that important town, to which are added memoirs of McKinlay the explorer and Dr. Nott*, Goodfellow & Hele, p. 110; Coombe, E.H., 1908, *History of Gawler*, Gawler Institute, p. 118

66 'Advertising', *Bunyip*, 15 May 1896, p. 3, viewed 25 July 2021, http://nla.gov.au/nla.news-article97578299

67 'Family Notices', *The Journal*, 18 November 1916, p. 2., viewed 28 July 2016, http://nla.gov.au/nla.news-article204680905

68 Loyau, G.E., 1880, *The Gawler handbook: a record of the rise and progress of that important town, to which are added memoirs of McKinlay the explorer and Dr. Nott,* Goodfellow & Hele, pp. 11–12; Ellis, D., & Ellis, A.L., 1968, *Gawler* 1838–1868, privately published, p. 12

69 DEWNR Fact sheet: Gawler Church Hill heritage area. [date unknown], viewed 15 Jul, 2015, her-fact-gawlerchurchhillsha-factsheet.pdf (environment.sa.gov.au)

70 Hennessy, H., 1991, 'Willaston – the beginning', paper submitted as part of Graduate Diploma in Local & Applied History, UNE, p. 9

71 Corporation of the Town of Gawler & Danver Architects, 1998, *Gawler Heritage Survey*, Danver Architects, pp. 139–154, 235–238, viewed 10 August 2016, https://data.environment.sa.gov.au/Content/heritage-surveys/2-Gawler-Heritage-Survey-1998.pdf

72 'At Home with God', *Australian Christian Commonwealth*, 6 November 1908, p. 13, viewed 28 November 2018, http://nla.gov.au/nla.news-article213589698; 'Obituary', *Chronicle*, 19 September 1908, p. 50, viewed 10 July, 2015, http://nla.gov.au/nla.news-article88304530

73 1935, 'Obituary', *Advertiser*, 26 March 1935, p. 17, viewed 17 May 2018, http://nla.gov.au/nla.news-article37276105

Chapter 3 - Birth, Growing Up, Education and Marriage

1 Jaensch, D., 'Coombe, Ephraim Henry (1858–1917)', *Australian Dictionary of Biography*, National Centre of Biography, Australian National University, first published 1981, viewed 2 August 2016, http://adb.anu.edu.au/biography/coombe-ephraim-henry-5768/text9777

2 'Editor's Notes', *Bunyip,* 12 February 1909: 2. Web. 25 Aug 2022 http://nla.gov.au/nla.news-article97730262

3 Thiele, C., 1975, *Grains of mustard seed,* South Australian Education Department

4 *Calton Henry*, n.d., Gawler History, viewed 2 July 2021, https://gawlerhistory.com/index.php/Calton_Henry

5 Coombe, E.H., 1908, *History of Gawler*, Gawler Institute, p. 143

6 Collinson, G., 1987, 'The Contribution of the Sunday School Movement to Mass Elementary Schooling in England 1780–1850', *Journal of Christian Education*, viewed 10 August 2016, Sage Pub Journals Database, doi.org/10.1177/002196578703000302

7 *To be a child: childhood in South Australia*, n.d. SA Nenory, State Library of South Australia, viewed 10 August 2016 https://www.samemory.sa.gov.au/site/page.cfm?u=1071

8 Coombe, E.H., 1908, *History of Gawler*, Gawler Institute, p. 14

9 'Mr. E.H. Coombe, M.P.', *Daily Herald*, 6 April 1917, p. 4, viewed 31 July 2016, http://nla.gov.au/nla.news-article105399920

10 Loyau, G.E., 1880, *The Gawler handbook: a record of the rise and progress of that important town, to which are added memoirs of McKinlay the explorer and Dr. Nott,* Goodfellow & Hele, p. 9

11 'The Week's News', *Adelaide Observer*, 6 December 1879, p. 7, viewed 19 September 2016, http://nla.gov.au/nla.news-article160127019

12 'Agricultural Education and Mr. Ridley', *Register*, 22 December 1879, p. 4, viewed 19 September 2016, http://nla.gov.au/nla.news-article43089689

13 'Family Notices', *Observer*, 13 March 1880, p. 20, viewed 10 August 2016, http://nla.gov.au/nla.news-article160130381; 'Family Notices', *The Express and Telegraph,* 9 March 1880, p. 2, viewed 9 July 2016, http://nla.gov.au/nla.news-article207586926; 'Family Notices', *South Australian Register*, 9 March 1880, p. 4, viewed 10 August 2016, http://nla.gov.au/nla.news-article43103387; 'Family Notices', *South Australian Register*, 20 March 1880, p. 2, viewed 10 August 2016, http://nla.gov.au/nla.news-article43111342; 'Family Notices', *The South Australian Advertiser*, 20 March 1880, p. 3, viewed 10 August 2016, http://nla.gov.au/nla.news-article73195397

14 'Family Notices', *Gawler Standard*, 10 September 1881, p. 2, viewed 10 January 2022, http://nla.gov.au/nla.news-article245315908

15 Advertising', *Argus*, 23 August 1881, p. 8, viewed 10 Jan 2022, http://nla.gov.au/nla.news-article5978723

16 'Social and Personal', *Bunyip*, 30 November 1923, p. 2, viewed 9 July 2016, http://nla.gov.au/nla.news-article97764471; 'Obituary', *Chronicle,* 5 May 1923, p. 19, viewed 9 July 2016, http://nla.gov.au/nla.news-article89243503; 'Editor's Notes', *Bunyip*, 18 January 1895, p. 2, viewed 15 January 2019, http://nla.gov.au/nla.news-article97573768

17 'Family Notices', *Bunyip*, 18 November 1904, p. 2, viewed 15 January 2019, http://nla.gov.au/nla.news-article97588751; 'Gawler', *Chronicle*, 12 November 1904, p. 13, viewed 15 January 2019, http://nla.gov.au/nla.news-article88376719

18 Carmichael, G., 1988, 'With this ring: First marriage patterns, trends and prospects in Australia', *Australian Family Formation Project Monograph No. 11*, Australian Institute of Family Studies, viewed 10 August 2016 https://aifs.gov.au/publications/ring-first-marriage-patterns-trends-and-prospect

19 'Country Correspondence', *Bunyip*, 11 October 1895, p. 3, viewed 27 December 2021, http://nla.gov.au/nla.news-article97569897; 'The Political Warfare', *Bunyip*, 14 February 1896, p. 3, viewed 27 December 2021, http://nla.gov.au/nla.news-article97575967; 'The Late Mr. E.J. Hiscock', *Adelaide Observer*, 22 December 1894, p. 16, viewed 27 December 2021, http://nla.gov.au/nla.news-article161814254

20 'Social And Personal', *Bunyip*, 30 November 1923, p. 2, viewed 9 July 2016, http://nla.gov.au/nla.news-article97764471

21 'A Tribute to Mr. E.H. Coombe', *Register*, 3 June 1914, p. 9, viewed 29 December 2020, http://nla.gov.au/nla.news-article59397721; 'Women's Christian Temperance Union', *Bunyip*, 5 September 1890, p. 3, viewed 31 December 2018, http://nla.gov.au/nla.news-article97232989; Burgess, H.T., 1907, *The cyclopedia of South Australia in two volumes: an historical and commercial review, descriptive and biographical, facts, figures, and illustrations: an epitome of progress*, Volume 2, Cyclopedia Co, p. 72

22 Jones, H., 1994, *In Her Own Name: A history of women in South Australia from 1836*, Wakefield Press, cited in http://www.slsa.sa.gov.au/women_and_politics/suffr2.htm; Lloyd, J.M., 2009, *Women and the shaping of British Methodism: persistent preachers*, 1807–1907, Manchester University Press

23 'Visit of Miss Jessie Ackermann', *Bunyip*, 2 October 1891, p. 4, viewed 31 December 2018, http://nla.gov.au/nla.news-article97233428; 'Pure Water for Adelaide', *Bunyip*, 16 August 1889, p. 2, viewed 31 December 2018, http://nla.gov.au/nla.news-article97227615

24 'The Barossa Election', *Bunyip*, 20 March 1896, p. 3, viewed 27 December 2021, http://nla.gov.au/nla.news-article97577488

25 'Advertising', *Bunyip*, 16 August 1889, p. 3, viewed 21 January 2019, http://nla.gov.au/nla.news-article97227609; 'W.C.T.U.', *Bunyip*, 5 December 1890, p. 2, viewed 21 January 2019, http://nla.gov.au/nla.news-article97232050; 'The Evening Meeting', *Bunyip*, 15 July 1892, p. 3, viewed 21 January 2019, http://nla.gov.au/nla.news-article97237200; 'Editor's Notes', *Bunyip*, 10 April 1896, p. 2, viewed 21 January 2019, http://nla.gov.au/nla.news-article97575862; no title, *Bunyip*, 24 April 1896, p. 2, viewed 21 January 2019, http://nla.gov.au/nla.news-article97576849; 'The Barossa Election', *Bunyip*, 20 March 1896, p. 3, viewed 21 January 2019, http://nla.gov.au/nla.news-article97577488; 'Summary Of Proceedings', *Bunyip*, 9 September 1898, p. 2, viewed 21 January 2019, http://nla.gov.au/nla.news-article97581881

26 'A New Bridge at Gawler', *Advertiser*, 23 January 1908, p. 9, viewed 16 June 2021, http://nla.gov.au/nla.news-article5122434

27 'Fails and Fetes', *Bunyip*, 26 November 1909, p. 3, viewed 17 December 2018, http://nla.gov.au/nla.news-article97730147; 'Catholic Bazaar', *Bunyip*, 20 October 1916, p. 2, viewed 17 December 2018, http://nla.gov.au/nla.news-article97733277

28 Burgess, H.T., 1907, *The Cyclopedia of South Australia in two volumes: an historical and commercial review, descriptive and biographical, facts, figures, and illustrations: an epitome of progress*, Volume 1, Cyclopedia Co, p. 145

29 Loyau, G.E., 1880, *The Gawler handbook: a record of the rise and progress of that important town, to which are added memoirs of McKinlay the explorer and Dr. Nott,*

Goodfellow & Hele, p. 31; Hirst, J.B., 1970, *Adelaide and the country, 1870–1914: a study of their social and political relationship*, p. 466 viewed 1 December 2020, http://hdl.handle.net/2440/20863; Phillips, S., & Pilkington, M., 1980, *Gawler's industrial buildings,* 1839–1939, University of Adelaide, Faculty of Architecture & Town Planning,

30 Hignett & Company, South Australia Heritage Unit, & Gawler Corporation, 1981, *Gawler Heritage Study: stage* 1, Hignett & Company, p. 4, viewed 4 December 2018 https://data.environment.sa.gov.au/Content/heritage-surveys/2-Gawler-Heritage-Study-Stage-One-1981.pdf; Phillips, S., & Pilkington, M., 1980, *Gawler's industrial buildings,* 1839–1939, University of Adelaide, Faculty of Architecture & Town Planning, p. 11

31 Coombe, E.H., 1908, *History of Gawler*, Gawler Institute, pp. 312–313, p. 201

32 Loyau, G.E., 1880, *The Gawler handbook: a record of the rise and progress of that important town, to which are added memoirs of McKinlay the explorer and Dr. Nott*, Goodfellow & Hele, p. 110

33 Day, I., 'The art of confectionery', n.d., from *The Pleasures of the Table*, by Brown, P., & Day, I., York Civic Trust, viewed 23 April 2018 http://www.historicfood.com/The%20Art%20of%20Confectionery.pdf

34 Coombe, E.H., 1908, *History of Gawler*, Gawler Institute, p. 124

35 Day, I., 'The art of confectionery', n.d., from *The Pleasures of the Table*, by Brown, P., & Day, I., York Civic Trust, viewed 23 April 2018 http://www.historicfood.com/The%20Art%20of%20Confectionery.pdf; Symons, M., 2007, *One continuous picnic: a gastronomic history of Australia*, Melbourne University Press, pp. 98–109

36 Huxley, M., 'Duffield, Walter (1816–1882)', *Australian Dictionary of Biography*, National Centre of Biography, Australian National University, first published 1972, viewed online 25 April 2018, http://adb.anu.edu.au/biography/duffield-walter-3449/text5239; Whitelock, D., 1985, *Adelaide 1836–1976: a history of difference 1985*, Adelaide from colony to jubilee: a sense of difference, Savvas Publishing; Burgess, H.T., 1907, *The cyclopedia of South Australia in two volumes: an historical and commercial review, descriptive and biographical, facts, figures, and illustrations: an epitome of progress*, Volume 1, Cyclopedia Co, p. 145; Smith, P.A., Pate, F.D., Martin, R., & Hills Face Zone Cultural Heritage Project, V*alleys of Stone: The archaeology and history of Adelaide's Hills Face*, Kopi Books: Miln Walker & Associates, pp. 375–376

37 'Advertising', *Gawler Standard*, 5 February 1881, p. 2, viewed 21 April 2019, http://nla.gov.au/nla.news-article245314951

38 'Eyes and Ears', *Gawler Standard*, 12 February 1881, p. 2, viewed 21 April 2019, http://nla.gov.au/nla.news-article245314971

39 'Assignments', 1881, 15 February, p. 4, viewed 31 December 2020, http://nla.gov.au/nla.news-article43166720

40 'Advertising', *Bunyip*, 4 February 1881, p. 3, viewed 7 July 2016, http://nla.gov.au/nla.news-article99826780; 'Advertising', *Bunyip*, 18 February 1881, p. 3, viewed 7 July 2016, http://nla.gov.au/nla.news-article99827206

41 1881, 'Eyes and Ears', *Gawler Standard*, 26 February, p. 3, viewed 21 April 2019, http://nla.gov.au/nla.news-article245315059; , 'Advertising', *Gawler Standard*, 26 February 1881, p. 3, viewed 22 April 2019, http://nla.gov.au/nla.news-article245315041

42 'Advertising', *Bunyip* 17 July 1869, p. 2, viewed 22 April 2019, http://nla.gov.au/nla.news-article97215290; 'Advertising', *Bunyip*, 23 March 1877, p. 3, viewed 22 April 2019, http://nla.gov.au/nla.news-article97220683

43 Walker, M., 2004, *The post, telegraph and telephone offices of South Australia and the Northern Territory*, Martin Walker, p. 334

44 The Colonial Mutual Life Assurance Society, image, Sands and McDougall's South Australian Directory for 1885, viewed 31 July 2016, https://images.slsa.sa.gov.au/almanacsanddirectories/1885sandsandmc/

45 'Advertising', *South Australian Register*, 18 January 1883, p. 2, viewed 13 January 2022, http://nla.gov.au/nla.news-article43467928

46 'Advertising', *South Australian Register*, 24 May 1883, p. 2, viewed 13 January 2022, http://nla.gov.au/nla.news-article41999537

47 *The Colonial Mutual Life Assurance Society*, image, Sands and McDougall's South Australian Directory for 1885, viewed 31 July 2016, https://images.slsa.sa.gov.au/almanacsanddirectories/1885sandsandmc/; , 'Advertising', *Bunyip*, 22 January 1886, p. 1, viewed 2 July 2016, http://nla.gov.au/nla.news-article97212772

48 *SA Newspapers: an early history*, n.d., SA Memory, State Library of South Australia, viewed 31 July, 2016 http://www.samemory.sa.gov.au/site/page.cfm?u=1473; Burgess, H.T., 1907, *The cyclopedia of South Australia in two volumes: an historical and commercial review, descriptive and biographical, facts, figures, and illustrations: an epitome of progress*, Volume 1, Cyclopedia Co, pp. 274 & 504

49 Coombe, E.H., 1908, *History of Gawler*, Gawler Institute, pp. 33, 115 & 313

50 Talbot, M.R., 1992,. *A chance to read: A history of the Institutes movement in South Australia*, Adelaide Libraries Board of South Australia, p. 15

51 Schumann & Associates, 2013, *Town of Gawler Cultural Heritage Collection Management Plan* 2013, Corporation of the Town of Gawler, p. 17

52 'The Transcontinental Railway', *Adelaide Observer*, 19 July 1902, p. 39, viewed 15 December 2021, http://nla.gov.au/nla.news-article161783101

53 Gawler Cultural Heritage Collection, *Burton & Warren Memorial Committee file*, viewed December 2021

54 *SA Newspapers: Journalists*, n.d., SA Memory, State Library of South Australia, viewed 31 July 2016, http://www.samemory.sa.gov.au/site/page.cfm?u=1535; Jaensch, D., 'Coombe, Ephraim Henry (1858–1917)', *Australian Dictionary of Biography*, National Centre of Biography, Australian National University, first published 1981, viewed 2 August 2016, http://adb.anu.edu.au/biography/coombe-ephraim-henry-5768/text9777,

55 'City Chatter', *Port Pirie Recorder and North Western Mail*, 15 June 1901, p. 3, viewed 11 January 2022, http://nla.gov.au/nla.news-article95275840

56 Prest, W., Round, K., & Fort, C.S., 2001, *The Wakefield Companion to South Australian history*, Wakefield Press, p. 401; Combe, G.D., & Playford, Sir T., 1957, *Responsible Government in South Australia*, Government Printer, Adelaide, p. 148

57 *Role description: Parliamentary Senior Reporter*, n.d., NSW Parliament, viewed 17 September 2016 https://www.google.com.au/url?sa=t&rct=j&q=&esrc=s&source=web&cd=&ved=2ahUKEwiL6Pqcq6b1AhWe4HMBHVgGAQQQFnoECBcQAQ&url=https%3A%2F%2Ffiles.jobs.nsw.gov.au%2Frba3gf&usg=AOvVaw0OJt2PQnfSdeox4ONF2-q6

61 'Obituary', *Advertiser*, 26 March 1935, p. 17, viewed 2 July 2016, http://nla.gov.au/nla.news-article37276105; 'A Reminder', *Bunyip*, 30 December 1910, p. 4, viewed 19 September 2016, http://nla.gov.au/nla.news-article97728652

58 'Advertising', *Bunyip*, 24 December 1886, p. 1, viewed 23 August 2016, http://nla.gov.au/nla.news-article97210297

59 'Advertising', *Bunyip*, 8 January 1892, p. 3, viewed 2 November 2020, http://nla.gov.au/nla.news-article97236691; 'Editor's Notes', *Bunyip*, 9 March 1894, p. 2, viewed 23 August 2016, http://nla.gov.au/nla.news-article97573569; Coombe, E.H., 1908, *History of Gawler*, Gawler Institute, p. 124

60 'Advertising', *Bunyip*, 10 July 1891, p. 3, viewed 10 January 2022, http://nla.gov.au/nla.news-article97232945; 'Mudla Wirra South', *Bunyip*, 17 July 1891, p. 3, viewed 10 January 2022, http://nla.gov.au/nla.news-article97233266; 'Advertising', *Bunyip*, 9 June 1893, p. 3, viewed 10 January 2022, http://nla.gov.au/nla.news-article97236277

62 'Correspondence', *Burra Record*, 15 August 1890, p. 3, viewed 17 September 2016, http://nla.gov.au/nla.news-article36030189; 'Scratchings in the City', *Kapunda Herald*, 22 July 1890, p. 3, viewed 17 September 2016, http://nla.gov.au/nla.news-article108353646

Chapter 4 - Journalism and Writing

1 Ewart, H.P., 2016, *Gentlemen squatters, 'self-made' men and soldiers: masculinities in nineteenth century Australia*, thesis, University of Adelaide, viewed 11 April 2019, p. 225, https://www.semanticscholar.org/paper/Gentleman-squatters%2C-%E2%80%98self-made%E2%80%99-men-and-soldiers%3A-Ewart/95eb9b58aeb94bf772f7ca37693215d2b5813169?utm_source=email; 'CIT', *Bunyip*, 23 February 1917, p. 3, viewed 18 December 2018, http://nla.gov.au/nla.news-article100413552

2 'Amalgamated Society of Engineers', *Bunyip*, 31 January 1890, p. 3, viewed 17 September 2016, http://nla.gov.au/nla.news-article97231362

3 'The Gawler Club', *Bunyip*, 14 March 1890, p. 4, viewed 10 August 2016, http://nla.gov.au/nla.news-article97234663; Coombe, E.H., 1908, *History of Gawler*, Gawler Institute, p. 404; , 'Union Cricket Club', *Bunyip*, 26 September 1890, p. 4, viewed 17 September 2016, http://nla.gov.au/nla.news-article97233313; 'Gawler Institute', *Bunyip*, 5 December 1890, p. 2, viewed 17 September 2016, http://nla.gov.au/nla.news-article97232053

4 Burgess, H.T., 1907, *The Cyclopedia of South Australia in two volumes: an historical and commercial review, descriptive and biographical, facts, figures, and illustrations: an epitome of progress*, Volume 2, Cyclopedia Co, p. 163

5 'Advertising', *Bunyip*, 4 April 1890, p. 3, viewed 19 September 2016, http://nla.gov.au/nla.news-article97231057; 'Progressive Land Tax', *Bunyip*, 16 May 1890, p. 2, viewed 19 September 2016, http://nla.gov.au/nla.news-article97231290; *Electoral district of Barossa*, n.d., viewed 19 September 2016, https://en.wikipedia.org/wiki/Electoral_district_of_Barossa; Powell, G., 2000, 'Downer, Sir John William', *The Biographical Dictionary of the Australian Senate*, Volume 1, Melbourne University Press, pp. 148–152, viewed 19 Sept 2016, http://biography.senate.gov.au/index.php/john-william-downer/

6 'Gawler', *South Australian Register*, 12 December 1890, p. 7, viewed 17 September 2016, http://nla.gov.au/nla.news-article47257677

7 1890, 'MEETING AT GAWLER', *The Express and Telegraph*, 30 September, p. 3, viewed 17 Sep 2016, http://nla.gov.au/nla.news-article208392552; 'Public Meeting In

The Institute Hall', *Bunyip*, 3 October 1890, p. 2, viewed 17 September 2016, http://nla.gov.au/nla.news-article97234052

8 'Municipality of Gawler', *Bunyip*, 21 June 1895, p. 4, viewed 17 December 2018, http://nla.gov.au/nla.news-article97572471

9 'Family Notices', *Bunyip*, 30 September 1892, p. 2, viewed 11 January 2022, http://nla.gov.au/nla.news-article97235496

10 Schiel, W., Cameron, S., Roberts, C., & Hall, R., 1998, 'Pertussis in South Australia 1893 to 1996', *Communicable Diseases Intelligence* Volume 22, Number 5, viewed 11 April 2019, http://www.health.gov.au/internet/main/publishing.nsf/Content/cda-pubs-cdi-1998-cdi2205-cdi2205c.htm

11 'Family Notices', *Bunyip*, 13 October 1893, p. 2, viewed 11 January 2022, http://nla.gov.au/nla.news-article97236359; 'Family Notices', *Bunyip*, 1 December 1893, p. 2, viewed 11 January 2022, http://nla.gov.au/nla.news-article97237691

12 *SA Newspapers: Country press*, n.d., SA Memory, State Library of South Australia, viewed 18 December 2018, https://www.samemory.sa.gov.au/site/page.cfm?u=1472

13 Honourable Fraternity of Humbugs, 1984, *The Bunyip: or Gawler Humbug Society's chronicle*, p. 2

14 'History of the Humbug Society and the *Bunyip*', 2020, Barnet, J., viewed 31 July 2016, https://gawlerhistory.com/index.php?title=Humbug_Society_in_Gawler&mobileaction=toggle_view_desktop

15 *SA Newspapers: Bunyip*, n.d., SA Memory, State Library of South Australia, viewed 31 July 2016, http://www.samemory.sa.gov.au/site/page.cfm?c=2596

16 *SA Newspapers: journalists*, n.d., SA Memory, State Library of South Australia, viewed 31 July 2016, http://www.samemory.sa.gov.au/site/page.cfm?u=1535; 'Mrs. J.M. Congreve', *Chronicle*, 27 December 1934, p. 14, viewed 31 July 2016, http://nla.gov.au/nla.news-article91074258; no title, *Bunyip*, 25 July 1890, p. 2, viewed 10 August 2016, http://nla.gov.au/nla.news-article97232629; Wall, B., 'Congreve, Henry John (Harry) (1829–1918)', *Australian Dictionary of Biography*, National Centre of Biography, Australian National University, first published 2005, viewed 28 December 2021, https://adb.anu.edu.au/biography/congreve-henry-john-harry-12853/text23207

17 'Mrs. William Barnet', *Observer*, 12 March 1921, p. 23, viewed 19 September 2016, http://nla.gov.au/nla.news-article165645428; Barnet, Hannah (1843–1921), Obituaries Australia, National Centre of Biography, Australian National University, viewed 5 February 2017, http://oa.anu.edu.au/obituary/barnet-hannah-23544

18 'SA Newspapers: Country Press', n.d., SA Memory, State Library of South Australia, viewed 18 December 2018, http://www.samemory.sa.gov.au/site/page.cfm?u=1472

19 'Fire At Gawler', *Advertiser*, 27 February 1885, p. 6, viewed 17 September 2016, http://nla.gov.au/nla.news-article35977258

20 Corporation of the Town of Gawler & Danver Architects, 1998, *Gawler Heritage Survey*, Danver Architects, pp. 177–178, viewed 10 August 2016, https://data.environment.sa.gov.au/Content/heritage-surveys/2-Gawler-Heritage-Survey-1998.pdf

21 *SA Newspapers: early history*, n.d., SA Memory, State Library of South Australia, viewed 18 December 2018, http://www.samemory.sa.gov.au/site/page.cfm?u=1473

22 'Biographical', *Register*, 6 May 1902, p. 7, viewed 23 August 2016, http://nla.gov.au/nla.news-article56561130

23 'Mr. E.H. Coombe, M.P.', *Daily Herald*, 6 April 1917, p. 4, viewed 23 August 2016, http://nla.gov.au/nla.news-article105399920

24 'Women's Suffrage', *Bunyip*, 24 October 1890, p. 2, viewed 17 September 2016, http://nla.gov.au/nla.news-article97231866

25 *Women's Suffrage: Women's Suffrage Petition – master photocopy, 1894 (GRG 92/5)*, n.d., State Records of South Australia, viewed 2 July 2021 https://archives.sa.gov.au/finding-information/discover-our-collection/other-topics/womens-suffrage

26 *Temperance Movement*, n.d, Wikipedia, viewed 17 September 2021, https://en.wikipedia.org/wiki/Temperance_movement

27 'The Federation Debates', *Bunyip*, 1 August 1890, p. 2, viewed 17 September 2016, http://nla.gov.au/nla.news-article97232227; 'Federation', *Bunyip*, 9 May 1890, p. 2, viewed 17 September 2016, http://nla.gov.au/nla.news-article97231442

28 Talbot, M.R., 1992, *A chance to read: A history of the Institutes movement in South Australia,* Adelaide: Libraries Board of South Australia

29 ibid, p. 99

30 Gooden, G.W. & Moore, T.L., 1903, *Fifty years history of the town of Kensington and Norwood, July 1853 to July 1903*, Webb & Son

31 Durward, E.L.D., 'Gill, Thomas (1849–1923)', *Australian Dictionary of Biography*, National Centre of Biography, Australian National University, first published 1983, viewed 2 January 2019, http://adb.anu.edu.au/biography/gill-thomas-6382/text10905

32 Burgess, H.T., 1907, *The cyclopedia of South Australia in two volumes: an historical and commercial review, descriptive and biographical, facts, figures, and illustrations: an epitome of progress*, Cyclopedia Co, Adelaide, Vol.1 p. 215 & Vol.2 p. 165, p. 281

33 Hunt, A.D., 'Burgess, Henry Thomas (1839–1923)', *Australian Dictionary of Biography, National Centre of Biography*, Australian National University, first published 1979, viewed 2 January 2019, http://adb.anu.edu.au/biography/burgess-henry-thomas-5427/text9205

34 'Gawler Institute', *Bunyip*, 28 April 1911, p. 3., viewed 29 Apr 2019, http://nla.gov.au/nla.news-article97564338; 'Advertising', *Bunyip*, 12 August 1910, p. 1., viewed 29 Apr 2019, http://nla.gov.au/nla.news-article97724464

35 'Gawler School Of Shorthand', *Bunyip*, 24 December 1897, p. 2, viewed 31 December 2020, http://nla.gov.au/nla.news-article97576429; 'Local Mems', *Bunyip*, 20 January 1905, p. 4, viewed 31 December 2020, http://nla.gov.au/nla.news-article97600631

36 Hirst, J.B., 'Martin, James (1821–1899)', *Australian Dictionary of Biography*, National Centre of Biography, Australian National University, first published 1974, viewed 17 April 2019, http://adb.anu.edu.au/biography/martin-james-4162/text6681

37 'Gawler Institute', *Bunyip*, 12 January 1906, p. 2, viewed 17 April 2019, http://nla.gov.au/nla.news-article97595954; Institutes Association of South Australia, *The South Australian Institutes' Journal,* May 24, 1906, p. 191

38 'Gawler Institute', *Bunyip*, 9 March 1906, p. 2, viewed 11 January 2022, http://nla.gov.au/nla.news-article97599732

39 'Gawler Institute', *Bunyip*, 20 April 1906, p. 4, viewed 11 January 2022, http://nla.gov.au/nla.news-article97600089

40 Institutes Association of South Australia, *South Australian Institutes' Journal*, April 1906, p. 174

41 'Gawler Institute', *Bunyip*, 29 April 1910, p. 3, viewed 29 December 2021, http://nla.gov.au/nla.news-article97728112; 'It Is Said–', *Bunyip*, 22 July 1910, p. 2, viewed 29 December 2021, http://nla.gov.au/nla.news-article97728267

42 'The *History of Gawler*', *Bunyip*, 29 July 1910, p. 2, viewed 1 January 2021, http://nla.gov.au/nla.news-article97728428

43 'Local Mems', *Bunyip*, 28 October 1910, p. 4, viewed 29 April 2019, http://nla.gov.au/nla.news-article97724700; 'Town Tattle', *Bunyip*, 5 August 1910, p. 2, viewed 29 April 2019, http://nla.gov.au/nla.news-article97730312

44 'Gawler Institute', *Bunyip*, 6 January 1911, p. 4, viewed 29 April 2019, http://nla.gov.au/nla.news-article97560506

45 'The *History of Gawler*', *Bunyip*, 30 December 1910, p. 2, viewed 29 April 2019, http://nla.gov.au/nla.news-article97728636; 'The *History of Gawler*', *Bunyip*, 1 September 1911, p. 3, viewed 29 April 2019, http://nla.gov.au/nla.news-article97568191

46 'Presentation to Mr. Coombe', *Chronicle*, 6 May 1911, p. 13, viewed 9 January 2022, http://nla.gov.au/nla.news-article88689272

47 'Gawler Institute', *Bunyip*, 9 September 1910, p. 2, viewed 29 April 2019, http://nla.gov.au/nla.news-article97730090; 'The *History of Gawler*', *Bunyip*, 5 May 1911, p. 4, viewed 29 April 2019, http://nla.gov.au/nla.news-article97563958

48 'The Late Mr.E.H. Coombe, M.P.', *Bunyip*, 13 April 1917, p. 1, viewed 15 December 2021, http://nla.gov.au/nla.news-article100412485

49 *Herald (Adelaide)*, n.d., Wikipedia, viewed 10 December 2018, https://en.wikipedia.org/wiki/The_Herald_(Adelaide); S*A Newspapers: SA Press: Daily Herald*, n.d., SA Memory, State Library of South Australia, viewed 18 December 2018; SA Newspapers: early history, n.d., SA Memory, State Library of South Australia, viewed 18 December 2018, http://www.samemory.sa.gov.au/site/page.cfm?c=2683

50 'Labour's New Editor', *Mail*, 25 April, p. 13, viewed 29 December 2021, http://nla.gov.au/nla.news-article59647228 1914

51 'South Australia', *The Australian Worker*, 6 July 1916, p. 17, viewed 29 December 2021, http://nla.gov.au/nla.news-article145765817

52 'Current Topics', *Australian Christian Commonwealth*, 13 April 1917, p. 9, viewed 24 October 2020, http://nla.gov.au/nla.news-article214063468

Chapter 5 - Parliamentary Career

1 Burgess, H.T., 1907, *The Cyclopedia of South Australia in two volumes: an historical and commercial review, descriptive and biographical, facts, figures, and illustrations: an epitome of progress*, Cyclopedia Co, Volume 1, p. 194

2 Bannon, J., 2009, *Supreme Federalist: The political life of Sir John Downer*, Wakefield Press, p. 24

3 Carroll, B., Fausboll, V., Davids, T.W.R, 1977, *Earning a Crust: An illustrated economic history of Australia*, Reed

4 Oldfield, A., 1992, *Woman suffrage in Australia: a gift or a struggle?*, Cambridge University Press; Barnard, M., 1976, *A History of Australia*, Angus & Robertson, pp. 143–144; 'The Picnic Of The Gawler Friendly Societies', *Bunyip*, 18 September 1869, p. 3, viewed 30 October 2018, http://nla.gov.au/nla.news-article97216555; 'Gawler Friendly Societies' Annual Picnic', *The South Australian Advertiser*, 28 September 1871, p. 2, viewed 30 October 2018, http://nla.gov.au/nla.news-article28604935; '1', *The South Australian Advertiser*, 25 May 1883, p. 6, viewed 30 October 2018, http://nla.gov.au/nla.news-article33762704; 'Gawler United Friendly

Societies' Demonstration', *South Australian Register*, 16 December 1887, p. 6, viewed 30 October 2018, http://nla.gov.au/nla.news-article46834209

5 Bannon, J., 2009, *Supreme Federalist: The political life of Sir John Downer*, Wakefield Press, p. 21

6 *Electoral district of Barossa*, n.d., Wikipedia, viewed 30 October 2018, https://en.wikipedia.org/wiki/Electoral_district_of_Barossa; Jaensch, D., History Trust of South Australia, & Electoral Commission of South Australia, 2007, *History of South Australian elections 1857–2006*, volume 1, viewed 2 January 2019, https://www.ecsa.sa.gov.au/index.php?option=com_content&view=article&id=205:information-resources&catid=10:about&Itemid=387; *Molly Byrne*, n.d., Wikipedia,viewed 2 January 2019, https://en.wikipedia.org/wiki/Molly_Byrne

7 'Current Topics', *Bunyip*, 16 March 1894, p. 2, viewed 19 January 2022, http://nla.gov.au/nla.news-article97572964; 'Gawler', *Advertiser*, 7 April 1894, p. 6, viewed 19 January 2022, http://nla.gov.au/nla.news-article25721439; 'Barossa Political Reform League', *Evening Journal*, 12 July 1894, p. 4, viewed 19 January 2022, http://nla.gov.au/nla.news-article202817150; 'Barossa Political Reform League', *Bunyip*, 13 July 1894, p. 3, viewed 19 January 2022, http://nla.gov.au/nla.news-article97570257; Country Correspondence', *Bunyip*, 10 August 1894, p. 3, viewed 19 January 2022, http://nla.gov.au/nla.news-article97569669; 'The Libel Law', *Bunyip*, 3 May 1895, p. 2, viewed 19 January 2022, http://nla.gov.au/nla.news-article97570809'; 'Current Topics', *Weekly Herald*, 9 August 1895, p. 2, viewed 19 January 2022, http://nla.gov.au/nla.news-article124811471

8 'Political Science Association' *Bunyip*, September 26 1884, p. 2, viewed January 19 2022, http://nla.gov.au/nla.news-article97210551

9 'Gawler', *South Australian Register*, 10 April 1894, p. 3, viewed 25 February 2018, http://nla.gov.au/nla.news-article53694909; 'Advertising', *Bunyip*, 6 July 1894, p. 3, viewed 10 January 2022, http://nla.gov.au/nla.news-article97573841; 'Editor's Notes', *Bunyip*, 9 June 1893, p. 2, viewed 1 January 2021, http://nla.gov.au/nla.news-article97236282; 'Barossa Political Reform League', *South Australian Chronicle*, 14 July 1894, p. 4, viewed 25 February 2018, http://nla.gov.au/nla.news-article92315487; 'Personalities', *Quiz and the Lantern*, 12 December 1895, p. 6, viewed 1 January 2021, http://nla.gov.au/nla.news-article166453841; Coombe, E.H., 1908, *History of Gawler*, Gawler Institute, pp. 312, 409; 'Editor's Notes', *Bunyip*, 24 January 1896, p. 2, viewed 3 January 2021, http://nla.gov.au/nla.news-article97576520; 'Advertising', *Bunyip*, 31 January 1896, p. 3, viewed 3 January 2021, http://nla.gov.au/nla.news-article97575575; 'Country News', *Adelaide Observer*, 1 February 1896, p. 11, viewed 3 January 2021, http://nla.gov.au/nla.news-article161834685; 'Political Platforms', *South Australian Register*, 4 February 1896, p. 7, viewed 3 January 2021, http://nla.gov.au/nla.news-article53669035; 'The New Factor In Politics', *Evening Journal*, 10 February 1896, p. 3, viewed 3 January 2021, http://nla.gov.au/nla.news-article199886319; 'Barossa', *Advertiser*, 10 April 1896, p. 7, viewed 3 January 2021, http://nla.gov.au/nla.news-article34543388; 'Barossa Election', *Bunyip*, 14 April 1899, p. 1, viewed 3 July 2021, http://nla.gov.au/nla.news-article97579136

10 'Mr. E H. Coombe at Gawler', *Bunyip*, 10 April 1896, p. 3, viewed 9 January 2022, http://nla.gov.au/nla.news-article97575876

11 Jaensch, D., History Trust of South Australia, & Electoral Commission of South Australia, 2007, *History of South Australian elections 1857–2006, volume 1*, viewed 2

January 2019, https://www.ecsa.sa.gov.au/index.php?option=com_content&view=article&id=205:information-resources&catid=10:about&Itemid=387

12 'Advertising', *Bunyip*, 28 March 1884, p. 3, viewed 2 January 2019, http://nla.gov.au/nla.news-article97213436

13 Bannon, J., 2009, *Supreme Federalist: The political life of Sir John Downer*, Wakefield Press, p. 132

14 Loughlin, G., 'Nesbit, Paris (1852–1927)', *Australian Dictionary of Biography*, National Centre of Biography, Australian National University, first published 1988, viewed 18 December 2018, http://adb.anu.edu.au/biography/nesbit-paris-7817/text13567

15 Best, M.R., 1986, *A Lost Glitter: Letters between South Australia and the Western Australian goldfields, 1895–1897*, Wakefield Press

16 'Town Talk', *Bunyip*, 1 May 1896, p. 2, viewed 3 January 2022, http://nla.gov.au/nla.news-article97576962

17 'The Barossa Election', *Bunyip*, 24 April 1896, p. 2, viewed 18 December 2018, http://nla.gov.au/nla.news-article97576868; 'The Political Situation', *Bunyip*, 24 April 1896, p. 3, viewed 18 December 2018, http://nla.gov.au/nla.news-article97576871; 'Advertising', *Bunyip*, 24 April 1896, p. 3, viewed 18 December 2018, http://nla.gov.au/nla.news-article97576855

18 *1896 South Australian referendum*, n.d., Wikipedia, viewed 3 July 2021, https://en.wikipedia.org/wiki/1896_South_Australian_referendum

19 'The Barossa Election', *Bunyip*, 24 April 1896, p. 2, viewed 1 January 2021, http://nla.gov.au/nla.news-article97576868

20 'A Reply To Criticisms', *Bunyip*, 24 April 1896, p. 2, viewed 30 October 2018, http://nla.gov.au/nla.news-article97576869; 'The Political Situation', *Bunyip*, 24 April 1896, p. 3, viewed 31 October 2018, http://nla.gov.au/nla.news-article97576871

21 'The New Factor In Politics', *Evening Journal*, 10 February 1896, p. 3, viewed 22 May 2018, http://nla.gov.au/nla.news-article199886319; 'The Political Warfare', *Bunyip*, 14 February 1896, p. 3, viewed 22 May 2018, http://nla.gov.au/nla.news-article97575967

22 Spence, C.H., Lyons, M., Wall, B., Magarey, S. & Beams, M., 2005, *Ever Yours, C.H. Spence: Catherine Helen Spence's An Autobiography (1825–1910), Diary (1894) and Some Correspondence (1894–1910)*, Wakefield Press, p. 198; *1896 South Australian colonial election*, n.d., Wikipedia, viewed 31 October 2018, https://en.wikipedia.org/wiki/South_Australian_colonial_election,_1896; Eade, S., 'Spence, Catherine Helen (1825–1910)', *Australian Dictionary of Biography*, National Centre of Biography, Australian National University, first published 1976, viewed 31 October 2018, http://adb.anu.edu.au/biography/spence-catherine-helen-4627/text7621

23 'The Elections', *Bunyip*, 1 May 1896, p. 2, viewed 19 January 2022, http://nla.gov.au/nla.news-article97576956

24 Bannon, J., 2009, *Supreme Federalist: The political life of Sir John Downer*, Wakefield Press, p. 135

25 'The Barossa Election', *Bunyip*, 12 June 1896, p. 3, viewed 15 June 2021, http://nla.gov.au/nla.news-article97575915

26 'Local Mems', *Bunyip*, 11 December 1896, p. 2, viewed 11 January 2022, http://nla.gov.au/nla.news-article97578410

27 'Barossa Election', *Bunyip*, 14 April 1899, p. 1, viewed 1 November 2018, http://nla.gov.au/nla.news-article97579136

28 'The Elections', *Bunyip*, 5 May 1899, p. 2, viewed 11 January 2022, http://nla.gov.au/nla.news-article97580206

29 'The Barossa Election', *Bunyip*, 12 May 1899, p. 3, viewed 1 November 2018, http://nla.gov.au/nla.news-article97581458; 'The Barossa Election', *Bunyip* 28 April 1899, p. 1, viewed 1 November 2018, http://nla.gov.au/nla.news-article97581093

30 'City Chatter', *Port Pirie Recorder and North Western Mail*, 15 June 1901, p. 3, viewed 11 January 2022, http://nla.gov.au/nla.news-article95275840; no title, *The Laura Standard*, 28 June 1901, p. 2, viewed 11 January 2022, http://nla.gov.au/nla.news-article188771657

31 'Obituary', *Register*, 5 August 1924, p. 9, viewed 30 December 2021, http://nla.gov.au/nla.news-article59026251; 'The Elections', *Bunyip*, 5 May 1899, p. 2, viewed 15 May 2020, http://nla.gov.au/nla.news-article97580206

32 'The Political Situation', *Bunyip*, 24 April 1896, p. 3, viewed 3 January 2021, http://nla.gov.au/nla.news-article97576871

33 'Gawler Institute', *Bunyip*, 16 February 1900, p. 4, viewed 15 December 2021, http://nla.gov.au/nla.news-article100579690

34 'Barossa Election', *Bunyip*, 14 April 1899, p. 1, viewed 1 November 2018, http://nla.gov.au/nla.news-article97579136; 'Barossa Election', *Bunyip*, 14 April 1899, p. 2, viewed 1 November 2018, http://nla.gov.au/nla.news-article97579134

35 'Local Mems', *Bunyip*, 28 April 1899, p. 2, viewed 1 November 2018, http://nla.gov.au/nla.news-article97581101; 'The Barossa Election', *Bunyip*, 12 May 1899, p. 3, viewed 1 November 2018, http://nla.gov.au/nla.news-article97581458

36 Jaensch, D., History Trust of South Australia, & Electoral Commission of South Australia, 2007, *History of South Australian elections 1857–2006, volume 1*, viewed 2 January 2019, https://www.ecsa.sa.gov.au/index.php?option=com_content&view=article&id=205:information-resources&catid=10:about&Itemid=387; *The Gross Defects of Plurality (First-Past-the Post) Electoral Systems*, n.d., Proportional Representation Society of Australia, viewed 1 November 2018, http://www.prsa.org.au/pluralit.htm#plumping; *Cumulative voting* ,n.d., Wikipedia, viewed 1 November 2018, https://en.wikipedia.org/wiki/Cumulative_voting

37 The Elections', *Bunyip*, 5 May 1899, p. 2, viewed 11 January 2022, http://nla.gov.au/nla.news-article97580206

38 'Advertising', *Bunyip*, 7 June 1901, p. 3, viewed 3 January 2021, http://nla.gov.au/nla.news-article100576745

39 'The Barossa Election', *Bunyip*, 24 May 1901, p. 3, viewed 15 May 2020, http://nla.gov.au/nla.news-article100580355

40 'The Barossa Election', *Bunyip*, 14 June 1901, p. 2, viewed 11 January 2022, http://nla.gov.au/nla.news-article100578669

41 'Declaration of the Poll', *Bunyip*, 14 June 1901, p. 2, viewed 3 January 2021, http://nla.gov.au/nla.news-article100578671

42 'Social to Mr. E.H. Coombe', *Bunyip (Gawler, SA: 1863–1954)*, 21 June 1901, p. 2., viewed 3 January 2021, http://nla.gov.au/nla.news-article100580542

43 'The New Member For Barossa', *Register*, 11 June 1901, p. 6, viewed 15 December 2021, http://nla.gov.au/nla.news-article56077448

44 *Hansard*, 23 July 1901, address in reply

45 *Hansard*, September 24 1901, p. 1081, Budget debate

46 *Hansard*, September 26 1901, p. 417, Budget speech

47 *Hansard,* September 26 1901, p. 407, second reading of the Angaston Railway Bill

48 *Hansard,* September 26 1901, p. 417, Budget speech

49 *Hansard,* December 12 1901, p. 1081, delay of reports

50 *Hansard,* Dec 12 1901, p. 1091, supply

51 Burgess, H.T., 1907, *The Cyclopedia of South Australia in two volumes: an historical and commercial review, descriptive and biographical, facts, figures, and illustrations: an epitome of progress*, Cyclopedia Co, Volume 1, p. 169, 192; *Electoral district of Barossa*, n.d., Wikipedia, viewed 30 October 2018, https://en.wikipedia.org/wiki/Electoral_district_of_Barossa; 'Parliamentary Electorates' *Chronicle*, 5 April 1902, p. 33, viewed May 16, 2020, http://nla.gov.au/nla.news-article87816882

52 Jaensch, D., History Trust of South Australia, & Electoral Commission of South Australia, 2007, *History of South Australian elections 1857–2006, volume 1*, viewed 2 January 2019, https://www.ecsa.sa.gov.au/index.php?option=com_content&view=article&id=205:information-resources&catid=10:about&Itemid=387

53 'Parliamentary Electorates', *Chronicle*, 5 April 1902, p. 33, viewed 11 January 2022, http://nla.gov.au/nla.news-article87816882

54 Rollison, K., 'Butler, Sir Richard (1850–1925)', *Australian Dictionary of Biography*, National Centre of Biography, Australian National University, first published 1979, viewed 30 October 2018, http://adb.anu.edu.au/biography/butler-sir-richard-5447/text9247

55 *William Gilbert (politician)*, n.d., Wikipedia, viewed 30 October 2018

56 Jaensch, D., 'Copley, William (1845–1925)', *Australian Dictionary of Biography*, National Centre of Biography, Australian National University, first published 1981, viewed 11 January 2022, https://adb.anu.edu.au/biography/copley-william-5775/text9791

57 'The Elections', *Bunyip*, 9 May 1902, p. 2, viewed 16 May 2020, http://nla.gov.au/nla.news-article97590375

58 'Mr. Coombe's Views', *Bunyip*, 11 April 1902, p. 4, viewed 16 May 2020, http://nla.gov.au/nla.news-article97594247; 'Tanunda Water Supply', *Bunyip*, 28 February 1902, p. 2, viewed 16 May 2020, http://nla.gov.au/nla.news-article97588350; 'Reticulation of Water from Barossa' *Bunyip*, 18 July 1902, p. 3, viewed May 16, 2020, http://nla.gov.au/nla.news-article97592620; 'Tanunda', *Bunyip*, 7 November 1902, p. 4, viewed May 16, 2020, http://nla.gov.au/nla.news-article97590434; 'Gawler Water Supply', *Bunyip*, 17 January 1902, p. 2, viewed 16 May 2020, http://nla.gov.au/nla.news-article97592137

59 'Town Tattle', *Bunyip*, 2 May 1902, p. 2, viewed 16 May 2020, http://nla.gov.au/nla.news-article97593473

60 'The Elections', *Bunyip*, 9 May 1902, p. 2, viewed 19 January 2022, http://nla.gov.au/nla.news-article97590375

61 *Statistical Record of the Legislature 1836–2007*, Parliament of South Australia, 2007, viewed 24 July 2021, https://web.archive.org/web/20190311113513/http://www.parliament.sa.gov.au/AboutParliament/From1836/Documents/StatisticalRecordoftheLegislature1836to20093.pdf

62 'The Elections', *Bunyip*, 9 May 1902, p. 2, viewed 11 January 2022, http://nla.gov.au/nla.news-article97590375

63 'Editor's Notes', *Bunyip*, 3 March, p. 2, viewed 17 May 2020, http://nla.gov.au/nla.news-article97600880 1905

64 Payton, P., 2016, *One and All: Labor and the radical tradition in South Australia,* Wakefield Press, p. 22; Jaensch, D., 1986, *The Flinders History of South Australia: Political history,* Wakefield Press, pp. 351–355

65 Jaensch, D., History Trust of South Australia & Electoral Commission of South Australia, 2007, *History of South Australian elections 1857–2006, volume 1,* p. 166, https://www.ecsa.sa.gov.au/index.php?option=com_content&view=article&id=205:information-resources&catid=10:about&Itemid=387

66 *1905 South Australian state election*, n.d., Wikipedia, viewed 30 October 2018, https://en.wikipedia.org/wiki/South_Australian_state_election,_1905; 'Electoral district of Barossa', n.d., Wikipedia, viewed 30 October 2018, https://en.wikipedia.org/wiki/Electoral_district_of_Barossa

67 'District Clerk's Silver Jubilee', *Bunyip*, 5 January 1906, p. 2, viewed 18 May 2020, http://nla.gov.au/nla.news-article97598712

68 'Gawler Liberal League', *Advertiser,* 11 May 1904, p. 7, viewed 15 December 2021, http://nla.gov.au/nla.news-article4968694

69 Loughlin, G., 'Nesbit, Paris', *Australian Dictionary of Biography,* volume 11, National Centre of Biography, Australian National University, first published 1988, https://adb.anu.edu.au/biography/nesbit-paris-7817

70 'Death of Mr. S.B. Rudall', *Advertiser,* 4 January 1945, p. 4, viewed 11 January 2022, http://nla.gov.au/nla.news-article43235491

71 'Editor's Notes', *Bunyip*, 20 January 1905, p. 2, viewed 11 January 2022, http://nla.gov.au/nla.news-article97600615

72 'Gawler Corporation', *Bunyip*, 12 January 1906, p. 4, viewed 18 May 2020, http://nla.gov.au/nla.news-article97595970; 'Local Mems', *Bunyip*, 24 March 1905, p. 4, viewed 17 May 2020, http://nla.gov.au/nla.news-article97603826

73 No title, *Bunyip*, 17 March 1905, p. 2, viewed 17 May 2020, http://nla.gov.au/nla.news-article97598290

74 'The Election Campaign', *Bunyip*, 28 April 1905, p. 3, viewed 17 May 2020, http://nla.gov.au/nla.news-article97602620

75 'Advertising', *Bunyip*, 19 May 1905, p. 3, viewed 17 May 2020, http://nla.gov.au/nla.news-article97600777

76 'Barossa District', *Bunyip*, 2 June 1905, p. 2, viewed 17 May 2020, http://nla.gov.au/nla.news-article97598761; 'Coming Events', *Bunyip*, 21 April 1905, p. 1, viewed 18 May 2020, http://nla.gov.au/nla.news-article97598668; 'Advertising', *Bunyip,* 28 April 1905, p. 3, viewed 18 May 2020, http://nla.gov.au/nla.news-article97602616

77 *Liberal and Democratic Union*, n.d., Wikipedia, viewed 30 Oct 2018, https://en.wikipedia.org/wiki/Liberal_and_Democratic_Union; Grainger, G., 'Peake, Archibald Henry (1859–1920)', *Australian Dictionary of Biography,* National Centre of Biography, Australian National University, first published 1988, viewed 13 January 2022, https://adb.anu.edu.au/biography/peake-archibald-henry-7995/text13929

78 *1906 South Australian state election*, n.d., Wikipedia, viewed 30 October 2018, https://en.wikipedia.org/wiki/South_Australian_state_election,_1906; 'The Open Column', *Bunyip*, 26 October 1906, p. 3, viewed 18 May 2020, http://nla.gov.au/nla.news-article97602916; 'The Open Column', *Bunyip*, 2 November 1906, p. 2, viewed 18 May 2020, http://nla.gov.au/nla.news-article97601990

79 'House of Assembly Election', *Bunyip*, 26 October 1906, p. 2, viewed 18 May 2020, http://nla.gov.au/nla.news-article97602874

80 'Gawler Institute', *Bunyip*, 2 November 1906, p. 4, viewed 19 May 2020, http://nla.gov.au/nla.news-article97602023

81 'The Barossa Election', *Bunyip*, 9 November 1906, p. 2, viewed 18 May 2020, http://nla.gov.au/nla.news-article97597181

82 'What Elections Cost', *Chronicle*, 12 January 1907, p. 38, viewed 10 December 2021, http://nla.gov.au/nla.news-article88131311

83 'State Politics', *Bunyip*, 11 June 1909, p. 2, viewed 9 January 2022, http://nla.gov.au/nla.news-article97723376

84 'The Wheat Trade', *Observer*, 20 November 1909, p. 13, viewed 10 January 2022, http://nla.gov.au/nla.news-article168282716; Thomas, D., 2006, *A Golden Era: Celebrating 50 years of bulk grain handling in South Australia*, ABB Grain Ltd Adelaide

85 'The Agricultural Conference', *Advertiser*, 25 August 1909, p. 10, viewed 9 January 2022, http://nla.gov.au/nla.news-article5755340

86 'Roseworthy College', *Chronicle*, 25 December 1909, p. 7, viewed 10 January 2022, http://nla.gov.au/nla.news-article88315269; 'Advertising', *Advertiser*, 23 December 1909, p. 2, viewed 10 January 2022, http://nla.gov.au/nla.news-article5211225; 'The Barossa Election', *Advertiser*, 17 March 1910, p. 13, viewed 10 January 2022, http://nla.gov.au/nla.news-article5245501

87 'Editor's Notes', *Bunyip*, 24 September 1909, p. 2, viewed 22 January 2022, http://nla.gov.au/nla.news-article97723615

88 'The Elections', *Bunyip*, 12 March 1915, p. 3, viewed 1 January 2022, http://nla.gov.au/nla.news-article97733616

89 'The Barossa Election', *Bunyip*, 4 March 1910, p. 2, viewed 20 May 2020, http://nla.gov.au/nla.news-article97727133

90 Jaensch, D., History Trust of South Australia & Electoral Commission of South Australia, 2007, *History of South Australian elections 1857–2006, volume 1*, p. 110, https://www.ecsa.sa.gov.au/index.php?option=com_content&view=article&id=205:information-resources&catid=10:about&Itemid=387

91 'The Barossa Election', *Bunyip*, 4 March 1910, p. 2, viewed 19 January 2022, http://nla.gov.au/nla.news-article97727133

92 'The Barossa Election', *Bunyip*, 8 April 1910, p. 2, viewed 19 January 2022, http://nla.gov.au/nla.news-article97728679

93 Jaensch, D., 1986, *The Flinders History of South Australia: Political history*, Wakefield Press, p. 227

94 'Complimentary Social to Mr. E.H. Coombe, M.P.', *Bunyip*, 29 April 1910, p. 2, viewed 10 January 2022, http://nla.gov.au/nla.news-article97728132

95 'Household Suffrage', *The Express and Telegraph*, 2 November 1910, p. 1, viewed 9 January 2022, http://nla.gov.au/nla.news-article209999712

96 Uhr, J., *Why We Chose Proportional Representation*', n.d., Parliament of Australia, viewed 17 September 2016, https://www.aph.gov.au/About_Parliament/Senate/Powers_practice_n_procedures/pops/pop34/c02

97 'Mr. Peake and Mr. Coombe', *Observer*, 18 November 1911, p. 47, viewed 9 January 2022, http://nla.gov.au/nla.news-article164738728

98 'A Democratic Liberal Union', *Register*, 5 November 1910, p. 11, viewed 17 September 2016, http://nla.gov.au/nla.news-article58160036; 'State Politics',

Advertiser, 10 December 1910, p. 10, viewed 9 January 2022, http://nla.gov.au/nla.news-article5220221

99 'BAROSSA' *Chronicle,* 27 January 1912, p. 41, viewed 14 August 2018 http://nla.gov.au/nla.news-article88698442

100 'Mr. Michael Lynch, Gawler', *Southern Cross*, 24 November 1933, p. 15, viewed 14 August 2018, http://nla.gov.au/nla.news-article167699118; 'Messrs. E.H. Coombe and M. Lynch At Gawler', *Bunyip*, 19 January 1912, p. 2, viewed 7 January 2019, http://nla.gov.au/nla.news-article97564829

101 Howell, P.A., 'Hague, William (1864–1924)', *Australian Dictionary of Biography*, National Centre of Biography, Australian National University, first published 1983, viewed 21 May 2020, http://adb.anu.edu.au/biography/hague-william-6518/text11189

102 *1912 South Australian state election*, n.d., Wikipedia, viewed 7 January 2019, https://en.wikipedia.org/wiki/1912_South_Australian_state_election; *Candidates of the 1912 South Australian state election*, n.d., Wikipedia, viewed 7 January 2019, https://en.wikipedia.org/wiki/Candidates_of_the_1912_South_Australian_state_election; *William Hague (Australian politician)*, n.d., Wikipedia, viewed 7 January 2019, https://en.wikipedia.org/wiki/William_Hague_(Australian_politician); *Rudall, Samuel Bruce*, n.d., Gawler Now and Then, viewed 7 January 2019, https://gawler.nowandthen.net.au/w/index.php?title=Rudall,_Samuel_Bruce; *Electoral district of Barossa*, n.d., Wikipedia, viewed 7 January 2019, https://en.wikipedia.org/wiki/Electoral_district_of_Barossa

103 'Messrs. E.H. Coombe AND M. Lynch at Gawler', *Bunyip*, 19 January 1912, p. 2, viewed 7 January 2019, http://nla.gov.au/nla.news-article97566626; 'The Barossa Election', *Bunyip*, 16 February 1912, p. 2, viewed 7 January 2019, http://nla.gov.au/nla.news-article97563660; 'Complimentary Social to Mr. E.H. Coombe', *Bunyip*, 22 March 1912, p. 2, viewed 7 January 2019, http://nla.gov.au/nla.news-article97566626

104 'The Barossa Election', *Bunyip*, 16 February 1912, p. 2, viewed 9 January 2022, http://nla.gov.au/nla.news-article97563660

105 'Labour's New Editor', *Mail*, 25 April 1914, p. 13, viewed 5 February 2017, http://nla.gov.au/nla.news-article59647228

106 'Mr. Coombe Attacks The Liberal Union', *Chronicle*, 17 February 1912, p. 14, viewed 13 January 2022, http://nla.gov.au/nla.news-article88698914

107 'Presentation To Mr. Coombe', *Chronicle*, 2 March 1912, p. 13, viewed 9 January 2022, http://nla.gov.au/nla.news-article88697720; 'Social to Mr. E.H.Coombe at Lyndoch', *Bunyip*, 26 April 1912, p. 4, viewed 22 January 2022, http://nla.gov.au/nla.news-article97568823

108 'The Country', *Advertiser*, 22 March 1912, p. 12, viewed 16 June 2021, http://nla.gov.au/nla.news-article5329328

109 'Social to Mr. E.H. Coombe', *Chronicle*, 30 Marc 1912 h, p. 13, viewed 8 January 2019, http://nla.gov.au/nla.news-article88693659; 'Complimentary Social to Mr. E.H. Coombe', *Bunyip*, 22 March 1912, p. 2, viewed 7 January 2019, http://nla.gov.au/nla.news-article97566626; 'Mr. S.H. James', *Chronicle*, 23 April 1931, p. 23, viewed 17 December 2021, http://nla.gov.au/nla.news-article90624185

110 'Local and General Topics', *Bunyip*, 23 February 1912, p. 2, viewed 16 June 2021, http://nla.gov.au/nla.news-article97560673; 'The Elections', *Daily Herald*, 27 February 1912, p. 7, viewed 16 June 2021, http://nla.gov.au/nla.news-article105218763

Chapter 6 - Move to Adelaide

1 'Gawler institute', *Bunyip*, 4 July 1913, p. 4, viewed 16 June 2021, http://nla.gov.au/nla.news-article97563162

2 'Gawler Union Parliament', *Bunyip*, 26 July 1912, p. 3, viewed 7 January 2019, http://nla.gov.au/nla.news-article97561480; 'Gawler Model Parliament', *Bunyip*, 29 August 1913, p. 2, viewed 7 January 2019, http://nla.gov.au/nla.news-article97561629

3 Linn, R., & Royal District Nursing Society of South Australia, 1993, *Angels of Mercy: District nursing in South Australia 1894–1994*, Royal District Nursing Society of SA (Inc.)

4 'Advertising', *The Mount Barker Courier and Onkaparinga and Gumeracha Advertiser*, 13 October 1911, p. 2, viewed 26 May 2020, http://nla.gov.au/nla.news-article147744932; 'Social Items', *The Mount Barker Courier and Onkaparinga and Gumeracha Advertiser*, 22 August 1913, p. 2, viewed 10 January 2022, http://nla.gov.au/nla.news-article146291237

5 'Electric Lighting', *Bunyip*, 16 August 1912, p. 2, viewed 13 January 2022, http://nla.gov.au/nla.news-article97567566

6 'The Locomotive Crisis', *Bunyip*, 13 September 1912, p. 3, viewed 7 January 2019, http://nla.gov.au/nla.news-article97568087

7 'Lyndoch Institute', *Bunyip*, 27 September 1912, p. 3, viewed 7 January 2019, http://nla.gov.au/nla.news-article97562887

8 'Willaston Going Ahead', *Bunyip*, 12 September 1913, p. 2, viewed 7 January 2019, http://nla.gov.au/nla.news-article97568485; 'A Greater Gawler', *Bunyip*, 31 October 1913, p. 5, viewed 7 January 2019, http://nla.gov.au/nla.news-article97564231; 'Marketing and Handling Wheat', *Bunyip*, 24 October 1913, p. 4, viewed 7 January 2019, http://nla.gov.au/nla.news-article97567130

9 'Meeting Of Board', *Bunyip*, 14 November 1913, p. 2, viewed 7 January 2019, http://nla.gov.au/nla.news-article97568379; 'The Hutchinson Hospital', *Bunyip*, 12 September 1913, p. 4, viewed 7 January 2019, http://nla.gov.au/nla.news-article97568493

10 'Conservatism', *Bunyip*, 4 October 1912, p. 2, viewed 7 January 2019, http://nla.gov.au/nla.news-article97566360; 'A Premising Invention', *Bunyip*, 10 May, p. 4, viewed 7 January 2019, http://nla.gov.au/nla.news-article97567222 1912; 'Railways and Land Settlement', *Bunyip*, 10 May, p. 2, viewed 7 January 2019, http://nla.gov.au/nla.news-article97567198 1912; 'The Coming Poll', *Bunyip*, 22 November 1912, p. 3, viewed 7 January 2019, http://nla.gov.au/nla.news-article97564402; 'To-Morrow's Poll', *Bunyip*, 6 December 1912, p. 4, viewed 7 January 2019, http://nla.gov.au/nla.news-article97566925

11 'Fruit Consumption', *Bunyip*, 11 April 1913, p. 2, viewed 7 January 2019, http://nla.gov.au/nla.news-article97560614

12 'Social and Personal Items', *Bunyip*, 12 December 1913, p. 2, viewed 7 January 2019, http://nla.gov.au/nla.news-article97561122

13 'Quoits', *Daily Herald*, 15 January 1914, p. 7, viewed 8 January 2019, http://nla.gov.au/nla.news-article105614231

14 'The Country', *Advertiser*, 27 February 1914, p. 7, viewed 8 January 2019, http://nla.gov.au/nla.news-article5417537

15 'A Surprise', *Bunyip*, 20 February 1914, p. 5, viewed 4 January 2019, http://nla.gov.au/nla.news-article97734627; 'Resignation of the Town Clerk', *Bunyip*, 6 March 1914,

p. 4, viewed 4 January, 2019, http://nla.gov.au/nla.news-article97741182; 'Town Clerk for 32 Years', *Bunyip*, 15 May 1914, p. 2, viewed 4 January 2019, http://nla.gov.au/nla.news-article97739081

16 'Choosing A Town Clerk', *Advertiser*, 1 April 1914, p. 6, viewed 13 January 2022, http://nla.gov.au/nla.news-article5422410

17 'Across The Bourne', *Bunyip*, 29 September 1922, p. 4, viewed 1 January 2022, http://nla.gov.au/nla.news-article97758627

18 'Resignation of the Town Clerk', *Bunyip*, 6 March 1914, p. 4, viewed 1 January 2022, http://nla.gov.au/nla.news-article97741182

19 'Advertising', *Bunyip*, 6 March 1914, p. 3, viewed 1 January 2022, http://nla.gov.au/nla.news-article97741190

20 'Local and General Topics', *Bunyip*, 20 March 1914, p. 2, viewed 5 January 2019, http://nla.gov.au/nla.news-article97738907

21 'Choosing A Town Clerk', *Advertiser*, 1 Apri 1914 l, p. 6, viewed 5 February 2017, http://nla.gov.au/nla.news-article5422410

22 'Choosing A Town Clerk', *Advertiser*, 1 April 1914, p. 6, viewed 5 February 2017, http://nla.gov.au/nla.news-article5422410

23 'An Open Letter', *Bunyip (Gawler, SA: 1863–1954)*, 10 April 1914, p. 3, viewed 23 September 2022, http://nla.gov.au/nla.news-article97736565

24 'Council Matters', *Bunyip*, 26 March 1915, p. 4, viewed 24 July 2021, http://nla.gov.au/nla.news-article97741075; 'The Open Column', *Bunyip*, 24 April 1914, p. 4, viewed 4 January 2019, http://nla.gov.au/nla.news-article97737957

25 'Mr. George Bright Dead', *Mail*, 31 March 1928, p. 4, viewed 4 January 2019, http://nla.gov.au/nla.news-article58548048

26 'Mr. Michael Lynch, Crawler,', *Southern Cross*, 24 November 1933, p. 15, viewed 4 January 2019, http://nla.gov.au/nla.news-article167699118

27 *Rudall, Joh,*', n.d., Gawler History, viewed 24 July 2021, https://gawlerhistory.com/Rudall_John

28 'The Open Column', *Bunyip*, 17 April 1914, p. 5, viewed 23 July 2021, http://nla.gov.au/nla.news-article97734739; 'The Open Column', *Bunyip*, 24 April 1914, p. 4, viewed 13 January 2022, http://nla.gov.au/nla.news-article97737957

29 'Gawler Corporation', *Advertiser*, 27 May 1914, p. 17, viewed 5 February 2017, http://nla.gov.au/nla.news-article6417877; 'Gawler Corporation', *Bunyip*, 12 June 1914, p. 2, viewed 4 January 2019, http://nla.gov.au/nla.news-article97731746; 'The Town Clerkship', *Bunyip*, 3 April 1914, p. 5, viewed 4 January 2019, http://nla.gov.au/nla.news-article97735098; 'Social and Personal Items', *Bunyip*, 15 May 1914, p. 2, viewed 4 January 2019, http://nla.gov.au/nla.news-article97739079

30 'Gawler Corporation', *Bunyip*, 3 July 1914, p. 2, viewed 5 January 2019, http://nla.gov.au/nla.news-article97733369; 'Gawler Corporation', *Bunyip*, 14 August 1914, p. 5, viewed 5 January 2019, http://nla.gov.au/nla.news-article97735920

31 'Electric Light Scheme', *Bunyip*, 16 October 1914, p. 3, viewed 5 January 2019, http://nla.gov.au/nla.news-article97733802; 'Electric Light Scheme', *Bunyip*, 6 November 1914, p. 2, viewed 5 January 2019, http://nla.gov.au/nla.news-article97737285

32 'The Town Clerk's Work', *Bunyip*, 5 February 1915, p. 3, viewed 5 January 2019, http://nla.gov.au/nla.news-article97737096; 'Gawler Corporation', *Bunyip*, 1 December 1916, p. 4, viewed 5 January 2019, http://nla.gov.au/nla.news-article97734360; 'Gawler Electric Light Undertaking', *Bunyip*, 9 July 1915, p. 3,

viewed 5 January 2019, http://nla.gov.au/nla.news-article97741066; 'Mayor's Annual Report', *Bunyip*, 8 December 1916, p. 3, viewed 5 January 2019, http://nla.gov.au/nla.news-article97736974

33 'Conscription Favored', *Bunyip*, 28 April 1916, p. 2, viewed 5 January 2019, http://nla.gov.au/nla.news-article97739009; 'Local Recruiting Centre', *Bunyip*, 24 March 1916, p. 2, viewed 5 January 2019, http://nla.gov.au/nla.news-article97736279

34 'The Open Column', *Bunyip*, 29 December 1916, p. 3, viewed 5 January 2019, http://nla.gov.au/nla.news-article97732168; 'The Patriotic Fund', *Bunyip*, 5 November 1915, p. 4, viewed 5 January 2019, http://nla.gov.au/nla.news-article97740653; 'Farewell To A Soldier', *Bunyip*, 12 November 1915, p. 2, viewed 5 January 2019, http://nla.gov.au/nla.news-article97732763

35 'Looking Backward', *Bunyip*, 4 January 1924, p. 3, viewed 7 January 2019, http://nla.gov.au/nla.news-article97763483

36 'Advertising', *Daily Herald*, 13 April 1914, p. 2, viewed 8 January 2019, http://nla.gov.au/nla.news-article125052558; 'Advertising', *Daily Herald*, 14 April 1914, p. 2, viewed 8 January 2019, http://nla.gov.au/nla.news-article125052705; 'Looking Backward', *Bunyip*, 1 January 1915, p. 2, viewed 29 July 2021, http://nla.gov.au/nla.news-article97735716

37 *The Herald (Adelaide)*, n.d., Wikipedia, viewed 8 January 2019, https://en.wikipedia.org/wiki/The_Herald_(Adelaide)

38 'The Address-In-Reply', *Herald*, 27 July 1901, p. 4, viewed 15 December 2021, http://nla.gov.au/nla.news-article110197443

39 SA Journalists: B, n.d., SA Memory, State Library of South Australia, viewed 8 January 2019, http://www.samemory.sa.gov.au/site/page.cfm?u=1534

40 Talbot, M.R., 1992, *A Chance to Read: A history of the Institutes movement in South Australia,* Libraries Board of South Australia, p. xiv

41 ibid., pp. 88, 90, 97

42 'Labor News', *Advertiser*, 24 December 1913, p. 18, viewed 1 January 2022, http://nla.gov.au/nla.news-article5398238; 'Enginedrivers and Firemen', *Daily Herald*, 22 May 1914, p. 2, viewed 1 January 2022, http://nla.gov.au/nla.news-article125058714; 'Railways and Tramways Employees', *Daily Herald*, 6 June 1914, p. 7, viewed 1 January 2022, http://nla.gov.au/nla.news-article125061117; 'A Likely Barossa Development', *The Journal*, 12 April 1917, p. 2, viewed 5 January 2022, http://nla.gov.au/nla.news-article204695727

43 'Local and General Topics', *Bunyip*, 24 April 1914, p. 2, viewed 8 October 2019, http://nla.gov.au/nla.news-article97737954; 'Local and General Topics', *Bunyip*, 1 May 1914, p. 2, viewed 24 July 2021, http://nla.gov.au/nla.news-article97732423; 'Mr. E.H. Coombe's Removal', *Observer*, 2 May 1914, p. 17, viewed 8 January 2019, http://nla.gov.au/nla.news-article163127686

44 'Labour's New Editor', *Mail*, 25 April 1914, p. 13, viewed 23 July 2021, http://nla.gov.au/nla.news-article59647228; 'Mr. E.H. Coombe', *Bunyip*, 1 May 1914, p. 2, viewed 23 July 2021, http://nla.gov.au/nla.news-article97732419; 'The Daily Herald', *Daily Herald*, 2 May 1914, p. 4, viewed 25 July 2021, http://nla.gov.au/nla.news-article125055618; 'Our New Editor', *Daily Herald*, 2 May 1914, p. 4, viewed 25 July 2021, http://nla.gov.au/nla.news-article125055671

45 'Town Topics', *Critic*, 6 May 1914, p. 3, viewed 23 July 2021, http://nla.gov.au/nla.news-article211449436; 'Town Tattle', *Bunyip*, 8 May 1914, p. 2, viewed 8 January 2019, http://nla.gov.au/nla.news-article97738388; 'City Scratchings',

Kapunda Herald, 15 May 1914, p. 3, viewed 23 July 2021, http://nla.gov.au/nla.news-article108277406; 'Mr. Peake and Mr. Coombe', *Daily Herald*, 9 June 1914, p. 4, viewed 9 December 2021, http://nla.gov.au/nla.news-article125061535

46 'The Daily Herald', *Daily Herald*, 2 May 1914, p. 4, viewed 29 December 2020, http://nla.gov.au/nla.news-article125055618

47 'The Elections', *Bunyip*, 12 March 1915, p. 3, viewed 1 January 2022, http://nla.gov.au/nla.news-article97733616

48 'Social and Personal Items', *Bunyip*, 8 May 1914, p. 2, viewed 8 January 2019, http://nla.gov.au/nla.news-article97738445; 'Mr. E.H. Coombe', *Bunyip*, 1 May 1914, p. 2, viewed 8 January 2019, http://nla.gov.au/nla.news-article97732419

49 'Back from England', *Bunyip*, 24 April 1914, p. 3, viewed 31 December 2021, http://nla.gov.au/nla.news-article97737985; 'District councils', *Bunyip*, 5 June 1914, p. 1, viewed 16 June 2021, http://nla.gov.au/nla.news-article97731286

50 'Local Mems', *Bunyip*, 10 April 1914, p. 4, viewed 9 January 2022, http://nla.gov.au/nla.news-article97736545

51 'Japanese Fair', *Bunyip*, 22 May 1914, p. 2, viewed 13 January 2022, http://nla.gov.au/nla.news-article97734919

52 'Complimentary social to Mr E.H. Coombe' (*concert program*), 1914 State Library of South Australia; 'Social to Mr. E.H. Coombe', *Bunyip*, 8 May 1914, p. 2, viewed 17 September 2016, http://nla.gov.au/nla.news-article97738391; 'Mr. E.H. Coombe to be Honoured', *Observer*, 9 May 1914, p. 17, viewed 8 January 2019, http://nla.gov.au/nla.news-article163128672; 'Farewell Social to Mr. E.H. Coombe', *Chronicle*, 6 June 1914, p. 47, viewed 8 January 2019, http://nla.gov.au/nla.news-article88844624

53 Clift, J., 2012, 'Edward Potter, J.P.F.G.S. Gawler', viewed 10 January 2022, https://drive.google.com/file/d/1fpdhHkr4uJYtBg_CYG2bbOGlMV8wby5n/view; 'Complimentary Social to Mr. E.H. Coombe, M.P.', *Bunyip*, 29 April 1910, p. 2, viewed 10 January 2022, http://nla.gov.au/nla.news-article97728132

54 'Personal', *The Journal*, 5 May 1914, p. 1, viewed 1 January 2022, http://nla.gov.au/nla.news-article204667261

55 'Bulk Handling of Wheat', *Daily Herald*, 25 March 1915, p. 3, viewed 1 January 2022, http://nla.gov.au/nla.news-article124927131; 'Patriotism and Patriotism', *Daily Herald*, 14 August 1914, p. 3, viewed 24 June 2020, http://nla.gov.au/nla.news-article105635590; 'The Prices Regulation Commission', *Daily Herald*, 20 April 1915, p. 3, viewed 24 June 2020, http://nla.gov.au/nla.news-article134404544

56 'Bulk Handling of Wheat', *Murray Pioneer and Australian River Record*, 4 June 1914, p. 2, viewed 23 July 2021 http://nla.gov.au/nla.news-article109205537

57 'Current Politics', *Register*, 26 May 1914, p. 10, viewed 23 September 2022, http://nla.gov.au/nla.news-article59405484; 'Candid Criticism', *Register*, 6 June 1914, p. 14. , viewed 23 Sep 2022, http://nla.gov.au/nla.news-article59405732

58 'Mr. Peake and Mr. Coombe', *Daily Herald*, 9 June 1914, p. 4, viewed 1 January 2022, http://nla.gov.au/nla.news-article125061535

59 'Effective Voting League', *Daily Herald*, 20 July 1914, p. 4, viewed 1 January 2022, http://nla.gov.au/nla.news-article105630588

60 'The Country', *Register*, 7 August, p. 5, viewed 23 July 1914 2021, http://nla.gov.au/nla.news-article56709417

61 'The Italian Disaster', *The Express and Telegraph*, 12 February 1915, p. 3, viewed 1 January 2022, http://nla.gov.au/nla.news-article210323247; 'Mr. E.H. Coombe's

Candidature', *Daily Herald*, 16 February 1915, p. 3, viewed 1 January 2022, http://nla.gov.au/nla.news-article124921092

62 Toft, M., Six o'clock Swill, History Trust of South Australia, viewed 20 Oct 2020, https://sahistoryhub.history.sa.gov.au/subjects/six-oclock-swill,

63 'Members Returned Unopposed', *Daily Herald*, 13 March 1915, p. 4, viewed 1 January 2022, http://nla.gov.au/nla.news-article124925338; 'Barossa District', *Chronicle*, 27 March 1915, p. 17, viewed 1 January 2022, http://nla.gov.au/nla.news-article95768821

64 'Campaign Aftermath', *Register*, 25 December 1919, p. 5, viewed 1 January 2022, http://nla.gov.au/nla.news-article63119698

65 'The Elections', *Bunyip*, 12 March 1915, p. 3, viewed 1 January 2022, http://nla.gov.au/nla.news-article97733616

66 'Labor's Triumph Complete', *Daily Herald*, 31 March 1915, p. 5, viewed 1 January 2022, http://nla.gov.au/nla.news-article124928059; 'THE STATE ELECTIONS', *Daily Herald*, 30 March 1915, p. 5, viewed 1 January 2022, http://nla.gov.au/nla.news-article124927976

67 Monteath, P., Paul, M., & Martin, R., 2014, *Interned: Torrens Island 1914–1915*, Wakefield Press, p. 94; Grainger, G., 'Vaughan, Crawford (1874–1947)', *Australian Dictionary of Biography*, National Centre of Biography, Australian National University, first published 1990, viewed 20 October 2020. http://adb.anu.edu.au/biography/vaughan-crawford-8909/text15651

68 'Victorian Allotments', *Pinnaroo and Border Times*, 10 November 1916, p. 3, viewed 27 July 2021, http://nla.gov.au/nla.news-article189163116

69 *Hansard*, 2 August 1916, p. 532

Chapter 7 - His final chapter

1 'South Australia', *Australian Worker*, 6 July 1916, p. 17, viewed 9 January 2022, http://nla.gov.au/nla.news-article145765817; , 'The Coombe Bomb', *Border Chronicle*, 11 August 1916, p. 6., viewed 9 January 2022, http://nla.gov.au/nla.news-article212861502

2 'Labour Plebicites', *Observer*, 23 December 1916, p. 23, viewed 22 November 2018, http://nla.gov.au/nla.news-article164178698

3 'Mr. E.H. Coombe, M.P.', *Daily Herald*, 11 January 1917, p. 6, viewed 28 July 2021, http://nla.gov.au/nla.news-article105385755; 'The Labor Split', *Advertiser*, 4 January 1917, p. 7, viewed 28 July 2021, http://nla.gov.au/nla.news-article5550036; 'Senate Plebiscite', *Daily Herald*, 9 February 1917, p. 4, viewed 28 July 2021, http://nla.gov.au/nla.news-article105390793; 'Senate Plebiscite', *Daily Herald*, 12 February 1917, p. 6, viewed 28 July 2021, http://nla.gov.au/nla.news-article105391252

4 'At Port Adelaide First Labor Meeting', *Daily Herald*, 31 March 1917, p. 5, viewed 4 January 2022, http://nla.gov.au/nla.news-article105399037

5 'Meeting At Port Adelaide', *Daily Herald*, 30 March 1917, p. 4, viewed 4 January 2022, http://nla.gov.au/nla.news-article105398804; 'Advertising', *Advertiser*, 29 March 1917, p. 2, viewed 4 January 2022, http://nla.gov.au/nla.news-article5573901; 'Advertising', *Daily Herald*, 30 March 1917, p. 2, viewed 4 January 2022, http://nla.gov.au/nla.news-article105398794

6 'Sad Sensation', *Daily Herald*, 31 March 1917, p. 5, viewed 4 January 2022, http://nla.gov.au/nla.news-article105399022

7 ibid.

8 'Mr. E.H. Coombe, M.P.', *Advertiser*, 31 March 1917, p. 15, viewed 4 January 2022, http://nla.gov.au/nla.news-article5574803

9 'Death of Dr. H.S. Covernton', *Advertiser*, 16 April 1940, p. 6, viewed 4 January 2022, http://nla.gov.au/nla.news-article48856060; *The South Australian Branch of the Australian Medical Association: A centenary history, 1979,* 1979, Australian Medical Association, privately published, p. 61, https://ama.com.au/sites/default/files/documents/AMA_SA_Centenary_History.pdf, viewed 15 Dec 2021; 'Social to Dr. and Mrs. Covernton', *Bunyip*, 15 August 1913, p. 3, viewed 7 June 2020, http://nla.gov.au/nla.news-article97560927; 'Hutchinson Hospital', *Observer*, 7 December 1912, p. 47, viewed 7 June 2020, http://nla.gov.au/nla.news-article163088340

10 Couper-Smartt, J., 'The Port Adelaide Casualty Hospital 1862–1980', South Australian Medical Heritage Society Inc, https://www.samhs.org.au/Virtual%20Museum/hospital-andother-orgs/PortAdelCasHosp/pachsp.html

11 'Mr. E.H. Coombe, M.P.', *Border Watch*, 4 April 1917, p. 3, viewed 4 January 2022, http://nla.gov.au/nla.news-article77663975; 'Mr. Coombe's Illness', *Daily Herald*, 2 April 1917, p. 4, viewed 4 January 2022, http://nla.gov.au/nla.news-article105399218; 'Personal', *Advertiser*, 2 April 1917, p. 6, viewed 4 January 2022, http://nla.gov.au/nla.news-article5574967; 'Mr. Coombe's Condition Critical', *Port Pirie Recorder and North Western Mail*, 2 April 1917, p. 2, viewed 4 January 2022, http://nla.gov.au/nla.news-article95452899

12 'Mr. E.H. Coombe, M.P.', *Daily Herald*, 3 April 1917, p. 4, viewed 5 January 2022, http://nla.gov.au/nla.news-article105399372; 'Death Of Mr. Coombe, M.P.', *Advertiser*, 6 April 1917, p. 6, viewed 4 January 2022, http://nla.gov.au/nla.news-article5576166

13 'Social And Personal', *Bunyip*, 6 September 1918, p. 2, viewed 5 January 2022, http://nla.gov.au/nla.news-article100415998

14 'Late Mr. E.H. Coombe', *Daily Herald*, 7 April 1917, p. 4, viewed 4 January 2022, http://nla.gov.au/nla.news-article105400017

15 'Laid To Rest', *Daily Herald*, 9 April 1917, p. 4, viewed 5 January 2022, http://nla.gov.au/nla.news-article105400235; ' Late Mr. Coombe, M.P.', *Mail*, 7 April 1917, p. 9, viewed 5 January 2022, http://nla.gov.au/nla.news-article59426186

16 'Mr. E.H. Coombe, M.P.', *Daily Herald*, 6 April 1917, p. 4, viewed 4 January 2022, http://nla.gov.au/nla.news-article105399920

17 'Mr. E.H. Coombe Suddenly Stricken with Illness', *Bunyip*, 6 April 1917, p. 2, viewed 4 January 2022, http://nla.gov.au/nla.news-article100415172; 'The Late Mr. E.H. Coombe, M.P.', *Bunyip*, 13 April 1917, p. 1, viewed 15 December 2021, http://nla.gov.au/nla.news-article100412485; 'Death Of Mr. E.H. Coombe', *Bunyip*, 13 April 1917, p. 2, viewed 15 December 2021, http://nla.gov.au/nla.news-article100412474; 'Death of Mr. E.H. Coombe', *Bunyip*, 13 April 1917, p. 2, viewed 15 December 2021, http://nla.gov.au/nla.news-article100412458; 'Late Mr. E.H. Coombe', *Daily Herald*, 11 April 1917, p. 4, viewed 4 January 2022, http://nla.gov.au/nla.news-article105400630; 'Death Of Mr. Coombe, M.P.', *Advertiser*, 6 April 1917, p. 6, viewed 4 January 2022, http://nla.gov.au/nla.news-article5576166

18 'Angaston's Regrets', *Daily Herald*, 7 April 1917, p. 4, viewed 5 January 2022, http://nla.gov.au/nla.news-article105400086; 'Advisory Council Of Education', *Daily Herald*, 3 May 1917, p. 4, viewed 5 January 2022, http://nla.gov.au/nla.news-article105404186; 'Death Of Mr. E.H. Coombe', *Register*, 6 Apri 1917 l, p. 7., viewed 5 January 2022, http://nla.gov.au/nla.news-article59970289; 'Family Notices',

Daily Herald, 9 April 1917 , p. 4, viewed 5 January 2022, http://nla.gov.au/nla.news-article105400190; 'Death Of Mr. E.H. Coombe', *Barrier Miner*, 8 April 1917, p. 1, viewed 9 January 2022, http://nla.gov.au/nla.news-article45390648; 'The Late Mr. Coombe', *Daily Herald*, 6 April 1917, p. 4, viewed 9 January 2022, http://nla.gov.au/nla.news-article105399858

19 'Family Notices', *Bunyip*, 5 Apri 1918 l, p. 2, viewed 26 July 2021, http://nla.gov.au/nla.news-article100414974

20 'The Price of Grapes in 1907', *Quiz*, 1 February 1907, p. 6, viewed 15 June 2020, http://nla.gov.au/nla.news-article166337237; 'Bits for Boniface', *Quiz*, 9 April 1909, p. 6, viewed 5 November 2019, http://nla.gov.au/nla.news-article168232970; Hoad, J.L., & Australian Hotels Association, South Australian Branch, 1986, *Hotels and Publicans in South Australia 1836–1984*, Gould Books, p. 48; 'Adelaide Wool Sales', *Kapunda Herald*, 29 November 1907, p. 2, viewed 5 November 2019, http://nla.gov.au/nla.news-article108443347; 'The Country', *Advertiser*, 24 February 1908, p. 8, viewed 5 November 2019, http://nla.gov.au/nla.news-article5126475; 'The Country', *Advertiser*, 29 April 1910, p. 9, viewed 5 November 2019, http://nla.gov.au/nla.news-article5262883; 'Rifle Shooting', *Observer*, 28 September 1907, p. 23, viewed 5 November 2019, http://nla.gov.au/nla.news-article163169895

21 'Social and Personal Items', *Bunyip*, 7 January 1916, p. 4, viewed 15 December 2021, http://nla.gov.au/nla.news-article97736500; 'A Likely Barossa Development', *The Journal*, 12 April 1917, p. 2, viewed 5 January 2022, http://nla.gov.au/nla.news-article204695727

22 'Labor Candidate For Barossa', *The Express and Telegraph*, 16 April 1917, p. 4, viewed 5 January 2022, http://nla.gov.au/nla.news-article209756281

23 'Social And Personal', *Bunyip*, 6 September 1918, p. 2, viewed 24 July 2021, http://nla.gov.au/nla.news-article100415998

24 'Local and General Topics', *Bunyip*, 18 May 1917, p. 2, viewed 5 January 2022, http://nla.gov.au/nla.news-article100412187

25 'Local And General', *Bunyip*, 15 June 1917, p. 2, viewed 5 January 2022, http://nla.gov.au/nla.news-article100418260

26 'Gawler Corporation', *Bunyip*, 13 April 1917, p. 4, viewed 5 January 2022, http://nla.gov.au/nla.news-article100412486; 'Gawler Corporation', *Bunyip*, 4 May 1917, p. 4, viewed 5 January 2022, http://nla.gov.au/nla.news-article100420406; 'Gawler Corporation', *Bunyip*, 18 May 1917, p. 4, viewed 5 January 2022, http://nla.gov.au/nla.news-article100412186

27 'Mudla Wirra South', *Bunyip*, 15 June 1917, p. 4, viewed 5 January 2022, http://nla.gov.au/nla.news-article100418275

28 'The E.H. Coombe Memorial', *Bunyip*, 22 June 1917, p. 3, viewed 26 July 2021, http://nla.gov.au/nla.news-article100412802

29 'The E.H. Coombe Memorial', *Bunyip*, 22 June 1917, p. 3, viewed 26 July 2021, http://nla.gov.au/nla.news-article100412802

30 'The E.H. Coombe Memorial', *Bunyip*, 20 July 1917, p. 2, viewed 5 January 2022, http://nla.gov.au/nla.news-article100416262; 'The E.H. Coombe Memorial', *Bunyip*, 17 August 1917, p. 2, viewed 5 January 2022, http://nla.gov.au/nla.news-article100419220

31 'The Coombe Memorial', *Bunyip*, 31 August 1917, p. 3, viewed 5 January 2022, http://nla.gov.au/nla.news-article100417313

32 'The Coombe Memorial', *Daily Herald*, 10 November 1917, p. 3, viewed 3 August 2021, http://nla.gov.au/nla.news-article105440075; 'The Coombe Memorial', *Bunyip*, 16 November 1917, p. 3, viewed 5 January 2022, http://nla.gov.au/nla.news-article100414562

33 'The Coombe Memorial', *Bunyip*, 4 January 1918, p. 2, viewed 5 January 2022, http://nla.gov.au/nla.news-article100418863

34 'E.H. Coombe Memorial', *Bunyip*, 1 March 1918, p. 2, viewed 5 January 2022, http://nla.gov.au/nla.news-article100411703

35 'Family Notices', *Express and Telegraph*, 2 September, p. 2, viewed 22 November 2018, http://nla.gov.au/nla.news-article209723176 1918; 'Social And Personal', *Bunyip*, 6 September 1918, p. 2, viewed 5 January 2022, http://nla.gov.au/nla.news-article100415998

36 'Local and General', *Bunyip*, 10 May 1918, p. 2, viewed 5 January 2022, http://nla.gov.au/nla.news-article100411643

37 'Coombe Memorial', *Bunyip*, 20 December 1918, p. 2, viewed 5 January 2022, http://nla.gov.au/nla.news-article100419667

38 'Tanunda Memorial', *Mail*, 27 December 1919, p. 2, viewed 3 August 2021, http://nla.gov.au/nla.news-article63768412

39 *Gawler South War Memorial*, n.d., Monument Australia, viewed 26 July 2021, https://monumentaustralia.org.au/themes/conflict/ww1/display/50739-gawler-south-war-memorial

40 *Gawler Institute Memorial Balcony*, n.d., Monument Australia, viewed 6 January 2022 https://monumentaustralia.org.au/themes/conflict/ww1/display/50736-gawler-institute-memorial-balcony

41 'Advertising', *Bunyip*, 23 May 1919, p. 3, viewed 26 July 2021, http://nla.gov.au/nla.news-article100417193; 1919, 'The E.H. Coombe Memorial', *Bunyip*, 6 June, p. 2, viewed 26 July 2021, http://nla.gov.au/nla.news-article100412578

42 'Coombe Memorial', *Bunyip*, 4 July 1919, p. 2, viewed 30 July 2021, http://nla.gov.au/nla.news-article100420289; 'Coombe Memorial', *Bunyip*, 19 September 1919, p. 2, viewed 26 July 2021, http://nla.gov.au/nla.news-article100412959; 'E.H. Coombe Memorial', *Bunyip*, 26 September 1919, p. 3, viewed 26 July 2021, http://nla.gov.au/nla.news-article100413325

43 'E.H. Coombe Memorial', *Murray Pioneer and Australian River Record*, 16 March 1928, p. 6, viewed 9 January 2022, http://nla.gov.au/nla.news-article109369094; 'Divorce Court', *Advertiser*, 11 December 1929, p. 28, viewed 31 December 2021, http://nla.gov.au/nla.news-article73788479

44 'Unveiling of Coombe Memorial at Tanunda' *Bunyip*, 7 March 1930, p. 10, viewed 17 September 2016 http://nla.gov.au/nla.news-article96666149

45 ibid.

46 Wohltmann, M., 2016, *A future Unlived: A forgotten chapter in South Australia's history*, Michael Wohltmann, p. 384

47 Hausler, A., Heuzenroeder, A., Ross, D., Leske, E., Saegenschnitter, G., Andretzke, C., et al, 2017, *The Barossa: Federation to the fifties: the twentieth century 1901–1950s*, Barossa Valley Archives and Historical Trust Inc Tanunda, p. 461

48 *Ephraim Coombe*, n.d., Monument Australia, viewed 22 November 2018, http://monumentaustralia.org.au/themes/people/government–state/display/51767-ephraim-coombe

49 Richardson, D., 'Henschke, Albert Julius (1888–1955)' *Australian Dictionary of Biography, Supplementary Volume,* 2005, Melbourne University Press, viewed 17 July 2015, http://adb.anu.edu.au/biography/henschke-albert-julius-12978

50 'Campaign Aftermath', *The Journal*, 24 December 1919, p. 1, viewed 6 January 2022, http://nla.gov.au/nla.news-article213272056

51 'Tanunda Memorial', *Mail*, 27 December 1919, p. 2, viewed 3 August 2021, http://nla.gov.au/nla.news-article63768412; 'Mr. Riedel's Version', *Mail*, 27 December 1919, p. 2, viewed 6 January 2022, http://nla.gov.au/nla.news-article63768408; 'Riedel's Circular', *Mail*, 27 December 1919, p. 2, viewed 6 January 2022, http://nla.gov.au/nla.news-article63768403

52 'Personal', *Critic*, 10 June 1914, p. 7, viewed 23 July 2021, http://nla.gov.au/nla.news-article211449855

53 *Coombe, South Australia*, n.d., Wikipedia, viewed 14 June 2021, https://en.wikipedia.org/wiki/Coombe,_South_Australia; 'Adelaide – Wolseley railway line', n.d., Wikipedia, viewed 14 June 2021, https://en.wikipedia.org/wiki/Adelaide%E2%80%93Wolseley_railway_line; 'Names Of Railway Stations', *Register*, 24 March 1915, p. 4, viewed 14 June 2021, http://nla.gov.au/nla.news-article60740013

54 'The Government Gazette', *Advertiser*, 23 March 1906, p. 6, viewed 14 June 2021, http://nla.gov.au/nla.news-article5017243; 'Lands For Closer Settlement', *Register*, 13 July 1906, p. 4, viewed 14 June 2021, http://nla.gov.au/nla.news-article57015761

55 *Bonython, Australian Capital Territory*, n.d., Wikipedia, viewed 14 June 2021, https://en.wikipedia.org/wiki/Bonython,_Australian_Capital_Territory

56 'Biographies of Our Chairmen (Cont.)', 1967, The Hutchinson Hospital (brochure), Max Wurcker Diazo Pty. Ltd. pp. 7, 30; 'Gawler Maternity Block', *Register*, 7 December 1926, p. 10, viewed 17 May 2021, http://nla.gov.au/nla.news-article54828661; 'Gawler the Colonial Athens', *Register*, 4 January 1927, p. 12, viewed 20 July, 2015, http://nla.gov.au/nla.news-article54886267

57 *Gawler's Changing Street Names*, Dr Wilmore, H., n.d., viewed 14 June 2021, https://gawlerhistory.com/Gawler%27s_Changing_Street_Names

58 Noye, R.J., *Dictionary of South Australian Photography 1845–1915*, 2007, Art Gallery of South Australia, Adelaide, pp. 195–196, viewed 6 Jan 2022, https://daao.library.unsw.edu.au/bio/version_history/edwin-marchant/biography/

59 'Farewell Social', *Bunyip*, 5 June 1914, p. 6, viewed 29 July 2021, http://nla.gov.au/nla.news-article97731317; 'Friendly Societies' Gratitude', *Bunyip*, 11 September 1914, p. 2, viewed July 29 2021, http://nla.gov.au/nla.news-article97731763

Chapter 8 - Conclusion

1 *South Australian Institutes' Journal*, 24 November 1915, p. 73

2 Ewart, H.P., 2016, *Gentlemen squatters, 'self-made' men and soldiers: masculinities in nineteenth century Australia*, thesis, University of Adelaide, p. 123, viewed 11 April 2019, https://www.semanticscholar.org/paper/Gentleman-squatters%2C-%E2%80%98self-made%E2%80%99-men-and-soldiers%3A-Ewart/95eb9b58aeb94bf772f7ca37693215d2b5813169?utm_source=email

3 'Mr. E H. Coombe at Gawler', *Bunyip*, 10 April 1896, p. 3, viewed 18 December 2018, http://nla.gov.au/nla.news-article97575876

4 Ewart, H.P., 2016, *Gentlemen squatters, 'self-made' men and soldiers: masculinities in nineteenth century Australia*, thesis, University of Adelaide, p. 123, viewed 11 April 2019 https://www.semanticscholar.org/paper/

Gentleman-squatters%2C-%E2%80%98self-made%E2%80%99-men-and-soldiers%3A-Ewart/95eb9b58aeb94bf772f7ca37693215d2b5813169?utm_source=email

5 'The Late Mr. E.H. Coombe, M.P.', *Bunyip*, 13 April 1917, p. 1, viewed 1 August 2021, http://nla.gov.au/nla.news-article100412485

6 'Death of Mr. Coombe, M.P.', *Advertiser*, 6 April 1917, p. 6, viewed 1 August 2021, http://nla.gov.au/nla.news-article5576166

7 'Henry George in Gawler', *Bunyip*, 2 May 1890, p. 3, viewed 1 August 2021, http://nla.gov.au/nla.news-article97233983, 'The Single Electoral Districts', *Bunyip*, 2 May 1890, p. 2, viewed 1 August 2021, http://nla.gov.au/nla.news-article97233966

8 'The Liberal and Democratic Union of South Australia', *Renmark Pioneer*, 9 October 1908, p. 4, viewed 1 August 2021, http://nla.gov.au/nla.news-article109522355

9 'Mr. Coombe, M.P.', *Register*, 5 April 1910, p. 11, viewed 9 January 2022, http://nla.gov.au/nla.news-article57376984

Appendix A

1 Molyneux, D., 2015, *Time for Play: Recreation and moral issues in colonial South Australia*, Wakefield Press, p. 9

2 Hignett & Company, South Australia Heritage Unit, & Gawler Corporation, 1981, Gawler heritage study: stage 1, Hignett & Company, pp. 4, 6, viewed 4 December 2018 https://data.environment.sa.gov.au/Content/heritage-surveys/2-Gawler-Heritage-Study-Stage-One-1981.pdf

3 'Cricket', *Bunyip*, 1 January 1875, p. 2, viewed 1 August 2021, http://nla.gov.au/nla.news-article97218186

4 'The Paris Exhibition And South Australian Exhibits', *Bunyip*, 19 October 1877, p. 2, viewed 1 August 2021, http://nla.gov.au/nla.news-article97219142

5 Coombe, E.H., 1908, *History of Gawler*, Gawler Institute, pp. 202, 267

6 'Editor's Notes', *Bunyip*, 11 September 1908, p. 2, viewed 18 January 2022, http://nla.gov.au/nla.news-article97724643

7 'CRICKET', *Gawler Standard*, 8 March 1878, p. 3, viewed 18 January 2022, http://nla.gov.au/nla.news-article245310472

8 'Fraternity', n.d., Wikipedia, viewed 4 December 2018, https://en.wikipedia.org/wiki/Fraternity; Independent Order of Rechabites', n.d., Wikipedia, viewed 4 December 2018 https://en.wikipedia.org/wiki/Independent_Order_of_Rechabites
Coombe, E.H., 1908, *History of Gawler*, Gawler Institute, pp. 202, 267

9 'Temperance Meeting At Gawler', *South Australian Register*, 3 June 1880, p. 2, viewed 2 December 2018, http://nla.gov.au/nla.news-article43110665

10 Coombe, E.H., 1908, *History of Gawler*, Gawler Institute, p. 244

11 Pers. comm. Geoff Sando

12 'Jubilee Demonstration', *Bunyip*, 12 August 1887, p. 2, viewed 18 December 2018, http://nla.gov.au/nla.news-article97229873; 'Country Intelligence', *Kapunda Herald*, 31 August 1888, p. 4, viewed 1 January 2021, http://nla.gov.au/nla.news-article108345628; 'Lost in London', *Bunyip*, 29 November 1889, p. 2, viewed 18 December 2018, http://nla.gov.au/nla.news-article97225174

13 Coombe, E.H., 1908, *History of Gawler*, Gawler Institute, p. 242

14 'Liquor Traffic Legislation', *Bunyip*, 10 October 1890, p. 2, viewed 17 September 2016, http://nla.gov.au/nla.news-article97231154

15 'Local Mems', *Bunyip*, 10 April 1914, p. 4, viewed 9 January 2022, http://nla.gov.au/nla.news-article97736545

16 'Breaking-Up for the Holidays', *Bunyip*, 23 December 1898, p. 2, viewed 31 October 2018, http://nla.gov.au/nla.news-article97579911; 'Country Schools of Mines', *Advertiser*, 15 December 1913, p. 7, viewed 7 December 2018, http://nla.gov.au/nla.news-article5394184; 'Advertising', *Bunyip*, 7 June 1895, p. 3, viewed 17 December 2018, http://nla.gov.au/nla.news-article97571493; 'GAWLER', *Daily Herald*, 10 January 1914, p. 8, viewed 8 January 2019, http://nla.gov.au/nla.news-article10561328

17 'Technical School Progress Throughout The Years', *Bunyip*, 29 April 1949, p. 10, viewed 18 December 2018, http://nla.gov.au/nla.news-article96856977

18 'The Choicest Gift', *Bunyip*, 21 August 1885, p. 2, viewed 28 December 2021, http://nla.gov.au/nla.news-article97212753

19 'INQUESTS', *Bunyip*, 21 February 1890, p. 2, viewed 17 September 2016, http://nla.gov.au/nla.news-article97231548; 'Sudden Death of Mrs. R.J. Fotheringham', *Bunyip*, 21 February, p. 2, viewed 17 September 2016, http://nla.gov.au/nla.news-article97231553; 'Coroner's Inquest', *Bunyip*, 14 March 1890, p. 2, viewed 10 August 2016, http://nla.gov.au/nla.news-article97234675; 'Gawler Agricultural Society', *Bunyip*, 31 January 1890, p. 2, viewed 17 September 2016, http://nla.gov.au/nla.news-article97231379; 'The Gawler Show', *Bunyip*, 26 September 1890, p. 2, viewed 19 September 2016, http://nla.gov.au/nla.news-article97233335

20 'Social at Gawler', *South Australian Chronicle*, 10 March 1894, p. 6, viewed 7 December 2018, http://nla.gov.au/nla.news-article92856421

21 No title, *Bunyip*, 3 March 1899, p. 2, viewed 9 January 2022, http://nla.gov.au/nla.news-article97579674

22 'Mr. E.H. Coombe, M.P.', *Daily Herald*, 6 April 1917, p. 4, viewed 23 August 2016, http://nla.gov.au/nla.news-article105399920; Burgess, H.T. , 1907, *The Cyclopedia of South Australia in two volumes: An historical and commercial review, descriptive and biographical, facts, figures, and illustrations: an epitome of progress,* Vol.1, Cyclopedia Co, pp. 165–166

23 Talbot, M.R., 1992, *A Chance to Read: A history of the Institutes movement in South Australia,* Libraries Board of South Australia, p. 90; 'Lyndoch Institute', *Bunyip*, 27 September 1912, p. 3, viewed 7 January 2019, http://nla.gov.au/nla.news-article97562887

24 'Adelaide Children's Hospital', *Bunyip*, 16 June 1899, p. 2, viewed 2 January 2019, http://nla.gov.au/nla.news-article97580077; 'Local and General Topics', *Bunyip*, 15 September 1911, p. 2, viewed 2 January 2019, http://nla.gov.au/nla.news-article97566946

25 Linn, R., 1993, *Angels of Mercy: District nursing in South Australia 1894–1994,* Royal District Nursing Society of SA (Inc.) Norwood, pp. 12, 19–20, 34

26 'Editor's Notes', *Bunyip*, 26 January 1900, p. 2, viewed 15 December 2021, http://nla.gov.au/nla.news-article100579459; 'Advertising', *Bunyip*, 19 January 1900, p. 3, viewed 15 December 2021, http://nla.gov.au/nla.news-article100578552; 'Editor's Notes', *Bunyip*, 27 April 1900, p. 2, viewed 15 December 2021, http://nla.gov.au/nla.news-article100576922; 'Advertising', *Kapunda Herald*, 25 May 1900, p. 2, viewed 15 December 2021, http://nla.gov.au/nla.news-article108318169; no title, *Bunyip*, 6 July 1900, p. 2, viewed 15 December 2021, http://nla.gov.au/nla.news-article100576528

27 *History of the State Library of South Australia: Board members & legislation*, n.d., State Library of South Australia, viewed 10 December 2018, http://guides.slsa.sa.gov.au/c.php?g=410288&p=2794469

28 Burgess, H.T. , 1907, *The Cyclopedia of South Australia in two volumes: An historical and commercial review, descriptive and biographical, facts, figures, and illustrations: an epitome of progress,* Vol.1, Cyclopedia Co, p. 409

29 'The Cottage Homes Fund', *Bunyip,* 2 March 1906, p. 2, viewed 11 January 2022, http://nla.gov.au/nla.news-article97596042

30 'Cricket', *Bunyip,* 26 May, p. 1, viewed 15 December 2021, http://nla.gov.au/nla.news-article97595727 1905; 'Presentation to Mr. E.H. Coombe, M.P.', *Bunyip,* 30 June 1905, p. 4, viewed 15 December 2021, http://nla.gov.au/nla.news-article97599468; 'The Late Mr. E.H. Coombe, M.P.', *Bunyip,* 13 April 1917, p. 1, viewed 15 December 2021, http://nla.gov.au/nla.news-article100412485

31 Coombe, E.H., 1908, *History of Gawler,* Gawler Institute, pp. 256–257; 'Mr. E H. Coombe at Gawler', *Bunyip,* 10 April 1896, p. 3, viewed 18 January 2022, http://nla.gov.au/nla.news-article97575876

32 'British and Foreign Bible Society', *Bunyip,* 2 October 1908, p. 2, viewed 7 December 2018, http://nla.gov.au/nla.news-article97729447; 'Gawler Town', *South Australian Weekly Chronicle,* 8 September 1860, p. 1, viewed 7 December 2018, http://nla.gov.au/nla.news-article90248684

33 'A history of agriculture in South Australia', n.d., Primary Industries and Recourses SA, viewed 18 Dec 2018, http://pandora.nla.gov.au/pan/131256/20111230-1019/www.pir.sa.gov.au/aghistory/left_nav/eras/1905-1925/key_people.html

34 'Ladies fish in "Boat Hole" on Outing', *Bunyip,* 13 May 1949, p. 1, viewed 18 December 2018, http://nla.gov.au/nla.news-article96855017

35 'Biographies of Our Chairmen (Cont.)', 1967, The Hutchinson Hospital (brochure), Max Wurcker Diazo Pty. Ltd. pp. 7, 30

36 'Bowls', *Bunyip,* 13 February 1914, p. 1, viewed 8 January 2019, http://nla.gov.au/nla.news-article97737308; , 'Bowls', *Bunyip,* 30 January 1914, p. 1, viewed 8 January 2019, http://nla.gov.au/nla.news-article97735572

37 'Personal', *Critic,* 5 April 1916, p. 6, viewed 27 July 2021, http://nla.gov.au/nla.news-article212164864; 'Davis, Browne, & Co.'s Great Sales-Promoting Contest', *Daily Herald,* 3 June 1916, p. 6, viewed 27 July 2021, http://nla.gov.au/nla.news-article124881183; 'Mr. Coombe's Trip', *Daily Herald,* 3 October 1916, p. 5, viewed 27 July 2021, http://nla.gov.au/nla.news-article124838086; 'Anti-Conscription', *Daily Herald,* 4 October 1916, p. 5, viewed 27 July 2021, http://nla.gov.au/nla.news-article124838426; 'Mr. Coombe's Tour', *Daily Herald,* 6 October 1916, p. 5, viewed 27 July 2021, http://nla.gov.au/nla.news-article124838756; 'Success For Antis', *Daily Herald,* 14 October 1916, p. 5, viewed 27 July 2021, http://nla.gov.au/nla.news-article124840060

38 'Education', *Daily Herald,* 10 March 1917, p. 6, viewed 9 January 2022, http://nla.gov.au/nla.news-article105395568

39 'A Storm in Parliament', *The South Eastern Times,* 14 November 1916, p. 3, viewed 27 July 2021, http://nla.gov.au/nla.news-article200030750; 'Mr. Coombe and National Service', *Register,* 10 November 1916, p. 6, viewed 9 January 2022, http://nla.gov.au/nla.news-article59913742; 'Mr. Coombe's Statement', *Daily Herald,* 10 November 1916, p. 6, viewed 27 July 2021, http://nla.gov.au/nla.news-article124844765; 'Suppressing the German Language', *Daily Herald,* 14 November 1916, p. 2, viewed

27 July 2021, http://nla.gov.au/nla.news-article124845267; 'The Referendum', *Register*, 21 November 1916, p. 7, viewed 27 July 2021, http://nla.gov.au/nla.news-article59904464; 'The Referendum', *Register*, 25 November 1916, p. 5, viewed 27 July 2021, http://nla.gov.au/nla.news-article59908684; 'Two Gawler Meetings Against Conscription', *Advertiser*, 11 October 1916, p. 9, viewed 9 January 2022, http://nla.gov.au/nla.news-article6458451

40 'Labour Plebicites [*sic*]', *Observer*, 23 December 1916, p. 23, viewed 22 November 2018, http://nla.gov.au/nla.news-article164178698

41 'Mr. E.H. Coombe, M.P.', *Daily Herald*, 11 January 1917, p. 6, viewed 28 July 2021, http://nla.gov.au/nla.news-article105385755; 'The Labor Split', *Advertiser*, 4 January 1917, p. 7, viewed 28 July 2021, http://nla.gov.au/nla.news-article5550036; 'Senate Plebiscite', *Daily Herald*, 9 February 1917, p. 4, viewed 28 July 2021, http://nla.gov.au/nla.news-article105390793; 'Senate Plebiscite', *Daily Herald*, 12 February 1917, p. 6, viewed 28 July 2021, http://nla.gov.au/nla.news-article105391252

Appendix B

1 Coombe, E.H., 1908, *History of Gawler*, Gawler Institute, p. 211; *Starr-Bowkett Society*, n.d., Wikipedia, viewed 15 July 2021, https://en.wikipedia.org/wiki/Starr-Bowkett_Society

2 Corporation of the Town of Gawler & Danver Architects, 1998, *Gawler Heritage Survey*, Danver Architects, pp. 177–178, viewed 10 August 2016, https://data.environment.sa.gov.au/Content/heritage-surveys/2-Gawler-Heritage-Survey-1998.pdf

3 Marsden, S., 2012, *A history of South Australian Councils to 1936*, Local Government of South Australia, https://www.lga.sa.gov.au/__data/assets/pdf_file/0025/468511/LGA-89938_-_2011_18_-_FINAL_History_of_SA_Councils.pdf

4 Lands Title Records

5 Wilmore, H., *Gawler's History in Maps and* Plans, 2021, public database, p. 20, viewed 21 January 2022, https://drive.google.com/file/d/1J-Ab3PjqDc3RpawvBV5YM_TVg5R0I0hR/view

6 'Family Notices', *Bunyip*, 7 November 1890, p. 2, viewed 9 January 2022, http://nla.gov.au/nla.news-article97234369

7 'Prompt Invigoration', *Bunyip*, 12 June 1896, p. 2, viewed 15 June 2021, http://nla.gov.au/nla.news-article97575913

8 'Family Notices', *Bunyip*, 30 September 1892, p. 2, viewed 9 January 2022, http://nla.gov.au/nla.news-article97235496

9 'This Week Mr. Chas. Deland Wanders up Lyndoch Road and out of Town', *Bunyip*, 26 November 1954, p. 14, viewed 26 November 2019, http://nla.gov.au/nla.news-article96904551

10 'Thomas Hutchinson Trust and related Trusts (Winding Up) Act 1995', n.d., Legislation SA, viewed 29 July 2021, https://www.legislation.sa.gov.au/LZ/C/A/Thomas Hutchinson Trust And Related Trusts (Winding Up) Act 1995/Current/1995.7.Auth.PDF

11 'Family Notices', *Advertiser*, 2 August 1902, p. 2, viewed 19 September 2016, http://nla.gov.au/nla.news-article4865503

12 'Concerning People', *Register*, 7 November 1901, p. 5, viewed 21 January 2022, http://nla.gov.au/nla.news-article55669828

13 'Mr. G. Penhall', *Chronicle*, 3 March 1938, p. 18, viewed 24 July 2021, http://nla.gov.au/nla.news-article92474357

14 'District Council Nominations', *Register*, 16 June 1914, p. 9, viewed 8 January 2022, http://nla.gov.au/nla.news-article59408322

15 Braithwaite, S., 2007, *Wandering Through Yesteryear: A family story for my grandchildren*, self-published

16 'The One Thing Needed', *Murray Pioneer and Australian River Record*, 12 January 1917, p. 7, viewed 28 July 2021, http://nla.gov.au/nla.news-article109218910

17 'The One Thing Needed', *Murray Pioneer and Australian River Record*, 12 January 1917, p. 7, viewed 28 July 2021, http://nla.gov.au/nla.news-article109218910; 'The War', *Bunyip*, 25 August 1916, p. 2, viewed 24 July 2021, http://nla.gov.au/nla.news-article97738328

18 'Late Social News', *The Journal*, 4 November 1916, p. 19, viewed 27 July 2021, http://nla.gov.au/nla.news-article204679417; 'Late Social News', *The Journal*, 16 December 1916, p. 19, viewed 27 July 2021, http://nla.gov.au/nla.news-article204683836

19 'A Soldier's Mother', *Murray Pioneer and Australian River Record*, 21 June 1918, p. 5, viewed 21 January 2022, http://nla.gov.au/nla.news-article109223263; 'Thirty-Two Soldier Trainees Placed', *Murray Pioneer and Australian River Record*, 29 August 1919, p. 5, viewed 21 January 2022, http://nla.gov.au/nla.news-article109225529; 1918, 'Motes From Berri', *Murray Pioneer and Australian River Record*, 8 November, p. 5, viewed 21 January 2022, http://nla.gov.au/nla.news-article109224448

20 'The One Thing Needed', *Murray Pioneer and Australian River Record*, 12 January 1917, p. 7, viewed 27 July 2021, http://nla.gov.au/nla.news-article109218910; 'Advertising', *Murray Pioneer and Australian River Record*, 19 April 1918, p. 5, viewed 28 July 2021, http://nla.gov.au/nla.news-article109222845

21 'Renmark Post Office Incident', *Murray Pioneer and Australian River Record*, 19 October 1917, p. 5, viewed 28 July 2021, http://nla.gov.au/nla.news-article109221399; 'Farriers And Settlers Association', *Murray Pioneer and Australian River Record*, 18 January 1918, p. 5, viewed 28 July 2021, http://nla.gov.au/nla.news-article109222051

22 'Advertising', *Murray Pioneer and Australian River Record*, 29 March 1918, p. 5, viewed 28 July 2021, http://nla.gov.au/nla.news-article109222626; 18, 'Social and Personal', *Bunyip*, 4 January, p. 2, viewed 21 January 2022, http://nla.gov.au/nla.news-article100418865

23 'Mr. G.A. Ash Honoured', *Murray Pioneer and Australian River Record*, 28 April 1922, p. 1, viewed 21 January 2022, http://nla.gov.au/nla.news-article109310127

24 'The Block E School', *Murray Pioneer and Australian River Record*, 5 September 1924, p. 16, viewed 21 January 2022, http://nla.gov.au/nla.news-article109320305

25 'A Pruning Bee', *Murray Pioneer and Australian River Record*, 15 July 1927, p. 6, viewed 21 January 2022, http://nla.gov.au/nla.news-article109361637; 'Country News', *Register*, 21 July 1927, p. 2, viewed 21 January 2022, http://nla.gov.au/nla.news-article55044030

26 'Family Notices' *Daily Herald*, 5 August 1919, p. 2, viewed November 22 2018, http://nla.gov.au/nla.news-article106472010

27 'Family Notices', *The Journal*, 5 August 1919, p. 1, viewed 22 November 2018, http://nla.gov.au/nla.news-article204718948

28 'Coombe S W', n.d., National Archives of Australia, B2455, viewed 12 December 2021, https://recordsearch.naa.gov.au/SearchNRetrieve/Gallery151/dist/JGalleryViewer.aspx?B=3404147&S=1&N=119&R=0#/SearchNRetrieve/NAAMedia/

ShowImage.aspx?B=3404147&T=P&S=6; 'W.C.T.U. First Annual Public Meeting', *Murray Pioneer and Australian River Record*, 12 October 1917, p. 3, viewed 21 January 2022, http://nla.gov.au/nla.news-article109221309

29 'Social and Personal', *Bunyip*, 30 November 1923, p. 2, viewed 9 July 2016, http://nla.gov.au/nla.news-article97764471; 'The Late Mrs. E.H. Coombe', *Murray Pioneer and Australian River Record*, 1 December 1923, p. 13, viewed 21 January 2022, http://nla.gov.au/nla.news-article109329656

Acknowledgements

1 Mostly Coombe – Migrants – Ephraim Coombe Extended Family', 1 March 2013, Mostly Coombe in Australia & Coumbe in North Hill, Cornwall Family History & Genealogy, http://coombe.id.au/mig/Ephraim_Coombe.htm

Index

Index

Index

Wakefield Press is an independent publishing and distribution company based in Adelaide, South Australia. We love good stories and publish beautiful books. To see our full range of books, please visit our website at www.wakefieldpress.com.au where all titles are available for purchase. To keep up with our latest releases, news and events, subscribe to our monthly newsletter.

Find us!

Facebook: www.facebook.com/wakefield.press
Twitter: www.twitter.com/wakefieldpress
Instagram: www.instagram.com/wakefieldpress

www.ingramcontent.com/pod-product-compliance
Lightning Source LLC
LaVergne TN
LVHW050955080826
845145LV00006B/1511

* 9 7 8 1 7 4 3 0 5 9 6 1 6 *